SURVIVING THE MONGOLS

The Institute of Ismaili Studies
Ismaili Heritage Series, 8
General Editor: Farhad Daftary

Previously published titles:

1. Paul E. Walker, *Abū Yaʿqūb al-Sijistānī: Intellectual Missionary* (1996)
2. Heinz Halm, *The Fatimids and their Traditions of Learning* (1997)
3. Paul E. Walker, *Ḥamīd al-Dīn al-Kirmānī: Ismaili Thought in the Age of al-Ḥākim* (1999)
4. Alice C. Hunsberger, *Nasir Khusraw, The Ruby of Badakhshan: A Portrait of the Persian Poet, Traveller and Philosopher* (2000)
5. Farouk Mitha, *Al-Ghazālī and the Ismailis: A Debate on Reason and Authority in Medieval Islam* (2001)
6. Ali S. Asani, *Ecstasy and Enlightenment: The Ismaili Devotional Literature of South Asia* (2002)
7. Paul E. Walker, *Exploring an Islamic Empire: Fatimid History and its Sources* (2002)

Surviving the Mongols

Nizārī Quhistānī and the Continuity of Ismaili Tradition in Persia

Nadia Eboo Jamal

I.B.Tauris *Publishers*
LONDON • NEW YORK
in association with
The Institute of Ismaili Studies
LONDON

Published in 2002 by I.B.Tauris & Co Ltd
6 Salem Rd, London W2 4BU
175 Fifth Avenue, New York NY 10010
www.ibtauris.com

in association with The Institute of Ismaili Studies
42–44 Grosvenor Gardens, London SW1W 0EB
www.iis.ac.uk

In the United States of America and in Canada distributed by
St Martin's Press, 175 Fifth Avenue, New York NY 10010

ISBN 1 86064 432 5 HB
1 86064 876 2 PB

A full CIP record for this book is available from the British Library
A full CIP record for this book is available from the Library of Congress

Library of Congress catalog card: available

Typeset in ITC New Baskerville by Hepton Books, Oxford
Printed and bound in Great Britain by MPG Books Ltd, Bodmin

The Institute of Ismaili Studies

The Institute of Ismaili Studies was established in 1977 with the object of promoting scholarship and learning on Islam, in the historical as well as contemporary contexts, and a better understanding of its relationship with other societies and faiths.

The Institute's programmes encourage a perspective which is not confined to the theological and religious heritage of Islam, but seek to explore the relationship of religious ideas to broader dimensions of society and culture. The programmes thus encourage an interdisciplinary approach to the materials of Islamic history and thought. Particular attention is also given to issues of modernity that arise as Muslims seek to relate their heritage to the contemporary situation.

Within the Islamic tradition, the Institute's programmes promote research on those areas which have, to date, received relatively little attention from scholars. These include the intellectual and literary expressions of Shiʿism in general, and Ismailism in particular.

In the context of Islamic societies, the Institute's programmes are informed by the full range and diversity of cultures in which Islam is practised today, from the Middle East, South and Central Asia and Africa to the industrialised societies of the West, thus taking into consideration the variety of contexts which shape the ideals, beliefs and practices of the faith.

These objectives are realised through concrete programmes and activities organised and implemented by various departments of the Institute. The Institute also collaborates periodically, on a programme-specific basis, with other institutions of learning in the United Kingdom and abroad.

The Institute's academic publications fall into a number of interrelated categories:

1. Occasional papers or essays addressing broad themes of the relationship between religion and society, with special reference to Islam.
2. Monographs exploring specific aspects of Islamic faith and culture, or the contributions of individual Muslim figures or writers.
3. Editions or translations of significant primary or secondary texts.
4. Translations of poetic or literary texts which illustrate the rich heritage of spiritual, devotional and symbolic expressions in Muslim history.
5. Works on Ismaili history and thought, and the relationship of the Ismailis to other traditions, communities and schools of thought in Islam.
6. Proceedings of conferences and seminars sponsored by the Institute.
7. Bibliographical works and catalogues which document manuscripts, printed texts and other source materials.

This book falls into category five listed above.

In facilitating these and other publications, the Institute's sole aim is to encourage original research and analysis of relevant issues. While every effort is made to ensure that the publications are of a high academic standard, there is naturally bound to be a diversity of views, ideas and interpretations. As such, the opinions expressed in these publications are to be understood as belonging to their authors alone.

Ismaili Heritage Series

A major Shiʿi Muslim community, the Ismailis have had a long and eventful history. Scattered in many regions of the world, in Asia, Africa, Europe and North America, the Ismailis have elaborated diverse intellectual and literary traditions in different languages. On two occasions they had states of their own, the Fatimid caliphate and the Nizari State of Iran and Syria during the Alamut period. While pursuing particular religio-political aims, the leaders of these Ismaili states also variously encouraged intellectual, scientific, artistic and commercial activities.

Until recently, the Ismailis were studied and judged almost exclusively on the basis of the evidence collected or fabricated by their enemies, including the bulk of the medieval heresiographers and polemicists who were hostile towards the Shiʿa in general and the Ismailis among them in particular. These authors in fact treated the Shiʿi interpretations of Islam as expressions of heterodoxy or even heresy. As a result, a 'black legend' was gradually developed and put into circulation in the Muslim world to discredit the Ismailis and their interpretation of Islam. The Christian Crusaders and their occidental chroniclers, who remained almost completely ignorant of Islam and its internal divisions, disseminated their own myths of the Ismailis, which came to be accepted in Europe as true descriptions of Ismaili teachings and practices. Modern orientalists, too, have studied the Ismailis on the basis of these hostile sources and fanciful accounts of medieval times. Thus, legends and misconceptions have continued to surround the Ismailis through the twentieth century.

In more recent decades, however, the field of Ismaili studies has been revolutionised due to the recovery and study of genuine Ismaili sources on a large scale – manuscript materials which in different ways survived the destruction of the Fatimid and Nizari Ismaili libraries. These sources, representing diverse literary traditions produced in Arabic, Persian and Indic languages, had hitherto been secretly preserved in private collections in India, Central Asia, Iran, Afghanistan, Syria and the Yemen.

Modern progress in Ismaili studies has already necessitated a complete re-writing of the history of the Ismailis and their contributions to Islamic civilisation. It has now become clear that the Ismailis founded important libraries and institutions of learning such as al-Azhar and the Dar al-ʿIlm in Cairo, while some of their learned *daʿis* or missionaries developed unique intellectual traditions amalgamating their theological doctrine with a diversity of philosophical traditions in complex metaphysical systems. The Ismaili patronage of learning and extension of hospitality to non-Ismaili scholars was maintained even in such difficult times as the Alamut period, when the community was preoccupied with its survival in an extremely hostile milieu.

The Ismaili Heritage Series, published under the auspices of the Department of Academic Research and Publications of The Institute of Ismaili Studies, aims to make available to wide audiences the results of modern scholarship on the Ismailis and their rich intellectual and cultural heritage, as well as certain aspects of their more recent history and achievements.

This book is dedicated
to my Grandparents

Contents

Foreword

In the course of their long history, the Ismailis have elaborated a diversity of literary and intellectual traditions and made important contributions to Islamic thought and culture. A distinct Nizārī religious tradition, based on the Persian language, developed during the Alamūt period (483–654/1090–1256) when the Ismailis of Persia had a state of their own centred on the stronghold of Alamūt. The Nizārīs lost their state and political prominence as a result of the Mongol invasions of Persia in 654/1256. But, in spite of the claims of the historian ʿAṭā' Malik Juwaynī, who was in the service of the Mongol conqueror Hülegü, the Persian Nizārī community was not totally extirpated by the Mongols. Countless numbers were massacred and the bulk of the Nizārī literature was destroyed . However, the all-important Nizārī imamate continued in the progeny of Imam Rukn al-Dīn Khurshāh (d. 655/1257), the last ruler of Alamūt, while certain aspects of the Nizārī *daʿwa* institution also survived.

With the fall of Alamūt, the Persian Nizārīs entered an obscure period of their history which lasted some two centuries until their Imams emerged at the village of Anjudān in central Persia, around the middle of the 9th/15th century, and initiated a revival in Nizārī *daʿwa* and literary activities. Many aspects of Nizārī Ismaili history during this interim period are still shrouded in mystery due to a lack of reliable sources. The Persian Nizārīs did not produce any doctrinal works in this period, and they observed *taqiyya*, dissimulating their beliefs and adopting Sufism and other forms of disguises to protect themselves against rampant persecution. As a result, many scattered Nizārī groups either disintegrated or fully assimilated themselves into other, dominant religious communities. Be that as it may, it is only in the last few decades that progress in Ismaili studies has enabled scholars to acquire a better understanding of at least the main trends in the history of Persian Nizārī Ismailism of the early post-Alamūt centuries. It is in such a context that the present book should be read and appreciated.

Ḥakīm Saʿd al-Dīn b. Shams al-Dīn Nizārī Quhistānī (645–720/1247–1320), who hailed from the region of Quhistān in south-eastern Khurāsān and as a boy witnessed the Mongol ravages in his native land, is the major Persian Ismaili poet of the early post-Alamūt period. He was perhaps also the first author to have adopted poetic forms of expression and Sufi idioms to convey his Ismaili ideas, which are in essence resonant with the teachings of the Alamūt period. In fact, Nizārī Quhistānī's writings reflect the earliest instance of a literary coalescence between Nizārī Ismailism and Sufism in Persia and as such, they represent the opening phase of a new Nizārī tradition which was fully developed by the time the Safawids established their rule over Persia in 907/1501.

By drawing extensively on Nizārī Quhistānī's unpublished collected works, the *Kulliyyāt*, particularly his versified *Safar-nāma*, and the findings of modern scholarship in the field, Dr Nadia Eboo Jamal has produced here the first thorough study of this poet in English as well as an important contribution to the history of the Persian Nizārī Ismailis in the aftermath of the Mongol debacle. She provides ample documentation of the way the Nizārīs of Persia succeeded, against all odds, not only to retain their distinct religious identity but to initiate yet another tradition which brought their community closer to Persian Sufism and enabled it to survive under highly adverse circumstances in post-Mongol Persia.

Farhad Daftary

Preface

This work was prepared originally for a doctoral thesis at the Department of Near Eastern languages and Literatures at New York University in 1996 and has been revised extensively for publication. Its main purpose is to examine the circumstances of the Ismaili community in the aftermath of the Mongol conquest of Persia in the mid–7th/13th century. Due to the tremendous upheaval caused in the community by this event, there is almost a complete lack of Ismaili sources for the next two centuries or so.

The only major Ismaili source material to have survived from the period of Mongol rule consists of the poetical works of Nizārī Quhistānī, who served as a local government official and court poet in the north-eastern Persian provinces of Khurāsān and Quhistān. These writings, in particular the poet's travelogue, the *Safar-nāma,* have been used in this study to explore the survival of the Ismaili community and the continuity of their traditions during the Mongol era. They also provide a unique insight into the interface between Ismailism and Sufism that emerged at this time. Since the works of Nizārī Quhistānī are largely unknown to the English-speaking world, this publication serves the additional purpose of introducing the reader to his life and poetry.

When undertaking the journey of writing a book, there are many friends and colleagues who hold one's hand along the way. Among these, I take great pleasure in recording my deep gratitude to the following in particular: Dr Robert McChesney who patiently supported me on my quest: Ghulam Abbas Hunzai and Dr Faquir Hunzai, true mentors and lasting friends; Dr Charles Melville, whose comments on the first draft of this book were invaluable; Mrs Zinat Safarha, a pure Sufi who shared her wisdom with me tirelessly; Dr Arzina Lalani, for her constant support, encouragement and advice; Dr Jalal Badakhchani, who not only assisted me in acquiring manuscripts for this work but has also helped me in numerous other ways; Dr Leonard Lewisohn for sharing his insightful comments, poetic skills and sense of humour; Dr Farhad Daftary, for believing in me and my work, and contributing a Foreword to this book; Kutub Kassam, who has painstakingly walked the journey with me; as well as all the other supporters I have encountered at The Institute of Ismaili Studies.

I would also like to recognise my wonderful friends who tirelessly supported me through good and bad times, and in particular my husband, a gem, and my amazing children, Nijhad and Shazia, who have watched me burn the midnight oil on many occasions without complaint.

Finally, it should be noted that the transliteration system adopted in this book is that of the new edition of *The Encyclopaedia of Islam*, with the usual modifications. Arabic and Persian terms common in English, such as Ismaili and Sufi, have not been transliterated. The following abbreviations have been used for sources:

EI2	*Encyclopaedia of Islam*, new ed.
JAOS	*Journal of the American Oriental Society*
JBBRAS	*Journal of the Bombay Branch of the Royal Asiatic Society*
JRAS	*Journal of the Royal Asiatic Society*
NS	New Series

NEJ

It is well that you should follow the Imamate,
For the Light of God is within his pure heart.
Through that Light you will be freed from darkness.
Follow that Light and may peace be with you!

Nizārī Quhistānī, *Dastūr-nāma*

Chapter 1

Introduction

> I say, therefore, that this thing involves the description of the greatest catastrophe and the most dire calamity (of the like of which days and nights are innocent) which befell all men generally, and the Muslims in particular; so that, should one say that the world, since God Almighty created Adam until now, hath not been afflicted with the like thereof, he would but speak the truth. For indeed history does not contain anything which approaches or comes near to it ... Nay, it is unlikely that mankind will see the like of this calamity until the world comes to an end and perishes, except for the final outbreak of Gog and Magog.[1]

These foreboding remarks of the Arab historian Ibn al-Athīr (d. 630/1233) vividly capture his impressions of one of the most catastrophic events to befall the Muslim world, constituted by the series of Mongol incursions which swept across a large part of Central Asia and the Middle East during the 7th/13th century. Ibn al-Athīr's words acquire particular poignancy when it is realised that he died in 630/1233, many years before the full onslaught of the Mongols actually materialised upon the largely Persian-speaking region from the Oxus to the Euphrates rivers,[2] culminating in the sack of Baghdad and destruction of the Abbasid caliphate in 656/1258. For the peoples of this region especially, the period of Mongol incursions was one of enormous human suffering and far-reaching social changes. The devastation of many towns and cities, the slaughter, enslavement and displacement of millions of people, and the subsequent death of countless others from war, famine or disease resulted in a marked decrease of population in the region. Economically, there was a rapid decline in agriculture as large areas of previously cultivated land reverted to nomadic pastoralism. Politically and religiously, by destroying the central caliphal state based in Baghdad and introducing their own laws and standards of politics, the Mongols challenged the established norms and practices of Muslim societies – thus disrupting the emergence of new patterns of thought and social organisation in the Muslim world at a time when Western Europe was making a historically decisive transition from feudalism to the construction of a new social, economic and political order.

The Mongol conquest of Persia was destructive to all its inhabitants, especially those communities who happened to offer any resistance to the conquerors. For the Nizārī Ismailis of Persia in particular, it was the single-most disastrous event in their history. It caused, within a short span of five or six years, a total upheaval of this Shiʿi community which, in the previous century, had succeeded in carving out its own autonomous territorial state of fortresses and citadels in parts of Persia and Syria. The capture and dismantling of many of these strongholds by the Mongols put a permanent end to the political aspirations and prominence of the Ismailis in the region. According to the sources which have come down to us, a large proportion of the Ismaili population was exterminated by the invaders, the Ismaili Imam of the time was taken into custody and later murdered, and the community ceased to exercise any influence, or even make its physical presence known publicly, for several centuries to come.

In view of these cataclysmic events, it is not surprising that the Persian Ismailis were unable to maintain any historical record of their own from the era of Mongol domination (654–754/1256–1353). Much of the Ismaili literature of the Alamūt period was destroyed with the collapse of their state and very little was written or preserved by the community in the following two centuries. Hence, what we know about the Ismailis is largely derived from non-Ismaili historians and chroniclers of the time, who were for the most part hostile to the Ismailis and whose accounts were written after the fall of the central Ismaili fortress of Alamūt in 654/1256.[3] The most famous of these historians, ʿAlāʾ al-Dīn ʿAṭā Mālik b. Muḥammad Juwaynī (d. 682/1283), was in fact present in the entourage of the Mongol ruler Hülegü at the capture of Alamūt. In his *Taʾrīkh-i jahān gushāy*,[4] he describes how he inspected the contents of its famed library, took a few texts and astronomical instruments which interested him, and consigned the rest to the flames.

Another major source is Rashīd al-Dīn Faḍl Allāh (d. 718/1318), who served as a physician, historian and chief minister to the Mongol ruler Ghāzān. He included a lengthy account of the Ismailis in his universal history, *Jāmiʿ al-tawārīkh*.[5] Rashīd al-Dīn appears to have had more information available to him than what we find in the extant text of Juwaynī and he preserves many details not previously recorded, possibly because he may have had independent access to other Ismaili sources. He also attempts to put forward a summary of the Ismaili doctrines of the time. Unlike Juwaynī whose narrative is distorted by his antipathy towards the Ismailis, Rashīd al-Dīn's account is somewhat more impartial; he is often reluctant to pass judgement and occasionally corrects Juwaynī where necessary.

In 1964, a third source came to light from a contemporary and collaborator of Rashīd al-Dīn called Jamāl al-Dīn Abu'l-Qāsim ʿAbd Allāh b. ʿAlī Kāshānī (al-Kāshānī) entitled *Zubdat al-tawārīkh*.[6] He was a relatively unknown chronicler, also in the employment of the Mongols, who collaborated with Rashīd al-Dīn in the compilation of the *Jāmiʿ al-tawārīkh*. There is much in common between Kāshānī's account of the Ismailis and that of Rashīd al-Dīn, indicating that both writers relied on the same sources, but Kāshānī also provides certain details not reported by the latter. Another account of the Ismailis is provided by the historian Shihāb al-Dīn ʿAbd Allāh b. Faḍl Allāh of Shīrāz, also known as Waṣṣāf or Waṣṣāf-i Ḥaḍrat, in his well-known history, *Tajziyat al-amṣār wa tajziyat al-aʿṣār* (also called *Taʾrīkh-i Waṣṣāf*).[7]

Perhaps the most comprehensive chronicler of the time to give attention to the Ismailis was Ibn al-Athīr (d. 630/1233) cited at the beginning of this chapter. In his work *al-Kāmil fi'l-taʾrīkh*,[8] this

Arab historian records much information about the Persian and Syrian Ismailis which is not found in other sources. He also reports many 'newsworthy' incidents involving skirmishes, massacres and other military engagements between the Mongols and the Ismailis; but he gives only sketchy information about these events, not going into the details of the circumstances surrounding them. Furthermore, his chronicle ends in the year 628/1230–31, two years before his death, so that he was unable to report the fall of Alamūt or the subsequent capture of Baghdad by the Mongols.

It is impossible to verify the accounts of these non-Ismaili historians and chroniclers against works by Ismaili authors since the bulk of their literature perished during the invasions. The few books that did survive were not easily accessible, being preserved until recently in private collections. In any case, since these are largely doctrinal in content they provide little historical information. The extreme scarcity of Persian Ismaili sources is a problem not confined to the period of Mongol rule; it extends, in fact, over four centuries until the rise of the Ṣafawids in the 10th/16th century. The decline in literary activity among the Ismailis may indeed reflect their disintegration as an organised community, but it is also likely to have been a result of the traditional Ismaili practice of *taqiyya*, 'protection' or precautionary dissimulation of belief, by which means individuals tried to conceal their religious identity in order to escape political and religious persecution.

In the absence of Ismaili sources, a number of orientalist scholars of the late 19th and early 20th centuries, relying largely on the histories and chronicles mentioned above, came to the conclusion that the Persian Ismailis had been totally exterminated by the Mongols. This was the view, for instance, of the distinguished French scholar Silvestre de Sacy (1758–1838), who was one of the earliest Europeans to study the Ismailis and also offer a satisfactory theory of the etymology of the term 'assassin'.[9] The same theory was advocated by the Austrian diplomat and historian Joseph von Hammer-Purgstall (1774–1856), the first Western author to devote an entire book to the Ismailis. But unlike de Sacy's sober and discriminating scholarship, von Hammer's work is marred by his uncritical acceptance of the anti-Ismaili prejudices of the sources he consulted.[10]

Among other scholars, however, it became increasingly clear that the old received image of a decimated Ismaili community was indefensible. Wladimir Ivanow (1886–1970), one of the pioneers of modern Ismaili studies, was the first to recognise that even though the political power of the Ismailis came to an end and the community was considerably diminished, a small minority did survive the massacres, as did also the Ismaili line of Imams.[11] His view was supported by Marshall G.S. Hodgson (1922–1968), the author of the most comprehensive study of the Ismailis of the Alamūt period to date,[12] and confirmed more recently by Farhad Daftary who writes:

> The Nizārīs of Persia, contrary to the declarations of Juwaynī and later historians, did in fact survive the destruction of their state and strongholds at the hands of the Mongols. Despite the Mongol massacres, the Persian Nizārī community was not totally extirpated ... and significant numbers survived the debacle in both Rūdbār and Quhistān.[13]

In spite of these corrections, the post-Alamūt period of Ismaili history remains extremely obscure and problematic, and there are many questions which remain unanswered. If, as seems to be the case, a large proportion of the Persian Ismailis were killed or displaced during the Mongol incursions of 651–654/1253–1256, what evidence is there of their continuity as an organised community in the second half of the 7th/13th century? What happened to the Ismaili *daʿwa*, the central religious and cultural organisation of the community? Did it collapse and disintegrate following the Mongol conquest or survive in a much diminished form? How did the Ismailis maintain their religious ethos and identity over long periods during which they were obliged to conceal their beliefs and practices? Where did the Ismaili Imams reside after the fall of Alamūt and how did they relate with their followers? What was the connection between the Ismailis and the Sufi fraternities which began to exercise increasing influence in the religious life of Persians during this period?

One of the few Ismaili authors who survived the Mongol conquest and whose works are accessible to us is the poet Saʿd al-Dīn b. Shams al-Dīn b. Muḥammad, more commonly known as Nizārī Quhistānī. Nizārī was born in 645/1247 in Bīrjand, a small town located south of Mashhad in the highlands of Quhistān in south-eastern Khurāsān, alongside the present border of Iran with Afghanistan. His poetical writings and links with Ismailism were discussed at length by medieval Persian authors,[14] and they have also attracted the attention of recent scholars in Iran, Russia and the West.[15] Both W. Ivanow and Jan Rypka regarded Nizārī as a much talented and underestimated poet, whose works deserve more examination.[16] The most comprehensive account of Nizārī Quhistānī is that by the Central Asian scholar Baiburdi, whose works have been an invaluable source of information for this study.[17]

Nizārī was about ten years old when the Mongols overwhelmed the Ismaili fortresses in Quhistān and massacred large numbers of Ismailis in the region, before proceeding to subjugate the rest of Persia under their rule. Hence, the major portion of Nizārī's life was spent in a political and social milieu dominated by the Īl-Khānid dynasty. After acquiring his education and developing the skills of a poet, he pursued administrative and poetic careers in the service of the local Sunni dynasties of the Karts and the Mihrabānids who ruled Khurāsān and Quhistān under Mongol patronage. Although the difficult circumstances of the time precluded Nizārī from expressing his Ismaili beliefs openly in his works, it is possible through an analysis of his poetical works to discern some information about the Persian Ismailis after the destruction of their political power. This evidence has often been overlooked or underestimated by historians, probably because of the poetic and mystical character of his works which have often been associated in Persian literary history with Sufism rather than as an expression of Ismaili religiosity. In fact, it is arguable that Nizārī Quhistānī provides a more accurate and reliable account of Ismaili activities during this period than any other contemporary Persian source.

This work represents the first study in English of Nizārī Quhistānī as an Ismaili poet in the social, cultural and political context of his time. It will focus, more specifically, on the poet's *Safar-nāma* (*Travelogue*) in which he describes his two-year journey from Quhistān to the Transcaucasian region, ostensibly for the purpose of supervising government revenue and expenditure, but perhaps to meet with leaders of the Ismaili community, including the Ismaili Imam of the time who was then residing in the Ādharbāyjān region. Through this exploration, an attempt will also be made to establish Nizārī's religious identity, his association with the Ismailis of his time, and to evaluate the evidence in his writings for the continuity of the Ismaili *da'wa* through the period of Mongol rule. Nizārī's poetical works will also be scrutinised for their reflection of the Ismaili doctrines of his time and the emergence of a close relationship between Persian Ismailism and Sufism.

The overall perspective of this work is both collective and individual, in that it is concerned with the fate of the Ismaili community on the one hand, as well as with the fortunes of a highly talented, individual Ismaili poet on the other, in their respective efforts to survive the calamity of the Mongol invasion. This dual focus is reflected in the structure of the book, which is divided into two parts: the first dealing with the historical evolution of the Ismaili community and, in particular, its *da'wa*; the second part is concerned chiefly with Nizārī Quhistānī and his efforts to make a living in a political and religious environment that was inimical to the Ismailis. As will become clear to the reader, the struggles of both the community and the individual to endure in a period of profound social change are very much interconnected. The historical experiences of one are often mirrored in the face of the other; and after an interval of disengagement and separation, the two eventually come together to confirm their common destiny and to reaffirm the same spiritual vision which has inspired this Muslim community from the beginning of its history.

PART ONE

The Ismaili Daʿwa: *Community, History and Destiny*

Chapter 2

The Early Ismaili and Fatimid Daʿwas

For the most part, the modern study of Ismaili history has been divided into a number of broad phases, such as the early Shiʿi, pre-Fatimid, Fatimid, Mustaʿlian and Nizārī periods, the last being further sub-divided into its Alamūt, post-Alamūt and other periods down to the contemporary era.[1] Such categorisations, usually based upon a combination of chronological, doctrinal, geographical and other factors, are conceived essentially on a linear conception of time progressing irreversibly from the past to the future. As such, it is in sharp contrast to the cyclical view of time and history in early Ismaili thought that presents a series of cosmic cycles which, in their turn, engender the configurations of terrestrial time and history. In its most developed form, the early Ismaili concept of cyclical time became the framework of a highly complex meta-historical system, integrating cosmology, prophetology, soteriology and eschatology within the perspectives of Shiʿi theology. A significant portion of this system of thought is clearly derived from the Qur'an, Prophetic Traditions and teachings of the early Shiʿi Imams, but it also consists of certain Gnostic and Neoplatonic ideas current among Muslims in the early centuries of Islam.

The Ismaili Vision of Time and History

In the Qur'an there are several verses relating to the notion of time (*dahr*), such as 7:54 which refers to God having created the heavens and the earth in 'six Days,' and 76:1 which raises the question whether there ever was a time in which man was 'a thing unremembered'.[2] On the subject of history, however, there are many Qur'anic verses which, taken together, represent a distinctive perspective of the historical process, encompassing the whole of humanity as well as all events of the past and the future. According to this view, history is not a neutral or random occurrence of events but a divinely ordered scheme of things, subject to the intervention of God in human affairs. Central to the divine purpose is the guidance of mankind, which is communicated through a long series of prophets and messengers, beginning with Adam and culminating with the Prophet Muḥammad. The message of Islam is accordingly conceived as the natural continuation and fulfilment of all preceding revelations and religions founded by the prophets. There are many passages in the Qur'an which rehearse the stories of these prophets and invite the faithful to learn from history the terrible end of those peoples and nations who failed to heed their divinely-inspired message.[3]

The Qur'an also warns of an all-consuming event to come in the future, the *qiyāma* or 'Resurrection,' when the souls of all human beings will be summoned before God to receive just recompense for their deeds on earth (3:185; 22:100–112; 39:67–75, etc.). The word *qiyāma* comes from the Arabic q-w-m, meaning 'to stand upright' or 'to rise'. Other synonymous terms used in the Qur'an for this eschatological event are *yawm al-qiyāma* (the Day of Judgement), *yawm al-ʿaẓīm* (the Great Day), *yawm al-hashr* (the Day of Gathering) and *al-sāʿa* (the Hour).[4] In the Qur'anic perspective, the *qiyāma* represents the final goal and consummation of history, the Last Day towards which the lives of all human beings are purposefully directed.

These scriptural perspectives on history and the decisive role of Islam in its unfolding exercised a strong influence on the tradition of Muslim historiography, and it also contributed to the development of a strong sense of historical and cultural identity which has persisted to this day in all Muslim societies. The emergence of this historical consciousness was particularly marked among the early Shiʿi groups in the second century of the Islamic era. The teachings of the Imams Muḥammad al-Bāqir (d.ca.121/738) and Jaʿfar al-Ṣādiq (d.148/765), in particular, appear to have inspired in their followers an intellectual ferment that was characterised by discussions of a variety of theological, philosophical, spiritual and esoteric issues.[5] These Imams were especially instrumental in establishing the principles of Shiʿi theology and jurisprudence, particularly the central doctrine of the Imamate (*imāma*) which, in its insistence on the historical necessity and continuity of divine guidance at all times, expresses both the spiritual and temporal aspirations of Shiʿi Islam.

While admitting with other Muslims the historical finality of the Qurʾanic revelation and the prophethood of Muḥammad, the Shiʿis maintain that divine guidance is an ongoing process that continues to reach mankind through the Prophet's descendants. Whereas the purpose of *nubuwwa* (prophecy) is to deliver a revelation to mankind in its external, exoteric (*ẓāhir*) form, the function of *imāma* (vicegerency) is to convey its inner, esoteric (*bāṭin*) understanding to successive generations of mankind to the end of time. Accordingly, the Shiʿis regard their Imams as the true successors of the Prophet of Islam, the inheritors of his spiritual knowledge (*ʿilm*), the bearers of the light (*nūr*) of God and His living proof (*ḥujja*) on earth. Hence, allegiance to these Imams becomes a fundamental requirement of Shiʿi Islam, for it is only through their mediation (*shafāʿa*) that believers can attain knowledge of God and salvation on the Last Day. More than any factor, it is this belief in a universal, divinely-ordained mission of their Imams that has imparted to the Shiʿi community a pronounced sense of historical purpose.

The religious and political implications of this historical outlook of early Shiʿism were worked out in their most comprehensive form by the emergent Ismailis of the 3rd/9th century and elaborated further under the Fatimids in the 4th/10th century. Building on the teachings of the Imams al-Bāqir and al-Ṣādiq, the early Ismaili thinkers developed a theory of universal history consisting of seven cycles of temporal time. Each cycle was inaugurated by a prophet-messenger called *nāṭiq* (literally, 'speaker') mentioned in the Qurʾan (Adam, Noah, Abraham, Moses, Jesus and Muḥammad), whose mission was to enunciate a revealed scripture with a new religious law (*sharīʿa*).[6] Each of these prophet-messengers was assisted by a deputy (Seth, Shem, Ishmael, Aaron, Simon and ʿAlī b. Abī Ṭālib respectively) called *waṣī* ('legatee'), with the mandate of safeguarding the divine message from corruption and conveying its esoteric interpretation (*taʾwīl*) to the faithful. The *waṣī* is also called *asās* ('foundation'), being the first of a series of Imams in each cycle of prophethood who inherit his spiritual knowledge and initiatory functions. The last Imam of the sixth cycle has the special status of *mahdī*, the messianic 'Saviour' of the Last Day, also called *qāʾim* or 'Resurrector'. Combining in himself the offices of both Prophet and Imam, the *qāʾim-mahdī* figure presides over the conclusive, seventh era leading to the end of time and history. One of the crucial roles of the *qāʾim* is to bring the great cycle of prophetic religions to a close and to reveal their inner truth to mankind as a whole.

The cyclical view of prophetic history was a much more elaborate system of thought than what is outlined above, since it was correlated with a variety of metaphysical, cosmological, eschatological and other ideas which cannot be examined here.[7] The important point to note is that it was the Ismaili belief in a divinely-ordained mission of their Imams, inherited from the Prophet Muḥammad, which became embodied in their central religious organisation of the *daʿwa*. In light of the importance of the Ismaili *daʿwa* for our study, it will be useful to examine briefly the development of this institution in the early centuries of Islam.

The *Daʿwa* in Early Islam

The term *daʿwa* is derived from the Arabic *daʿā*, which means 'to call,' 'to summon' or 'to invite.' It is used in the Qurʾan in multiple ways (8:21; 14:44; 30:25), but the verse which came to be understood to express the concept of *daʿwa* in its most emphatic sense is the one addressed to the Prophet: 'Call unto the way of thy Lord with wisdom and fair exhortation, and reason with them in the best of ways' (16:125). The religious usage of *daʿwa* denotes an invitation to mankind by God and His messengers to believe in the true religion.[8] As such the mission of each prophet is considered to be the *daʿwat al-Islām*, 'the call to the submission of God' (3:19). The Prophet Muḥammad was said to have been aided by twelve companions who assisted him in his work and helped to spread the divine message, just as Moses was supported by twelve 'chiefs' (*nuqabā*, sing. *naqīb*), and Jesus by his twelve disciples. In this general sense, the *daʿwa* may be understood as the responsibility of all prophets and messengers to disseminate the message of God and to call people to the true path.

In the early part of the 2nd/8th century, the term *daʿwa* began to acquire a distinct political colouring when it was employed by various movements championing the cause of an individual or family claiming descent from the Prophet's family (*ahl al-bayt*) and their right to leadership of the Muslim community. It was in this religio-political sense that the term *daʿwa* and *dāʿī* ('caller' or 'summoner') came to be utilised commonly by some Shiʿi groups, united in their opposition to the Umayyad dynasty. There is no need for us to review the social, economic, political and religious circumstances which contributed to the rise of these early Shiʿi movements.[9] Suffice it to note that the massacre by Umayyad troops in 681/680 of the Prophet's grandson, al-Ḥusayn, together with many of his family and followers, at Karbalāʾ in Iraq was an important factor in the consolidation of Shiʿi Islam. In addition to inspiring a series of uprisings against the Umayyads, it also generated a strong current of messianic expectations in the general public, focusing on a *mahdī* to come from the Prophet's family who would deliver them from their oppressors and establish a new era of peace and justice.

One of the earliest *daʿwa* movements to emerge was that of the Hāshimids led by the Abbasid family who claimed descent from an uncle of the Prophet Muḥammad. The Abbasid *daʿwa* was able to attract mass popular support, especially among the Shiʿa of Persia and Iraq, which led eventually to the overthrow of the Umayyad state in 132/750. Upon seizing power, however, the Abbasids disassociated themselves from their Shiʿi supporters and began to regard them with open hostility which soon turned to persecution. In contrast to such Shiʿi groups as the Tawwābūn, Kaysāniyya and Zaydiyya who advocated armed revolt against the Abbasids, the Ḥusaynids who descended from the Prophet's grandson al-Ḥusayn refrained from supporting any overt political activity. By disengaging themselves from politics, the Ḥusaynid Imams were able to devote themselves to intellectual and spiritual matters. Thus, al-Ḥusayn's son, Zayn al-ʿĀbidīn (d. 95/714), one of the few survivors of the massacre at Karbalā', retired to Medina where he devoted himself to a life of piety and teaching. His eldest son, Muḥammad al-Bāqir, articulated the principles of Shiʿi theology and law,[10] which were later consolidated and systematised by his successor, Jaʿfar al-Ṣādiq. Through their engagement with the critical intellectual issues facing the early Muslim community, these Ḥusaynid Imams laid the foundations of a distinctive Shiʿi legal and theological system.

Early Shiʿi sources convey the picture of a wide and knowledgeable circle of Imam al-Bāqir's adherents, clearly illustrating the existence of a rudimentary organisation that enabled him to communicate with his followers.[11] The emergence of a distinctive *daʿwa* organisation of the Shiʿa, however, is first recorded to have occurred under the Imam Jaʿfar al-Ṣādiq. With the growing number of his disciples and followers, the need arose apparently for him to introduce some form of internal organisation to his community. This became necessary not merely to facilitate the Imam's communication with his followers from his residence in Medina but also to maintain consistency in the dissemination of his teachings. Accordingly, Jaʿfar al-Ṣādiq is known to have appointed a number of his close disciples, including Abu'l-Khaṭṭāb and al-Mufaḍḍal b. ʿUmar, as *dāʿīs* to guide his followers in Kūfa and other places. We are also told by the North African Fatimid jurist al-Qāḍī al-Nuʿmān in his book, *Iftitāḥ al-daʿwa*, that the Imam al-Ṣādiq despatched two *dāʿīs*, Abū Sufyān and al-Hulwānī, as far as the Maghrib.[12] But at this early stage of Shiʿism the organisation of the *daʿwa* appears to have been limited in scope and only later did it evolve into the elaborate system of the Ismailis. It is with the Ismailis that the term *daʿwa* has become most closely associated historically, and it is to this organisation that we must now turn our attention. As the early history of the Ismailis has been the subject of many studies, the following discussion will be confined mainly to those aspects which have a bearing on their *daʿwa*.[13]

The Emergence of the Ismaili *Daʿwa*

Following the death of the Imam Jaʿfar al-Ṣādiq in 148/765, there occurred a major schism among his followers regarding his succession. Most Shiʿi sources agree that al-Ṣādiq had earlier appointed by *naṣṣ* (designation) his eldest son Ismāʿīl to succeed him. Some sources maintain that Ismāʿīl predeceased his father by a few years, while according to others Jaʿfar arranged a mock-funeral to conceal his son's whereabouts from the Abbasids and that Ismāʿīl was later seen in Baṣra. There was also considerable confusion as to whether or not the late Imam had made a second *naṣṣ* in favour of any of his surviving three sons, ʿAbd Allāh al-Afṭaḥ, Mūsā al-Kāẓim and Muḥammad b. Jaʿfar. Consequently, a number of rival groups emerged supporting or disputing the claims of the brothers to the Imamate. Eventually a majority came to acknowledge Ismāʿīl's younger half-brother, Mūsā al-Kāẓim, as their next Imam. He became the forebear of several generations of Imams until the twelfth in the series, Muḥammad b. al-Ḥasan, who disappeared in mysterious circumstances in 260/873–4. The Ithnāʿashariyya (literally 'Twelvers'), as this community of Shiʿis came to be known, believe that their last Imam is living in occultation (*ghayba*) and will return at the end of time as the *mahdī*, the messianic saviour of mankind.[14] The Ithnāʿasharīs constitute the largest Shiʿi Muslim community today, concentrated mainly in Iran, Iraq, Lebanon, Pakistan and India.

In contrast to those Shiʿis who supported the claim of one or another of Jaʿfar al-Ṣādiq's surviving sons to the Imamate, there were other smaller groups of his disciples residing mostly in the city of Kūfa, who had been especially close to Ismāʿīl during his lifetime and held fast to al-Ṣādiq's designation of him as his successor. Initially some of them refused to acknowledge Ismāʿīl's death before his father, arguing that the late Imam's *naṣṣ*, being divinely-guided, could not be revoked or altered in any way.

Another group, having accepted the fact of Ismāʿīl's untimely death, maintained that al-Ṣādiq had subsequently appointed his grandson, Muḥammad b. Ismāʿīl, to succeed him. They asserted further that after al-Ḥusayn, the Imamate could only be passed in direct succession from father to son. Although the origins of the Ismaili movement remain extremely complex and obscure, there is general agreement among scholars that it was from a coalescence of these minor groups, adhering to the Imamate of Ismāʿīl and his son, that Ismaili Shiʿism took root and began to flourish in the course of the next century.[15]

There is little information available on the activities of Muḥammad b. Ismāʿīl following the recognition of Mūsā al-Kāẓim as Imam by the majority of his grandfather's followers. In Ismaili sources, he is reported to have left Medina to visit his supporters in Iraq and Persia. Thereafter, he is believed to have gone into concealment, his whereabouts known to only a few trusted disciples, on account of which he came to be known among his followers as *al-maktūm*, 'the hidden'. His successors are reported to have continued to live in anonymity for the next century and a half, disguising their true identity under various pseudonyms and personae of wealthy merchants or landowners so that their activities could go undetected by Abbasids agents who were constantly in search of them. This policy of secrecy and concealment undoubtedly enabled the Ismaili Imams to escape the fate of their relatives in the Ithnāʿasharī line of Imams of whom several are known to have been murdered by the Abbasid authorities.

It is with the 'disappearance' of Muḥammad b. Ismāʿīl that later Ismaili writers begin their reckoning of the *dawr al-satr* or 'cycle of concealment,' during which there was little direct contact with their Imams. Although very little is known about the biographies of these early Ismaili Imams, there is a good deal of circumstantial evidence to show their active involvement in organising and directing the Ismaili *daʿwa*. According to the sources, Muḥammad b. Ismāʿīl is known to have despatched a number of his *dāʿīs* to preach in Khūzistān and surrounding areas of Persia in the name of the hidden Imam. But it was in the time of his son and successor, ʿAbd Allāh (also known as al-Wafī Aḥmad), that the *dāʿīs* began to achieve a measure of success. This appears to have aroused the hostility of local authorities and attempts by the Abbasids to have him arrested, causing the Imam to move to Iraq. Subsequently he migrated to Syria where, around 257/870, he settled in the town of Salamiyya. The choice of this small and relatively unknown location for his residence appears to have been determined by ʿAbd Allāh's need for anonymity and security in a place far from the major urban centres where the visits of his leading *dāʿīs* could not be easily noticed by the authorities. It was from here that ʿAbd Allah and his successors, Aḥmad (al-Taqī Muḥammad), al-Ḥusayn (Raḍī al-Dīn) and ʿAbd Allāh al-Mahdī (known as ʿUbayd Allāh in non-Ismaili sources), were able to establish the headquarters of the Ismaili *daʿwa*.[16]

Thus it was that in the second half of the 3rd/9th century the Ismaili *daʿwa* emerged in the Muslim world in its characteristic form of an organised movement of religious, political and social reform. From the few sources which have survived from this period of Ismaili history (such as the works of al-Sijistānī, Abū Ḥātim al-Rāzī and Jaʿfar b. Manṣūr al-Yaman) it is evident that the Ismaili *daʿwa* was consciously structured upon the paradigmatic image of a spiritual hierarchy (*ḥudūd al-dīn*) of angelic and human intermediaries (*wasāʾiṭ*) between God and humans.[17] Extending from the heavens to the mundane world, the *ḥudūd* consisted of parallel cosmic and terrestial hierarchies, acting in concert to fulfil the Word of God on earth. Each earthly rank (*ḥadd*), from the Prophet and Imam down to the chief *dāʿī*, was believed to be supported by their angelic counterparts in the celestial world.

Such was the vision of a universal, divinely-ordained mission, at once anchored in and transcending the passage of historical time, which the Ismaili *daʿwa* attempted to embody and translate into social reality. This it did principally by summoning people to the knowledge of God through the Imams and disseminating their teachings to the community of believers at large. This function is reflected in the terms used by the early Ismaili authors to designate their *daʿwa* as well as the community as a whole, such as *ahl al-daʿwa* (people of the mission), *al-daʿwa al-hādiya* (the rightly-guiding mission) and *daʿwat al-ḥaqq* (summons to truth) Apparently the term al-Ismāʿīliyya was seldom used by them and it rarely occurs in medieval Ismaili texts; nor did they employ names like Sabaʿiyya (Seveners) and Bāṭiniyya (Esotericists) by which they became known to the public at large. An important corollary of the spiritual mission of the early Ismaili *daʿwa* was the establishment of a stable and suitable environment for the Imam to come out of concealment as the head of an independent Islamic state. It was with a combination of these objectives that the earliest Ismaili *dāʿīs* were despatched to different locations on their proselytising missions.

We have little biographical data about the earliest Ismaili *dāʿīs* apart from their names and scanty details of their activities in the provinces, where they seemed to have concentrated on converting local populations, although sometimes they also targeted local rulers and princes receptive to their teachings.[18] The paucity of information may be because these *dāʿīs* operated secretly in Abbasid territories and the people they converted were obliged to practise *taqiyya* to avoid persecution by their opponents. It could also be, as Paul Walker has noted, 'because the *dāʿīs* in these regions never achieved any lasting political success and therefore little is known about the efforts of its non-literary members.'[19] However, there is more information on the *dāʿīs* who flourished in the latter part of the century when the Ismaili *daʿwa* was attracting widespread support in the Muslim world. Among the most notable of these men were Ḥamdān Qarmaṭ, ʿAbdān, Zikrawayh b. Mihrawayh, Abū Saʿīd al-Jannābī, ʿAlī b. Faḍl and Ibn al-Ḥawshab (Manṣūr al-Yaman). Through their energetic activities, the Ismaili *daʿwa* became well established in parts of Syria, Iraq, Persia, Baḥrayn and Yemen, as well as in regions as far apart geographically as Transoxania in Central Asia, Sind in north-western India and the Maghrib in North Africa. In those locations where the *dāʿīs* acquired a large enough following, they usually proceeded to establish a *dār al-hijra*, an 'abode of emigration' where they could be secure from their persecutors; but most of these fortified positions could not be sustained for long and had soon to be abandoned. In many of these areas, it seems that the *dāʿī* often became the effective head of his local community, exercising a considerable degree of political and juridical authority over it either directly or through his subordinates.

One of the few first-hand accounts of the operation of the early Ismaili *daʿwa* which has survived to our day is the *Kitāb al-ʿĀlim wa'l-ghulām* (*Book of the Master and the Disciple*) by Jaʿfar b. Manṣūr al-Yaman.[20] According to this work, which is composed in the form of a dramatic dialogue and based on the archetypal theme of a young man's quest for truth, the recruitment of a new member into the *daʿwa* was carefully planned, involving the development of a close personal bond between the *dāʿī* and his disciple, followed by graduated instruction in Ismaili doctrines and culminating in an initiation ceremony based on strict vows of loyalty and secrecy. The crucial aspect of this process was the commissioning of the young man by his senior *dāʿī* with the divine 'trust,' that is, the obligation of every member of the *daʿwa* to transmit the knowledge he has received to other people in his family, community and society. The entire dialogue indicates the primacy of the religious and pedagogic function of the Ismaili *daʿwa*. Compared with the task of inducting individuals into the path of esoteric Islam, the organisation's political ambitions represented an instrumental goal.

The *dawr al-satr* may thus be regarded as the formative period of the Ismaili *daʿwa* during which there was a gradual structuring and expansion of the organisation, resulting in the conversion of large numbers of people in different parts of the Muslim world to the Ismaili cause during the 3rd/9th and 4th/10th centuries. One of the factors which contributed to the popular appeal of the early Ismaili *daʿwa* was the expectation it promoted of the return of Muḥammad b. Ismāʿīl as the *mahdī* or *qāʾim* to liberate humanity from injustice and oppression. This message appears to have attracted a large following among socially deprived people in rural and urban areas, especially the bedouins, peasants and artisans whose economic conditions had deteriorated under the Abbasids. The Ismaili *daʿwa* was also supported by those sympathetic to the ʿAlids who harboured deep resentment against the Abbasids for repudiating the Shiʿism which they had originally espoused, and who now sought a more forceful assertion of their rights.

As noted, the socio-political programme of the Ismaili *daʿwa* was contingent on its spiritual message which offered the faithful access to the esoteric truths of religion via the mediation of their Imam, a symbolic hermeneutics (*taʾwīl*) of the Qurʾan and an ethical understanding of the prescriptions of the *sharīʿa*, together with diverse philosophical and cosmological speculations. In this respect, the teachings of the Ismaili *daʿwa* differed from the increasingly legalistic interpretation of faith espoused by the Sunni Abbasid state. The fact that the Ismaili message had considerable appeal to the more educated classes in urban areas too, is evident from the highly influential encyclopaedic work of philosophic, gnostic and mystical thought produced in the 4th/10th century, the *Rasāʾil Ikhwān al-Ṣafāʾ (Epistles of the Brethren of Purity)*, whose Ismaili inspiration, if not authorship, is well recognised in modern scholarship.[21]

The Advent of the Fatimid *Daʿwa*

The pivotal event in early Ismailism came around the year 286/899 when the head of the Ismaili *daʿwa*, ʿAbd Allāh (ʿUbayd Allāh), claimed the Imamate for himself as a descendant of Imam Jaʿfar al-Ṣādiq. According to him, it had become necessary in the past for himself and his forefathers to conceal their ʿAlid ancestry to avoid persecution by the authorities. By thus asserting his Imamate in his correspondence with various *dāʿīs*, shortly after having assumed the leadership of the Ismaili *daʿwa*, ʿAbd Allāh is said to have closed the cycle of concealment (*dawr al-satr*) and commenced a new historical cycle of manifestation (*dawr al-ẓuhūr*), during which the identity of the Ismaili Imams became publicly known to all their followers.

The assertion by ʿAbd Allāh of his Imamate was, however, not unanimously accepted by the rank and file of the Ismaili *daʿwa*. Coming after more than a century during which his predecessors had claimed to be the *ḥujja* or 'proof' of the hidden Imam, it precipitated an internal crisis in some sections of the *daʿwa*. Among the senior *dāʿī*s at least, their concerns appear to have centred around two principal issues: the legitimacy of ʿAbd Allāh's claim to the Imamate and its implications for their belief in the return of Muḥammad b. Ismāʿīl as the messianic *mahdī-qāʾim*, a doctrine to which the *daʿwa* had hitherto given unqualified acceptance.[22] The fact that the majority of the Ismaili *daʿwa* acknowledged the Imamate of ʿAbd Allāh suggests that his claim was supported by persuasive argument and evidence. Nonetheless, there was a minority who held fast to their belief in the imminent return of Muḥammad b. Ismāʿīl.

As is well known, this latter group seceded from the mainstream Ismaili community and came to be known as the Qarmaṭīs after one of their leaders, Ḥamdān Qarmaṭ. In the following years the Qarmaṭīs turned into a highly radicalised movement, launching a series of violent rebellions against the Abbasids in Iraq and Syria. The turbulence caused by these events soon became dangerous to ʿAbd Allāh's own security, causing him to flee Salamiyya in 289/902 shortly before the Qarmaṭīs sacked the town and killed his relatives. Accompanied by his son, Abu'l-Qāsim, and a small entourage of followers, ʿAbd Allāh took a westward course via Palestine and Egypt to the city of Sijilmāsa in the Maghrib (in present-day Morocco). There he settled down in the guise of a merchant, but was shortly afterwards arrested and imprisoned by the local Aghlabid authorities who ruled the region nominally for the Abbasids.

In spite of this setback, ʿAbd Allāh's decision to move to North Africa had been well calculated because it was in the Maghrib that the Ismaili *daʿwa* had achieved its most enduring success under the *dāʿī* Abū ʿAbd Allāh al-Shīʿī. Originally from Yemen, this *dāʿī* was sent by his superior Ibn Ḥawshab to the Maghrib in 280/893, where he was able to convert the Kutāma Berbers to the Ismaili cause in the name of the *mahdī*. Having won their support, Abū ʿAbd Allāh began a campaign of territorial expansion which culminated in 296/909 with his capture of the Aghlabid capital of Qayrawān (in present-day Tunisia) and the release of the Imam from prison in Sijilmāsa.[23] In the following year ʿAbd Allāh was officially proclaimed the first Imam-caliph of the Fatimid dynasty (named after Fāṭima, the Prophet's daughter married to the Imam ʿAlī). He also assumed the regal title of *al-Mahdī biʾllāh,* by which he is commonly known in history, and also conferred on his eldest son Abu'l-Qāsim the title of al-Qā'im bi Amr Allāh. By adopting these honorific names, al-Mahdī acknowledged the strong messianic and eschatological expectations associated with him. It was in these circumstances that the Fatimid state was founded and, in the course of the next sixty years, expanded into one of the major political powers in medieval Islam.[24]

Since the Fatimids derived their authority ultimately from their claim to be the Prophet's descendants and inheritors of his temporal and spiritual legacy, they regarded the revival and reunification of the Muslim world as an essential part of their mission. For this purpose it was necessary to have a powerful state as well as an active *daʿwa* capable of summoning people to their cause. The first three Fatimid Imam-caliphs, al-Mahdī (d. 322/934), al-Qāʾim (d. 334/946) and al-Manṣūr (d. 341/953), were preoccupied with consolidating their power, especially against the opposition of local Sunni and Khārijī populations, as well as attempts of the Abbasids, the Umayyads of Spain and the Byzantines to destabilise the Fatimid state. Furthermore, the Ismaili *daʿwa,* which had not yet recovered from the Qarmaṭī schism in the eastern part of the Muslim world, was further divided in the Maghrib by doctrinal disputes among the new converts recruited locally to its ranks. For these reasons, the early Fatimid Imam-caliphs decided to exercise strict control of the *daʿwa* and its activities,[25] and it was not until the reign of the Imam al-Muʿizz (d. 365/975) that a gradual revitalisation and reformation of the *daʿwa* began to take place.

A major factor in the revival of the Fatimid *daʿwa* was the articulation of Ismaili doctrines in a coherent and systematic form by al-Qāḍī al-Nuʿmān (d.363/974), the chief Fatimid *dāʿī,* theologian and judge. In his works, written under the guidance of al-Muʿizz, the Qāḍī undertook the task of formulating the principles of Ismaili Shiʿism in the context of the political realities and intellectual discourse of his time. Perhaps the most lasting contribution of al-Qāḍī al-Nuʿmān was his monumental work on Ismaili law, the *Daʿāʾim al-Islām* (*Pillars of Islam*),[26] in which he emphasised the legitimacy of the Fatimid dynasty and the validity of Ismailism as a Shiʿi *madhhab* ('persuasion' or school of religious law) in Islam. Basing his interpretations on the Qurʾan, Prophetic Traditions and the teachings of the early Shiʿi Imams, he advocated a balanced observation of the *ẓāhirī* (exoteric) and *bāṭinī* (esoteric) aspects of the faith. On the basis of these doctrinal formulations, the Qāḍī was authorised by the Imam al-Muʿizz to organise a regular programme of public education on Ismaili law and doctrines, as well as special lectures on esoteric teachings called *majālis al-ḥikma* (sessions of wisdom) which were held exclusively for Ismailis in the caliph's palace.[27]

The most decisive factor in the regeneration of the Ismaili *daʿwa* was the Fatimid occupation of Egypt in 358/969, which marked the emergence of local dynasty into a major political, economic and military power, and made it possible for the Fatimids to mount a serious challenge to the Abbasid dominance of the Muslim world. It was probably with this objective that the Imam al-Muʿizz embarked upon an ambitious programme of social, cultural and economic development, which included the founding of their new capital city of Cairo, al-Qāhira al-Muʿizziyya (the Victorious City of al-Muʿizz) with its great mosque of al-Azhar, the establishment of schools, colleges, libraries and hospitals, the building of roads and bridges, as well as expansion of trade. In order to avoid the religious and sectarian conflicts of the kind they had encountered in the Maghrib, the Fatimids sought to foster religious tolerance between the Muslim, Jewish and Christian communities of Egypt, as well as between the Sunni and Shiʿi Muslims. The Fatimids also adopted a generous policy of patronising the arts and the sciences, which encouraged scholars, poets and artists to come to Cairo. These reforms had in due course the effect of generating a level of material prosperity unprecedented since the Arab invasion of Egypt three centuries earlier, and transforming Cairo into one of the leading intellectual and cultural centres of the Muslim world. The increasing revenues of the state enabled the Fatimids to raise a powerful army and naval force to extend their territories eastward into Palestine, Syria and the Hijaz.

While the Fatimid policy of territorial expansion had to be necessarily based on strategic calculations of changing political, economic and military circumstances, it required of the dynasty, first and foremost, to win the hearts and minds of ordinary people to the Ismaili cause both within and outside its territories. Since the role of the *daʿwa* was obviously crucial to this process the Fatimid Imam-caliphs undertook a number of measures, among which the most far-reaching perhaps was the development of the *daʿwa* into one of the major public institutions of state, parallel to the administrative and military hierarchies. As was the case in the Maghrib, the chief *dāʿī* (given the title of *bāb*, 'gateway') held the position of the chief judge (*qāḍī al-quḍāt*), but now with the official responsibility of administering the state's religious and legal policies for all the communities of Muslims, Christians and Jews. The complexity of these tasks must have required a considerable reorientation in the attitudes of the *daʿwa* and the recruitment of a professional class of non-Ismaili jurists and Sunni *ʿulamāʾ*. The question of how and to what extent the Ismaili *daʿwa* was able to adapt itself into the role of a public institution and respond to the needs of a multi-faith society is an aspect of Fatimid history on which there has been little research to date.[28]

In addition to institutionalising the *daʿwa*, the Fatimids placed increasing emphasis on the training of Ismaili *dāʿīs* and public education more generally. In 378/988, the Imam al-ʿAzīz biʾllāh (d. 386/996) authorised the expansion of al-Azhar mosque into an educational centre for the study of a variety of religious sciences. In 396/1005 the Imam al-Ḥākim bi-Amr Allāh (d. 411/1021) established a separate institution, the Dar al-ʿIlm (House of Knowledge), one of whose main functions appears to have been the training of an elite cadre of *dāʿīs* with advanced knowledge of the 'non-religious sciences' such as philosophy, medicine, astronomy, mathematics and philology. A still more specialised and exclusive form of education for the Ismailis was conveyed through a revival of the *majālis al-ḥikma* which were held weekly in the Fatimid palaces. The sources also report other *majālis* organised specially for women, court officials and other audiences associated with the *daʿwa*.

Although there is little information on the curriculum content and scope of these training programmes for the *daʿwa*, it seems that a good proportion of the students who came to Cairo for advanced studies were recruited from different countries on the basis of their intellectual merit and commitment to the faith. The few years of their residence in Cairo constituted a period of intensive study and intellectual inquiries, after which the *dāʿīs* usually returned to their home countries to continue their mission. According to a unique Fatimid treatise on the *daʿwa* that has survived, *al-Risāla al-mūjaza* by the *dāʿī* Aḥmad al-Naysābūrī (or Nīshābūrī) who flourished towards the end of the 4th/10th century, the fully-trained *dāʿī* was supposed to possess a number of exceptional virtues and qualities, including the following:

> The *dāʿī* must combine in himself all the ideal qualities and talents which may separately be found in the people of different professions and standing. He must possess the good qualities of an expert lawyer (*faqīh*) because he must often act as a judge; he must possess patience (*ṣabr*), good theoretical education (*ʿilm*), intelligence, psychological insight, honesty, high moral character, sound judgement, etc. He must possess the virtues of leaders, such as a strong will, generosity, administrative talent, tact and tolerance. He must be in possession of the high qualities of the priest, because he has to lead the esoteric prayers of his followers. He must be irreproachably honest and reliable, because the most precious thing, the salvation of the souls of many people, is entrusted to him. He should be a real *mujāhid*, a warrior for the religious cause, in his heart, ready to sacrifice his life and everything for the religion.[29]

To what extent the academic programmes of the Fatimid *daʿwa* were actually modelled on this profile of the ideal *dāʿī* is difficult to say, but al-Naysābūrī's portrait captures vividly the intellectual, ethical and spiritual perspectives which informed the organisation and contributed to its success in many parts of the Muslim world. This first-hand report also stands in sharp contrast to the simplistic view of the Ismaili *dāʿī* often conveyed in Western scholarship as a 'propagandist,' 'political agent' or 'revolutionary' intent on subverting authorities everywhere – a retroactive image that appears to be inspired more by modern-day political movements than the realities of Muslim history. What is often overlooked in most studies is the profoundly intellectual and spiritual character of the Ismaili *daʿwa* whose primary concern was to invite people to seek knowledge and the salvation of their souls; nor is there adequate recognition of the internal function of the *daʿwa* within the Ismaili community as an institution of learning and scholarship. In fact, it is the Ismaili *daʿwa*'s emphasis on intellectual and spiritual accomplishments which accounts for the emergence of a number of highly learned jurists, theologians, philosophers and poets who made important contributions to Ismaili thought and various areas of Islamic culture more generally. Among the most prominent of these scholar-*dāʿīs* whose works have survived to epitomise Fatimid intellectual achievement, mention may be made of Jaʿfar b. Manṣūr al-Yaman (d.c.345/956), al-Qāḍī al-Nuʿmān (d.363/974), Abū Yaʿqūb al-Sijistānī (d.c.386/996), Ḥamīd al-Dīn al-Kirmānī (d.c.412/1021), al-Mu'ayyad fī'l-Dīn al-Shīrāzī (470/1078) and Nāṣir-i Khusraw (d.c. 465/1072).

It was also largely due to these Ismaili scholars that the spiritual hierarchy (*ḥudūd al-dīn*) of the *daʿwa* became fully elaborated in its theoretical form. The formal structure of the organisation in Egypt was a development of the early system of the pre-Fatimid era. As noted, the Ismaili *daʿwa* was conceived as a single, integrated order of ranks extending from the earth to the heavens, whose horizontal axis was represented by human personalities and its vertical axis by celestial beings. The entire system was symbolically correlated with the medieval cosmological scheme of spheres, stars and planets. In keeping with the *daʿwa*'s claim of continuing the prophetic mission, the *ḥudūd al-dīn* was headed upon the earthly plane in the current era of Islam by the Prophet Muḥammad as the *nāṭiq*, the law-announcing 'speaker' or messenger-prophet. He was followed by the Imam ʿAlī as *waṣī*, the Prophet's immediate successor, also designated as *ṣāmit*, 'the silent one' because of his esoteric function. The ranks of the *nāṭiq* and the *waṣī* corresponded upon the cosmological level of the *ḥudūd* with the Universal Intellect (*ʿaql*) and Soul (*nafs*). As was the case before, the Fatimid Imam-caliph was the absolute head of the *daʿwa* for his period of office and all senior appointments in the hierarchy had to be personally approved by him. Under the Imam was ranked the *dāʿī al-duʿāt*, the administrative head of the *daʿwa*, also referred to in Ismaili sources as the *bāb* (gateway) due to his proximity to the Imam. Although there is much variation in the sources regarding the number, designations and functions of different ranks in the hierarchy, the basic structure of the *ḥudūd al-dīn* can be summarised in a simplified form as follows from the *Rāḥat al-ʿaql* (*Peace of the Intellect*) of the Fatimid theologian and philosopher Ḥamīd al-Dīn al-Kirmānī.[30]

1. *Nāṭiq* – the messenger-prophet who inaugurates a new historical era with a religious law (*sharīʿa*); the proclaimer or enunciator of divine revelation (*tanzīl*) which he communicates to people in its *ẓāhir* (exoteric) form.
2. *Waṣī* – the Prophet's 'legatee' and successor, also designated as *asās* (the founder) and *ṣāmit* (the silent one); the fountainhead of *ta'wīl* (esoteric exegesis) and *bāṭin* (inner meaning) of the Prophetic revelation.
3. *Imām* – successor of the *waṣī* with spiritual and temporal authority over the community; the current Imam who has full knowledge of the exoteric and the esoteric aspects of faith.
4. *Bāb* – the 'gateway' to the Imam with the position of chief *dāʿī* (*dāʿī al-duʿāt*) in his capacity as the administrative head of the *daʿwa*;
5. *Ḥujja* – the 'proof' of the Imam, one of the twelve regional chiefs of the *daʿwa*; also called *naqīb*, *lāḥiq* or *yad* in early Ismaili literature.
6. *Dāʿī al-balāgh* – chief assistant to the *ḥujja*, responsible for communicating with the *daʿwa* headquarters in the Fatimid capital.
7. *Dāʿī al-muṭlaq* – the leading *dāʿī* in the field with full authority to initiate into the higher, esoteric, level of Ismaili doctrines.
8. *Dāʿī al-maḥṣūr* – assistant to the above with authority limited to initiate into the lower, exoteric, level of Ismaili doctrines.
9. *Maʿdhūn al-akbar* – the chief 'licentiate' with the duty of administering the oath of allegiance (*ʿahd* or *mīthāq*) to an initiate.

10. *Maʿdhūn al-maḥṣūr*– assistant to the above whose function was to invite individuals to the faith.

The initiatory, hierarchical and organisational character of the *daʿwa* should not mislead us to believe that it was an elitist institution set apart from ordinary members of the Ismaili community. All converts to the faith were required to be formally initiated into the *daʿwa* and take an oath of allegiance to the Imam of the time. By performing this solemn act, they were called *mustajīb* (literally 'respondent') or *muʾmin* (believer),[31] a status that did not represent a distinct rank of the hierarchy but which required total submission (*taslīm*) to the Imam and his *daʿwa*. In fact, for the vast majority of the Ismailis in different parts of the Muslim world, it was precisely through the vehicle of the *daʿwa* that they were able to confirm and perpetuate a spiritual bond with the Imam whom they were never likely to meet physically in person. In other words, the *daʿwa* personified and embodied the living presence of the Imam and his teachings. Thus, every Ismaili, from the humble peasant or householder to the most senior *dāʿī*, could count himself or herself as part of the *ahl al-daʿwa*.

At the administrative level, the operation of the Fatimid *daʿwa* appears to have organised its activities according to the division of the world into twelve regions or *jazāʾir* ('islands,' sing. *jazīra*). Each *jazīra* was headed by a *ḥujja* who, while, having considerable independence within his area of jurisdiction, was required to report to the *daʿwa* headquarters. S.M. Stern mentions regular correspondence and arrival of envoys in Cairo sent by *dāʿīs* in distant provinces, bringing with them contributions (*aʿmāl* or *qurbān*) collected from the community.[32] But in practice it is unlikely that *ḥujjas* were appointed for all the regions at any one time, since the fortunes of the Fatimid *daʿwa* prospered or declined in different areas according to local circumstances, and in some places its network was permanently uprooted.[33]

The long reign of nearly six decades by the Imam-caliph al-Mustanṣir bi'llāh, who came to the throne in 427/1036, marked a major watershed in the history of the Fatimid dynasty. In addition to the loss of Fatimid territories in the Maghrib, the Egyptian economy was devastated by a great famine that lasted for several years due to the low water level of the Nile. The most serious threat to the Fatimids, however, came from military rebellions and ethnic conflicts between various mercenary factions in the army comprised of Berbers, Turks, Daylamīs, Sudanese and Armenians, the majority of whom had no ties to the Ismaili faith. As a result of these upheavals, there was a significant increase in the power of the victorious Armenian troops led by Badr al-Jamālī who began to exercise undue influence over the military and civilian administrations, including interference in the affairs of the *daʿwa* itself. Although peace and prosperity were restored during the final two decades of al-Mustanṣir's reign, by the time he died in 487/1094 the new military commander, Badr's son al-Afḍal, had acquired sufficient power to determine al-Mustanṣir's succession by supporting his younger son, al-Mustaʿlī, instead of his eldest son and designated successor, Nizār. The latter fled the capital to Alexandria where he was proclaimed caliph with the title of al-Muṣṭafā li-Dīn Allāh, but after a short period he was captured and executed in Cairo. There are different versions of the events leading to this crisis, but its consequences were far-reaching for the Ismailis.[34] It precipitated a major schism between the followers of Nizār and al-Mustaʿlī, and split the *daʿwa* into rival factions adhering to different lines of Imams. It also dealt a severe blow to the authority of the Fatimid dynasty, reducing the Mustaʿlī caliphs in Cairo to figureheads under a succession of military dictators and contributing eventually to the collapse of the state in 567/1171, when Ṣalāḥ al-Dīn (Saladin) seized absolute power to establish the Ayyubid dynasty in Egypt and restored Sunni Islam as the official religion of state.

Chapter 3

The Nizārī Ismaili Daʿwa

The division of the Fatimid *daʿwa* between the Nizārīs and Mustaʿlīs had a profound effect in all regions where Ismailism had previously operated as a unified, centrally organised movement. Whereas most Ismailis in Egypt, Yemen, India and Syria accepted al-Mustaʿlī as the new Imam-caliph, in Persia, Iraq and parts of Syria the *daʿwa* upheld the succession of Nizār, and by so doing effectively terminated its relations with Cairo. From this time on, the Nizārī Ismailis began to operate their own independent *daʿwa* which, while retaining the original spiritual and political vision of the Fatimids, developed its own distinctive intellectual and literary traditions. It is the *daʿwa* of the Nizārī Ismailis, rather than the one of the Mustaʿlīs, which will concern us mainly in this chapter.[1]

Ḥasan-i Ṣabbāḥ and the Rise of the Nizārī Ismaili *Daʿwa*

Unlike the Mustaʿlī Ismailis of Egypt who were unable to free themselves from military dictatorship and internal factionalism, the Nizārīs succeeded in maintaining the cohesiveness and dynamism which the Fatimid *daʿwa* had attained before the death of the Imam-caliph al-Mustanṣir. To a large extent, this was due to the *dāʿī* Ḥasan-i Ṣabbāḥ, who occupies a singular place in Nizārī Ismaili history as the leading organiser of the Nizārī *daʿwa*. The main source on Ḥasan's life, the *Sargudhasht-i Sayyidnā* (*Biography of our Master*) has not survived, but some extracts of it are preserved in non-Ismaili sources, especially the histories of Juwaynī and Rashīd al-Dīn.

Born in the middle of the 5th/11th century to a Twelver Shiʿi family in Qumm, central Persia, Ḥasan acquired his early education in the neighbouring city of Rayy, which was then a major centre of Ismaili activity. At the age of seventeen he was converted to Ismaili Shiʿism and admitted to the Fatimid *daʿwa*. The young man's intelligence and talents quickly brought him to the notice of the chief *dāʿī* of the region, ʿAbd al-Malik b. ʿAṭṭāsh, who sent him in 469/1076 to Cairo where he spent three years during al-Mustanṣir's reign. The precise nature of Ḥasan's education and activities in Egypt are not clear, but it appears that his open support for the Imam's heir-apparent Nizār incurred the animosity of the military commander and vizier Badr al-Jamālī, who had him expelled from the country around 474/1081.

Upon returning to Persia, Ḥasan spent the next nine years travelling extensively in his capacity as a *dāʿī*, visiting centres of Ismaili population throughout the country which was then under the rule of the Saljūqs. A powerful dynasty of Turkish origin from Central Asia, the Saljūqs had seized power from the Būyids in Baghdad in 447/1055, together with effective control of the Abbasid caliphate. As staunch defenders of Sunni Islam, the Saljūq sultans sought to impose their version of Islam on all Muslims in their domains and persecuted the Shiʿis, especially the Ismailis, with unremitting energy. They also pursued an aggressive policy of war and polemics against the Fatimids of Egypt, later succeeding in expelling their forces from Syria and Palestine. In Persia, which the Saljūqs had occupied before entering Baghdad, the Turkish invaders were much detested for their oppressive rule, among both its Sunni and Shiʿi inhabitants.

Ḥasan-i Ṣabbāḥ's travels in this highly volatile political and religious environment convinced him that the Ismailis were dangerously exposed, which required the *daʿwa* to take urgent action to protect the community. For this reason he began to look for a strong, defensible position where he could establish a base for his operations. His choice fell upon Alamūt, a remote and nearly impregnable mountain-fortress in the Rūdbār region of

Daylam in northern Persia, held by forces loyal to the Saljūqs. After converting its garrison and the local population to the Ismaili cause, Ḥasan and a small number of his fellow *dāʿīs* seized Alamūt without bloodshed in 483/1090. The success of this bold venture provided the springboard for the Persian Ismailis in the following years to seize control of a large number of other strategically placed fortresses, towns and villages in the surrounding areas of Rūdbār as well as Quhistān in southern Khurāsān. The inability of local Saljūq leaders to stem this movement forced the Saljūq Sultan Malik Shāh to send a number of military expeditions against the Ismailis, which were largely unsuccessful. The Ismailis continued to reinforce and extend the areas under their control, thus creating in the space of a few years what amounted to an autonomous territorial state of their own, consisting of large and small fortresses scattered across parts of northern and eastern Persia within the Saljūq domain.

The Ismaili rising against the Saljūqs does not seem to have been a spontaneous event but a planned and co-ordinated movement masterminded by Ḥasan-i Ṣabbāḥ and his fellow *dāʿīs*, probably well in advance of the occupation of Alamūt. It is also possible that this policy had been approved at the time by the Fatimid *daʿwa* headquarters in Egypt. According to Nizārī sources, the line of their Imams did not terminate with the murder of Nizār but continued through one of his sons or grandsons whom his supporters had escorted out of Egypt to Persia. But his identity and whereabouts were apparently kept hidden from the public, possibly because of the Saljūq threat to the community. In the physical absence of the Imam, Ḥasan-i Ṣabbāḥ was recognised as his *ḥujja* or 'proof' and acting head of the Nizārī *daʿwa*. Thus began, in the Ismaili reckoning of their history, a new cycle of hidden Imams similar to the *dawr al-satr* in the pre-Fatimid period, with the *ḥujja* and the *daʿwa* becoming the crucial chain of links between the Imam and his followers.

In the course of the next two decades, Ḥasan-i Ṣabbāḥ continued with his policy of intensifying *daʿwa* activity and consolidating the Ismaili state in Daylamān and Quhistān, as well as extending its influence to the Khūzistān and Fārs provinces of Persia, as far as Iraq and Syria. In spite of many massacres of Ismaili populations in urban areas and the fall of some of their strongholds, such as Shāhdiz near Iṣfahān in 500/1107, the Nizārī *daʿwa* was undeterred in its quest for independence from Saljūq rule. It is estimated that at the height of their power, the Ismailis may have controlled nearly 200 castles and fortresses, as well as numerous towns and villages in surrounding areas.[2] Most of these strongholds were located strategically, some on massive rocky peaks rising high above a flat plateau, reinforced by massive walls, battlements, watchtowers, tunnels and other fortifications, rendering them extremely difficult to assault by mounted or infantry troops. The Ismailis also went to great lengths to make their citadels self-sufficient in food and water by building irrigation channels and underground water cisterns, thus enabling them to withstand prolonged sieges. In fact, the largest of these centres apart from Alamūt, such as Lamasar in Rūdbār, Girdkūh near Dāmghān and Qāʾin in Quhistān, became virtually self-contained fortified cities, each one representing a *dār al-hijra*, a place of refuge for Ismailis escaping from persecution and massacres in different parts of the country. The major fortresses also possessed well-equipped libraries to enable learning and scholarship to continue unimpeded by the upheavals of war and isolation from the rest of the world.

There can be little doubt that it was largely due to this extensive network of strongholds that the Ismailis were able to withstand repeated military offensives by a succession of Saljūq leaders over a long period of time. This remarkable achievement may also be accounted for by the outstanding leadership of Ḥasan-i Ṣabbāḥ and a number of other capable *dāʿīs*, such as Kiyā Buzurg-Ummīd, Ḥusayn Qāʾinī, Raʾīs Muẓaffar and Aḥmad b. ʿAṭṭāsh. Under their direction, the *daʿwa* operating at the local level was able to mobilise the Ismaili community into a powerful force of resistance against the Saljūqs with a strong sense of solidarity, purpose and sacrifice. Although we have no accounts of the immense organisational and logistical efforts involved in this process, it would not have been possible without a highly disciplined *daʿwa* organisation drawing upon the full human and material resources of a community united under a common cause.

To some extent, the success of the Ismailis was also due to the gradual weakening in the power of the Saljūq rulers, caused by dynastic and territorial disputes which broke out periodically among various Turkish princes and warlords, especially after the death of Sultan Malik Shāh in 465/1073. Another factor in favour of the Ismailis was the tacit support they received from various classes in Persian society who detested the Turkish Saljūqs as alien conquerors of their homeland.[3] The authority of the Saljūqs was further undermined by the Ismailis through assassination of some of their leading opponents in the administration and the military. It is not necessary to review the many myths and legends which arose in medieval Muslim and European worlds regarding this aspect of the Ismaili struggle, which Daftary has analysed at length.[4] Suffice it to note that the Ismailis used multiple strategies, military and diplomatic, as a means of deterring Saljūq leaders from their policy of exterminating the community. As a general rule, the Ismailis preferred a policy of diplomacy and negotiation with their opponents rather than all-out military confrontations.[5]

By the time Ḥasan-i Ṣabbāḥ died in 518/1124, he had succeeded in establishing an independent Ismaili state consisting of a network of strongholds scattered across Persia. A man of charismatic personality, intense piety, military genius and single-minded devotion to his cause, Ḥasan was able to organise the Nizārī *daʿwa* into a powerful force through strategies which have rarely been utilised so effectively before or after him. But his talents were not confined to military matters, for he was also an accomplished scholar, writer and poet, who composed a highly original treatise on the doctrine of *taʿlīm*, the authoritative knowledge of the Imam. Unfortunately Ḥasan's original text in Persian has survived only in a fragmentary form summarised in Arabic by the heresiographer ʿAbd al-Karīm al-Shahrastānī in his *Kitāb al-Milal wa'l-niḥal* (*Book of Religions and Sects*)[6] under the title of *al-Fuṣūl al-arbaʿa* (*Four Chapters*). Ḥasan's interpretation of *taʿlīm* formed the centrepiece of what al-Shahrastānī designated as *al-daʿwa al-jadīda* (the new teachings) of the Nizārī Ismailis, as distinct from *al-daʿwa al-qadīma* (the old teachings) of Fatimid times. However, Ḥasan was not introducing a new doctrine but reformulating an old Shiʿi precept that had been outlined by the early Shiʿi Imams. The widespread dissemination of Ḥasan's teachings is well attested to by the popular usage of the term 'Taʿlīmiyya' for the Persian Ismailis as well as the polemical response Ḥasan's teachings provoked from Sunni theologians, notably the famous Abū Ḥāmid Muḥammad al-Ghazālī who denounced the doctrine of *taʿlīm* as heretical in several of his treatises.[7]

Consolidation and Expansion of the *Daʿwa*

For the next forty years after Ḥasan-i Ṣabbāḥ's death, his policy of territorial expansion was continued by his successors at Alamūt. In addition to reinforcing their main positions in Rūdbār and Quhistān, the Ismailis managed to secure or build new strongholds at Manṣurā, Ṣaʿādatkūh, Maymūndiz and other places. The historian Rashīd al-Dīn reports that by the middle of the 6th/12th century, the Ismailis controlled many districts of Persia and Iraq, and had even extended their *daʿwa* activities into Georgia.[8]

It was probably due to this expansion of Ismaili influence as much as the weakening of their own authority that the Saljūq sultans appear to have eventually come to acknowledge the political reality of Ismaili territorial independence. The precarious balance of power between the protagonists resulted occasionally in their collaboration when it was mutually beneficial to both parties. Although such alliances between Saljūq and Ismaili officials had occurred previously at a local level during the time of Ḥasan-i Ṣabbāḥ, the Saljūq sultan Sanjar (d. 552/1157) now found it expedient to negotiate directly with the Ismaili leadership for assistance in dealing with their political rivals or common foes.[9] As a result, an unofficial truce prevailed between the two sides and there was a marked falling off in military offensives between them.

As noted in the previous chapter, the Fatimid *daʿwa* had been active in Syria from its earliest days. Not long after the Nizārī-Mustaʿlī split, the majority of Syrian Ismailis were won over to the Nizārī cause by the *dāʿīs* Abū Ṭāhir al-Ṣāʾigh and Bahrām, despatched from Alamūt in the first decade of the 6th/12th century.

They began their activities in the urban areas of Aleppo and Damascus, but following massacres of Ismaili populations in these cities instigated by the local Sunni *ʿulamāʾ*, the Syrian Ismailis too were forced, like their Persian co-religionists, to withdraw to the remote and mountainous areas of the country. By the middle of the century they managed to gain control of a number of fortresses, including Qadmūs and Maṣyāf, in the Jabal Bahrāʾ region of central Syria (known today as the Jabal Anṣāriyya), to create an autonomous territorial zone of their own. The Syrian *daʿwa* was directed by the headquarters in Alamūt, which appointed its leadership and also conveyed instructions to the Syrians from Alamūt.[10] A number of Syrian Ismailis are also known to have visited Alamūt where they received specialised training in the *daʿwa*.

The most prominent leader to emerge among the Syrian Ismailis in the latter part of the 6th/12th century was Rāshid al-Dīn Sinān, one of the most outstanding figures of the early Nizārī *daʿwa*. Formerly a schoolmaster from Baṣra, Sinān was recruited into the Nizārī *daʿwa* and sent to Alamūt for further training. Upon his appointment as head of the Syrian *daʿwa* soon after 557/1162, Sinān was confronted by the expansionist policies of the Zangid ruler of Aleppo, Nūr al-Dīn, and the Ayyubid general Ṣalāḥ al-Dīn, who were seeking to establish their hegemony over Syria, in addition to the increasing threat of the Crusaders encroaching upon the Syrian highlands from their positions in Jerusalem and Tripoli. By skilfully exploiting the hostilities between them, and through a mixture of diplomacy and war, Sinān was able to consolidate and extend the Ismaili state in Syria to the peak of its power.

In contrast to these political and military activities of the Nizārī Ismaili *daʿwa*, its organisational features and religious teachings are less well documented. As was the case in Fatimid times, the Nizārī *daʿwa* in Persia and Syria fulfilled multiple religious, legislative, administrative and military functions. There is some evidence to indicate that while Ḥasan-i Ṣabbāḥ and his successors retained the formal hierarchical structure of the Fatimid *daʿwa*, they reduced the number of ranks in its *ḥudūd*, probably to ensure a more direct chain of command and communication from Alamūt in a time of warfare. We also note the introduction of the terms *rafīq* (friend, companion or comrade) and *fidāʾī* (one who offers his life for a cause) to designate individuals of the *daʿwa* with specific functions related to the struggle.

As mentioned, while the hidden Imam continued to be recognised as the supreme head of the *daʿwa*, the leadership was exercised in his absence by Ḥasan-i Ṣabbāḥ and his successors. As the *ḥujja* of the Imam, they supervised the administration of the *daʿwa* and made all the major decisions and appointments. The command of the major fortresses and strongholds was usually exercised by a senior *dāʿī* (*dāʿī al-kabīr*), under whom operated a network of local *dāʿī*s in towns and villages, with a regular system of communication maintained between them. Among the senior *dāʿī*s, the one in Quhistān held the special status of *muḥtashim* (governor) with considerable personal authority, probably because of the large Ismaili presence in that province.

The Advent of the *Qiyāma*

The most important event for the Nizārī Ismailis of the Alamūt period was undoubtedly the re-appearance of their Imam and his declaration of *qiyāma* on the 17th of Ramaḍān 559/8 August 1164, the anniversary of the death of the first Shiʿi Imam ʿAlī. On this day, the fourth leader of the Nizārī state and *daʿwa*, Ḥasan (who is always referred to in Ismaili sources as Ḥasan *ʿalā dhikrihi'l-salām*, meaning 'on whose mention be peace'), met with representatives of the community summoned from different areas to Alamūt to convey a special message he had received from the hidden Imam. In the course of a symbolic ceremony held at the foot of the fortress, Ḥasan delivered a sermon in Arabic in which he announced the advent of the *qiyāma*, the long-awaited Day of Resurrection. A similar ceremony was held later at the fortress of Mu'minābād in Quhistān, where the same address was repeated with the additional claim that Ḥasan was the *khalīfat Allāh*, God's vicegerent on earth, a status reserved only for the Imams in Shiʿi theology, as well as being the *qāʾim-i qiyāmat* (Lord of the Resurrection).

The declaration of the *qiyāma* is one of the most obscure and misunderstood aspects of Ismaili history, partly because there are no contemporary accounts of it in Ismaili or non-Ismaili sources of the time. Much of the information we have about it is derived from highly hostile and prejudicial accounts given by Juwaynī and other anti-Ismaili authors writing nearly a century after the event. In spite of these shortcomings in the sources, most contemporary scholars, with a few notable exceptions,[11] have tended to reproduce their versions of the event in a more or less uncritical way.

The earliest Ismaili discussions of the *qiyāma* are preserved in literature produced in the final decades of the Alamūt period, but their understanding of the event seems to be derived from the time of Ḥasan's son and successor as Imam, Nūr al-Dīn Muḥammad, who interpreted and elaborated the spiritual meaning of his father's teachings.[12] In these sources, the *qiyāma* enunciated at Alamūt is presented as the conclusion of the preceding cycle of concealment (*satr*) and the dawn of a new era of manifestation (*kashf or ẓuhūr*). It was also interpreted as an existential event, signifying the rebirth of the soul from a state of ignorance and darkness to one of divine knowledge and illumination. This mystical state is not accessible to everyone, nor attainable solely by observing the outward forms of ritual worship, but requires the individual to pursue a more interiorised spiritual life and dedicated search for truth.

Even more crucial for the realisation of *qiyāma* is the spiritual mediation of the perfect 'man of God' (*mard-i khudā*), the locus (*maẓhar*) of the divine word (*kalima*) on earth, that is, the Imam of the time; for it is only through his intervention that the knowledge of God becomes possible. In this sense, the doctrine of *qiyāma* was a reassertion of the cardinal Shiʿi precept of the Imam as the intermediary between man and God, the recognition of whom is essential for the believers to achieve salvation. According to the Ismaili authors of this period, the essential function of the Imam is to inspire a regeneration of human souls from a state of potentiality to actuality, and from darkness to light. By recognising the Imam's inner spiritual reality, the believer is brought closer to the truth (*ḥaqīqa*). Such a soul can be said to have reached the state of *qiyāma*, attained salvation and admitted to the Garden of Paradise, even while he is physically present on the earth.

This multifaceted understanding of the *qiyāma* is further reflected in Ismaili sources through their classification of mankind into three categories according to the individual's status vis-à-vis the Imam of the time. The *ahl al-taḍādd* (people of opposition) are the vast majority of common people who are either ignorant of the existence of the Imam or stand in active opposition to him. The ordinary members of the Ismaili community constitute the *ahl al-tarattub* (people of gradation) who acknowledge and accept the Imam but do not as yet fully perceive his true spiritual reality. Finally, there are the *ahl al-waḥda* (people of union), those few individuals who have become one with the Imam spiritually and thus attained the stage of *qiyāma*. These spiritually advanced people represent the super-elite (*akhaṣṣ-i khāṣṣ*) of the Imam's followers, whose souls have been resurrected and tasted the fruits of Paradise.[13]

Community and *Daʿwa* in the Age of *Qiyāma*

It is probably significant that the *qiyāma* was announced just a few years after the death of the Sultan Sanjar in 552/1157 when the Saljūq empire was beginning to disintegrate and a number of independent principalities were emerging in the Persian world. But whatever sense of security and independence the Ismailis may have derived from this turn of events was short-lived, because they soon found themselves confronting new enemies with the rise of the Khwārazm-shāhs and the Ghūrids in eastern Persia. In their efforts to replace the Saljūqs as the dominant power, both dynasties launched offensives against the Ismailis in the Daylam and Quhistān regions.

The rapidly changing political situation in Persia was alarming as much for the Ismailis as the Abbasid caliph al-Nāṣir who was seeking to recover his own political and religious authority from the Saljūqs in Baghdad. As a result, he favoured a policy of forging a broad alliance of political and religious forces, including the Ismailis, under his leadership. As a result of the caliph's overtures to the Ismaili Imam Jalāl al-Dīn Ḥasan, who had succeeded his father Nūr al-Dīn Muḥammad in 607/1210, they seem to have negotiated an extraordinary peace agreement, according to which al-Nāṣir accepted Ismaili sovereignty over their lands and conceded further territory to them; in return the Ismailis apparently agreed to adopt the *sharīʿa* in its Sunni form.[14] This policy of accommodation had its obvious political and military advantages for both sides as it enabled them to resist their common enemies with a united front. For the Persian Ismailis, their outward confession of Sunnism did not represent the abandonment of their beliefs but simply another period of *satr* in their vision of cyclical history, requiring the community to observe its traditional practice of *taqiyya* in times of adverse circumstances.

The history of the Nizārī Ismailis in the first half of the 7th/13th century consists mainly of shifting alliances, evolving policies and intermittent warfare, which are fully narrated in the works of Hodgson and Daftary. The continuity and vitality of the Nizārī *daʿwa* during this time of relative stability is reflected in the Ismaili capture of a number of strongholds in Qūmis, Ṭārum and the Zagros mountains, as well as major advances in the Badakhshān region of Central Asia and the north-western parts of India, where large numbers were converted to Ismaili Islam.[15]

Contrary to the view of some scholars that the threefold classification of mankind mentioned above replaced the hierarchical structure of the Nizārī *daʿwa*, it is clear that the institution continued to flourish to the end of the Alamūt period, but in a reconfigurated form. This is evident from the works of the foremost Ismaili thinker and writer of the time, Naṣīr al-Dīn al-Ṭūsī (d. 672/1274). In his *Rawḍat al-taslīm* (*Paradise of Submission*), he enumerates a hierarchy of seven ranks: *mutaʿalim* (learner), *muʿallim* (teacher), *dāʿī*, *bāb-i bāṭin* (gate of the hidden), *zabān-i ʿilm* (tongue of knowledge), *ḥujjat-i aʿẓam* (greatest proof) and *dast-i qudrat* (hand of power).[16] There is some evidence that the *ḥujja* may have assumed a higher spiritual profile in the community because, as the Imam's chief *dāʿī*, he came to be regarded as belonging to the elite class of liberated souls.

During the final decades of the Alamūt period, there was a brief renaissance of Ismaili intellectual and literary activity that was inspired to a large extent by the doctrine of *qiyāma*. By far the most outstanding thinker of the Alamūt period was Naṣīr al-Dīn al-Ṭūsī, who composed a number of important treatises on Nizārī Ismaili doctrines. In addition to the *Rawḍat al-taslīm* mentioned above, there also exists his unique autobiographical essay, the *Sayr wa sulūk* (*Contemplation and Action*), in which he describes the course of his early education, his search for knowledge and truth, meetings with Ismaili *dāʿīs* and conversion to the Ismaili faith around 624/1227.[17] Following his admission to the *daʿwa*, al-Ṭūsī occupied himself for the next three decades with philosophical and scientific studies at the Ismaili stronghold of Qaʾīn in Quhistān and subsequently at Alamūt. Through these studies, al-Ṭūsī was able to emerge in the later years of his life as one of the great Muslim Shiʿi scholars of his time, making major contributions to the sciences of theology, philosophy, mathematics and astronomy. The intellectual life of the Ismailis was further stimulated by a number of non-Ismaili scholars who visited their fortresses from time to time, attracted by their libraries and the opportunities they offered for learning in a climate of intellectual freedom.

The apparent stability and culture of learning in the Ismaili state was, however, deceptive because from the early decades of the 7th/13th century, the Persian-speaking world was confronted by the looming threat of one of the most powerful and destructive forces ever to erupt in human history. Having already ravaged large parts of China and Central Asia, the Mongols were now making preparations to launch a major assault on the very heartlands of the Muslim world.

Chapter 4

The Mongol Catastrophe

From very early times, predating the rise of Islam, there has been a continuous movement of nomadic horsemen from the inner Asian steppes into the Persian-speaking world. But it was only with the arrival of the Saljūq Turks at the beginning of the 5th/11th century that they were able to establish dynastic rule over the region. Although these nomadic Turkmen were already Muslim at the time of their arrival, they came initially as 'marauders and plunderers,' compelled more by the need for new pastures for their animals than the cause of holy war.[1] But as we have seen in previous chapters, having established their political and military ascendancy over much of Persia, Iraq and Syria, and reduced the Abbasid caliphate to a nominal status under their protection, the Saljūqs later became staunch defenders of Sunni Islam and sought to impose it aggressively on all Muslims living in their territories.

The Mongols were a different breed of conquerors altogether: they had no affiliation to Islam nor did they seek to impose their own mixture of Shamanist and Buddhist beliefs on the Muslims; their political and military objectives were more far-reaching and the ferocity of their conquests unprecedented in history. The transformation of the Mongol tribes into a powerful, all-conquering force was mainly due to Chingiz Khān (d.625/1227), under whose leadership the Mongols carved out a vast Eurasian empire stretching from the Sea of Japan to the shores of the Caspian Sea and from the Volga plains of Russia to the river basin of Transoxania.

By 618/1221, Chingiz Khān had destroyed the empire of the Khwārazm-shāhs of Central Asia, capturing Bukhārā, Samarqand and Balkh, slaughtering their inhabitants *en masse* and reducing these once prosperous cities to ruin.[2] In the following years, the same terrible fate befell upon the cities of Marw and Nīshāpūr in the Khurāsān province of north-eastern Persia. The relentless advance of the Mongols was continued by Chingiz Khān's successors Ögedei, Güyük and Möngke who were determined to extend their control over the whole of western Asia. To this end, in 650/1252 Möngke despatched his brother Hülegü to spearhead the conquest of the Persian-speaking lands south and west of the Oxus river.

According to Rashīd al-Dīn, one of the first priorities of Hülegü was the destruction of Ismaili strongholds in northern and eastern Persia, followed by the suppression of the Kurds and Lurs in Iraq, and finally to secure the allegiance of the Abbasid Caliph al-Mustaʿṣim in Baghdad by force if necessary. Hülegü's instructions with regard to the Ismailis were later versified by a Persian chronicler:

> Overthrow Girdkūh and Lamasar;
> turn their heads down and their bodies up.
> Let there not remain in the world
> a single castle, not even one heap of earth.[3]

The Ismailis had recognised the danger of the Mongols from the early decades of the 7th/13th century when an increasing number of Muslim refugees sought refuge in their sanctuaries, fleeing from the Mongol incursions into Central Asia. In response to this threat, the Imam Jalāl al-Dīn Ḥasan sent emissaries to Chingiz Khān to express his goodwill as early as 616/1219.[4] Jalāl al-Dīn was, in fact, one of the first Muslim rulers to negotiate peaceful terms with the Great Khān and his overtures were probably responsible for the fact that the Mongols avoided attacking Ismaili positions during the first phase of their expansion westward from Transoxania to Ādharbāyjān and the Caucasus. In 635/1238, the Ismaili Imam and the Abbasid Caliph al-Mustanṣir sent a joint embassy to King Henry III of England and King Louis IX of France to seek an alliance of Christian and Muslim nations against the

Mongols.[5] These European nations were, however, in no mood to support the Muslims whom they mistrusted as much as they feared the Mongols. In 644/1246, the Imam Jalāl al-Dīn took another initiative for peace by despatching a mission on behalf of all Muslim leaders to the new Mongol overlord Güyük on the occasion of his enthronement ceremony in the Khangay mountains of Mongolia. But the appeals of this delegation, led by two senior Ismaili *dāʿīs*, the governors of Quhistān Shihāb al-Dīn and Shams al-Dīn, were rejected by the Khān. Rashīd al-Dīn reports that Güyük's animosity towards the Ismailis was provoked by complaints he had received from Mongol commanders as well as Sunni scholars at his court about their military and political activities.

Ismaili relations with the Mongols deteriorated further during the reign of Möngke whose suspicions of the Ismailis had been reinforced by a number of Sunni *ʿulamāʾ* at his court who desired their downfall. His resolve to take action against the Ismailis seems to have taken shape especially when the chief *qāḍī* of Qazwīn appeared before him wearing a coat of mail, explaining that he always wore armour under his clothing for fear of the 'heretics' of Alamūt. There were undoubtedly other, more strategic considerations which led Möngke to order Hülegü that the extermination of the Ismailis should be his first task in the invasion of Persia.[6] The initial encounter between the Ismailis and the Mongols occurred in 651/1253 when an advance guard under the command of Ket-Buqa seized several Ismaili strongholds in Quhistān, putting their inhabitants to the sword, before laying siege to the fortress of Girdkūh.[7] According to Ḥamd Allāh Mustawfī, some 12,000 Ismailis were killed in the town of Tūn alone on the orders of Hülegü.[8] In a final attempt to avert a full-scale Mongol onslaught, the Ismailis are known to have despatched a group of *fidāʾīs* to assassinate Möngke, as reported by the Franciscan friar William of Rubruck, who was in Mongolia at this time on a diplomatic mission for the King of France.[9] The failure of this attempt, if that was indeed the case, made it all but certain that the Mongol retribution upon the Ismailis would be uncompromising in its ferocity and ruthlessness.

The Destruction of the Ismaili State

It was in the year 654/1256 that Hülegü crossed the Oxus river into Khurāsān at the head of a large army converging from different directions on the Ismaili strongholds of Quhistān. When the Mongols captured Tūn once again, Hülegü ordered the slaughter of all its people, except for younger women and children.[10] This massacre had the intended effect of persuading the Ismaili governor of Quhistān, Shams al-Dīn, to surrender to the Mongol commander in person. It also led the Imam Rukn al-Dīn Khurshāh, who had succeeded his father 'Alā' al-Dīn in the previous year at the age of twenty-five and was residing at the fortress of Maymūndiz near Alamūt, to send his brother Shāhanshāh with a message of his submission to Hülegü. But this was not sufficient for the Mongol lord who demanded that Rukn al-Dīn surrender in person and instruct his followers to demolish all their fortresses in the country. There ensued a further series of inconclusive negotiations between them which exasperated Hülegü, causing him to execute many of the Ismaili envoys sent to him. Finally, in November 1256 Hülegü arrived before Maymūndiz and laid siege to the fortress, demanding Rukn al-Dīn's immediate submission. When the Imam still declined, the Mongols commenced battle by using mangonels and ballista to bombard the Ismaili defences with fire and stone.

As the fighting intensified, there was much debate taking place inside Maymūndiz among the senior *dā'īs* and advisers of Rukn al-Dīn Khurshāh about the best course of action, some calling for continued resistance while others counselling surrender on the terms set out by Hülegü. The latter group, led by the scholar Naṣīr al-Dīn al-Ṭūsī, eventually prevailed and the Imam came down from the fortress with his family, chief *dā'ī* and other officials to present himself before Hülegü. In spite of this, a section of the garrison refused to surrender and put up a fierce resistance against the Mongols for three days and nights until they were hunted down and killed. In accordance with the terms agreed with Hülegü, Rukn al-Dīn issued orders to his followers to destroy all their fortifications. As a result, a large number of Ismaili castles and fortresses were demolished by the occupants in the following days and weeks, with the exceptions of Lamasar and Maymūndiz where only some walls and turrets were destroyed. Shortly thereafter, the massive citadel of Alamūt too surrendered when the Mongols converged upon it, dismantling its walls and setting fire to its buildings. Juwaynī, who accompanied Hülegü throughout his campaign as his official historian and adviser, was able to visit the library of Alamūt before its destruction and recorded his impression in these memorable words:

> I went to examine the library from which I extracted whatever I found in the way of copies of the Qur'an and other choice books ... I likewise picked out the astronomical instruments such as *kursis* (part of an astrolabe), armillary spheres, complete and partial astrolabes, and others that were there. As for the remaining books, which related to their heresy and error, and were neither founded on tradition nor supported by reason, I burnt them all. And although the treasuries were copious (with) gold and silver goods without limit, I recited over them the words: 'O yellow, be yellow, and O white, be white,' and magnanimously shook my sleeve upon them.[11]

The only Ismaili stronghold to hold out successfully against the Mongols was Girdkūh, near Dāmghān, whose resistance was not overcome for another thirteen years until 669/1270 when its defenders succumbed to disease and want of clothing. The example of Girdkūh has led some scholars to speculate whether Rukn al-Dīn Khurshāh took the right decision in surrendering his major fortresses such as Alamūt and Maymūndiz. It has been observed and further confirmed by modern archaeological research that these strongholds were virtually impregnable and self-sustaining, with the resources to survive long periods of siege and warfare, as was demonstrated during the Ismaili struggle against the Saljūqs.[12] The ambiguous role of Naṣīr al-Dīn al-Ṭūsī in the Imam's decision to surrender has also come under critical scrutiny, especially in light of the fact that immediately after the fall of Maymūndiz and Alamūt, he disassociated himself from the Ismailis, joined Hülegü's personal entourage as a senior adviser and subsequently went on to become one of the leading officials of the Mongol Īl-Khānid state in Persia.[13]

Having thus achieved his first objective of destroying the power of the Ismailis and compelling the surrender of Rukn al-Dīn Khurshāh, Hülegü detained the Imam under house arrest at his encampment near Hamadān in order that all the remaining Ismaili fortresses would be destroyed. In the following year, the Imam requested to go to Mongolia to visit the Khān. When this was approved by Hülegü, Rukn al-Dīn set off in 1257 accompanied by nine companions and a guard of Mongol troops. But on arrival in Karakorum, Möngke refused to meet him because of the continuing resistance of the Ismailis of Girdkūh and Lamasar, and ordered his return to Persia. It was in the course of this return journey, as the party rested for the night in the Khangay mountains of northwestern Mongolia, that Rukn al-Dīn and his companions were taken away one by one and brutally murdered by their Mongol guards. In the words of Juwaynī: 'He and his followers were kicked to a pulp and then put to the sword, and of him and his stock no trace was left, and his kindred became but a tale on men's lips and a tradition in the world.'[14]

Both Rashīd al-Dīn and Juwaynī report that shortly afterwards, the Imam's family exiled in the northern Persian town of Qazwīn, was executed. The Mongols also killed all the Ismailis held in their custody and others in the vicinity of their fortresses.[15] In Quhistān, for instance, 12,000 men were gathered in large assemblies before being slaughtered. According to Juwaynī, 'they spared no one over ten years except for younger women,' which Rashīd al-Dīn corrects to read 'except artisans'.[16] Hodgson reports that 'The slave markets of Khurāsān were glutted with Ismā'īlī women and children, denied the privileges of Muslims.'[17] It is impossible to tell how many lost their lives in these atrocities which took place over a number of months or possibly years. Even though one has to be sceptical of the actual numbers of those killed as reported by Juwaynī and Rashīd al-Dīn, such brutality towards civilians was typical of the Mongol conduct throughout their conquests of Asia and Europe. It is reasonable to conclude that a large number of Ismailis, if not the major portion of the community, was indeed killed or driven into exile. The fact that these massacres violated Hülegü's agreement with the Ismailis was of no consequence for the Mongols because, according to Juwaynī's chilling testimony: 'It had been laid down in the original *yasa* of Chingiz Khān and also in the decree of Mengü Qa'an that none of these people should be spared, not even a babe in its cradle.'[18]

The Post-Alamūt Period

It was in these tragic circumstances that the Nizārī Ismailis of Persia, who had successfully challenged the military might of the Saljūqs, the Khwārazm-shāhs, the Ghūrids and diverse other opponents for 166 years, were overwhelmed by the world-conquering forces of the Mongol invaders within a matter of a few months. There is perhaps no better summation of the significance of the Ismaili struggle for sovereignty than Hodgson's remarks on the collapse of the Ismaili dream:

> That this handful of villagers and small townsmen, hopelessly outnumbered, should again and again reaffirm their passionate sense of grand destiny, reformulating it in every new historical circumstance with unfailing imagination, power and persistent courage – that they should be able to keep alive not only their own hopes but the answering fears and covert dreams of all the Islamic world for a century and a half – this in itself is an astonishing achievement.[19]

For the Mongol invaders of Persia, the extermination of the Ismailis was a small but necessary step to their goal of capturing Baghdad, which they achieved in 656/1258, subjecting the city to an unprecedented scale of devastation and slaughter, murdering the Caliph al-Mustaʿṣim and thus terminating the Abbasid dynasty. The Mongols subsequently advanced to conquer Syria, but their westward expansion was decisively checked in 658/1260 when they were defeated at the Battle of ʿAyn Jalut in Palestine by the Mamlūk armies of Egypt led by the Sultan al-Muẓaffar Quṭūz.[20]

The destruction of the Ismaili state in Persia was not an isolated phenomenon but part of a larger pattern of change that engulfed the Muslim world during the 7th/13th century. Nor was the destruction and bloodshed confined to the Ismailis but visited upon millions of other Muslims from the Central Asian steppes to the shores of the Mediterranean Sea. The consequences of these events have been debated for long by scholars of Islamic history, a discussion of which falls outside the purview of our study.[21] What is of particular relevance here is the lasting impact of the Mongol catastrophe on the Ismaili community as a whole and the Nizārīs of Persia in particular, who were never again able to exercise the same degree of political, intellectual and religious influence which they did in the preceding four or five centuries of Islam. Nonetheless and contrary to the reports of Muslim historians of this time, the Ismaili community was not altogether wiped out in Persia, nor was the Nizārī line of Imams terminated by the murder of Rukn al-Dīn Khurshāh and his family by the Mongols.

The few centuries after the fall of Alamūt are considered the darkest period in Ismaili history, primarily because of the paucity of historical data about the community during this long span of time. From the Ismaili perspective of their history, this period resembled that which followed the end of the Fatimid state in that there ensued in both cases the beginning of a cycle of concealment (*dawr al-satr*), during which the Ismailis had little direct contact with their Imams. The young son and successor of Rukn al-Dīn Khurshāh, by the name of Shams al-Dīn Muḥammad, is reported to have been concealed by a group of *dāʿīs* in a safe place before the Mongols occupied their fortresses, and was subsequently taken to Ādharbāyjān where the Ismaili *daʿwa* had been active for a long time.

As for the circumstances of Persian Ismailis who survived in the immediate aftermath of the Mongol conquest, the sources are equally meagre. Needless to say, the collapse of the Ismaili state and the murder of their Imam must have left these Ismailis demoralised and in a fragmented condition. As was the case with many other Persians of the time (including scholars and Sufis), a portion of the Ismaili survivors may have fled the country to seek a new life in Afghanistan, India or other neighbouring regions. Some may have found refuge in the Daylam region of northern Persia, while others remained in their own local areas. The displacement of the Ismailis was part of a large-scale migration of people moving from rural to urban areas in search of security and a better livelihood.

Given the repressive policies of both the Mongols and the Sunni *ʿulamāʾ* towards them, it became difficult for the Ismailis to profess their faith, forcing them to live in a clandestine manner by practising *taqiyya* and concealing their beliefs. To this end, many Ismailis may have adopted Sufism or integrated themselves within their local Sunni communities. As Daftary has pointed out, this practice is very likely to have resulted in the course of time in a complete absorption of the Ismailis in their host communities in many regions and the eventual loss of their Ismaili identity.[22]

All these factors may have contributed to a significant decline in Ismaili population, but large numbers of them appear to have survived in the Quhistān and Rūdbār regions. In fact, the Ismailis were sufficiently recovered within a few decades to make several attempts to recapture Alamūt; in 674/1275–76 they even managed to reoccupy the fortress briefly before being driven out by the Mongols. According to von Hammer, the people of Quhistān were still devoted to Ismailism seventy years after the fall of Alamūt, and that the Īl-Khānid ruler Abū Saʿīd (716/1316–736–1335), together with Shāh ʿAlī Sijistānī, the ruler of Quhistān, sent a team of Sunni *ʿulamāʾ* to Qāʾin to convert them.[23] Similarly, in Syria the Nizārī Ismailis continued to maintain their identity and the foundations of their *daʿwa*, in spite of coming under the rule of the Sunni Mamlūks. When the famous traveller Ibn Baṭṭuṭa passed through Syria in 726/1326, he reported that the Ismailis controlled several fortresses, which they were allowed to keep by the Mamlūk authorities.[24]

We also know that there was a major revival of the community in the latter part of the 9th/15th century when the Ismaili Imams re-emerged in Anjudān, central Persia. Under the more favourable rule of the pro-Shiʿi Ṣafawid dynasty (907–1135/1501–1722), the Ismaili Imams were able to reinvigorate their *daʿwa* in the region. Isfizārī observes that the Ismailis of Tūn, Nahārjān and Muʾminābād in Quhistān were sufficiently organised at this time to forward their religious dues to the Imams.[25] The Ismaili *daʿwa* also extended its activities in the eastern Islamic world, especially in Central Asia and the Indian subcontinent. In all these areas, however, the *daʿwa* had to adopt new patterns of organisation and propagation appropriate to local social and cultural conditions, which were in many ways different from that of the Alamūt period. Thus, whereas in Persian-speaking lands the *daʿwa* adopted a mode of operation which was akin to that of the Sufi *ṭarīqa*s, in north-western India it was led by peripatetic *pīr*s, preacher-saints and poet-singers in the tradition of Bhakti devotees.[26] The revival of the *daʿwa* was also accompanied by a renaissance of Ismaili literature in Persian and Indic languages.[27]

For scholars and students of Ismaili history, the post-Alamūt period of Ismailism in Persia presents many questions and problems, not least because of the paucity of source materials which has precluded any focused research to date on this obscure age of several centuries. The present study is intended to fill this gap in scholarship to some extent by investigating more closely the impact of the Mongol conquest on the Ismailis of north-eastern Persia and how this may have affected their *daʿwa* organisation. By so doing we shall also scrutinise some of the strategies the Ismailis may have used to maintain their beliefs and sense of identity as a distinctive Muslim community. Our primary point of reference will be the poet Nizārī Quhistānī, who lived in the years immediately after the fall of Alamūt and whose writings constitute the main source of information on the Ismailis of this period. It is to an examination of these and related issues that we now turn our attention in the second part of our study.

PART TWO

Nizārī Quhistānī: The Search for Meaning and Identity

Persia and Adjacent Regions in the 7th/13th Century

Chapter 5

The Poet Nizārī Quhistānī

The life of Nizārī Quhistānī was spent almost entirely under Mongol rule in Persia and he was witness to the enormous destruction caused by the Mongol invaders of his homeland, including the massacres of his own community of Ismailis. Nizārī was born in 645/1247 in the town of Bīrjand in the south-eastern part of the mountainous region of Quhistān in Khurāsān province, where he also received his early education. Later on, in the second half of the 7th/13th century, he appears to have achieved considerable poetic fame at the courts of the local rulers governing Khurāsān and Quhistān on behalf of the Mongols. But in the course of his career, he became increasingly dissatisfied with and critical of the policies of the ruling classes, which led eventually to his dismissal from service and exile in the countryside. Reduced to poverty, Nizārī lived the remainder of his life in obscurity, continuing to write until his death in 720/1320.

In spite of the outstanding quality of Nizārī's poetry, recognised by Persian and European scholars alike, his name seldom appears in biographies, histories and anthologies of Persian poetry and literature. This neglect may be partly due to the rarity of his poetical works, which did not become fully accessible to scholars until the last century. As a matter of fact, there is only one complete surviving copy of his collected works, the *Kulliyyāt*, which is now preserved in St. Petersburg.[1] According to Ivanow, the reason why Nizārī's poems were so little read and copied in Persia is because the depth of his thought and religious convictions are hidden behind a veil of Sufi symbolism whose meaning few could understand and the poems therefore did not appeal to everybody.[2] However, it is more likely that the political and religious climate of Nizārī's time, which was extremely hostile towards the Ismailis, discouraged the study and dissemination of his works. This antipathy is expressed, for instance, in the *Dīwān* of a minor poet, Kātibī (d. 838/1434–35) of Nīshāpūr or Turshīz, who advised his son to emulate famous poets like Firdawsī, Rūmī and 'Aṭṭār but not Nizārī who, he claimed, 'was unhappy till the end of his life because of his connection to the Imam.'[3] In spite of his criticism, we may consider Kātibī's mention of the Ismaili poet alongside the great Persian masters as an admission on his part of the exemplary quality of Nizārī's writings.

Who Was Nizārī Quhistānī?

The earliest references to Nizārī Quhistānī in Persian sources come more than a century after his death, when the Tīmurids displaced the Mongols as the rulers of greater Persia. The renewed interest in his works can possibly be explained by the emergence of Harāt as a centre of art and literature under the Tīmurid prince Bāysunghur (d. 837/1433), who was a generous patron of the arts and commissioned the copying of works by many poets and scholars working in his library.[4] By the turn of the century, especially under the reign of Bayqarā (d. 912/1506), Harāt became a centre for many Persian and Turkish poets, artists, architects and scholars. Among the most distinguished figures who settled in the city was the famous poet and mystic 'Abd al-Raḥmān Jāmī (d. 898/1492) who was the first major literary figure to recognise Nizārī's poetic skills by remarking that the poetry of Ḥāfiẓ, the master of the Persian lyric, is close in character to that of Nizārī Quhistānī. He added, however, that 'in the verse of Nizārī there is a lot of "fat and lean", but in the verse of Ḥāfiẓ there is less.'[5]

It is probable that one of these copies of Nizārī's works made in Harāt was acquired by the above-mentioned Kātibī in the same period. Although he seems to have had no doubt about Nizārī's religious convictions, the poet's identity was by no means clearly established in the literary circles of the time. Amīr Dawlatshāh (d.893/1488) in his famous anthology of poets, the *Tadhkirat al-shuʿarāʾ* (*Memoirs of the Poets*), discusses various views held among the scholars of Harāt on Nizārī, some claiming he was a Sufi and others that he was an Ismaili. Dawlatshāh also reports two theories on Nizārī's *takhalluṣ* (pen-name): the first, that he was so-called because of his lean build, ascribing the name to the Arabic word *nazr* or *nazīr*, meaning 'little' or 'insignificant'; the second, which was Dawlatshāh's own view, that the poet had adopted this *nom de plume* in honour of the Imam Nizār and was thus demonstrating his allegiance to the Ismaili faith. On the whole, Dawlatshāh is sympathetic towards Nizārī, whom he describes as 'a gentle-tempered man with great wisdom (*mard-i ḥakīm*), an adept in spiritual realities.'[6]

Another well-known Persian author who commented on Nizārī was the historian Muḥammad b. Khwāndshāh, better known as Mīrkhwānd (d. 903/1498), who spent most of his life in Harāt under the patronage of Mīr ʿAlī Shīr Navāʾī, the vizier of the Tīmurid ruler Bayqarā. He too discussed the poet's pen-name and subscribed to Dawlatshāh's view that it was derived from the Nizārī Ismaili Imam.[7] Mīrkhwānd's grandson, Ghiyāth al-Dīn Khwānd Amīr (d.942/1535–36), who served as a historian and biographer in the court of the Ṣafawid ruler Ismāʿīl, also endorsed the same theory.[8] But the fruitless nature of this line of inquiry was apparent to the geographer Amīn Aḥmad Rāzī, who argued in 1003/1594 that it is was not important whether Nizārī was an Ismaili or not, since he was one of the best representatives of Persian poetry.[9] Yet another Persian scholar to have to have examined Nizārī's poetry was the 11th/17th-century critic Luṭf ʿAlī Beg Ādhār who chose to discuss Nizārī's connection with Sufism rather than Ismailism.[10]

Given the nature of these speculations in the sources, it is not surprising that the question of Nizārī's religious persuasion has continued to be debated among modern scholars in Persian, European and American circles. Among the former, Mujtahid Zāda Bīrjandī, who wrote a biography of Nizārī with specimens of his verses, observes that opinion on the poet is divided between those claiming that he was a Twelver Shiʿi and the other insisting on his Ismaili identity. He is quite adamant that the latter group is incorrect because Nizārī's Ismaili expressions were written under duress. He argues that the poet was held against his will by the Ismailis of Quhistān and persuaded to write in favour of them, in the same way that the philosopher Nasīr al-Dīn al-Ṭūsī was alleged to have been held prisoner in their fortresses.[11] However, this view is flatly rejected by two other Persian scholars, ʿAlī Riḍā Mujtahid Zāda in his work on Nizārī and ʿAbbās Iqbāl in his survey of Persian poetry during the Mongol period, both concluding that the poet was of Ismaili persuasion.[12]

Although there is still some difference of opinion on the derivation of Nizārī's name, the general consensus among modern Iranian scholars is that Nizārī Quhistānī was definitely an Ismaili. This has been stated emphatically by Zabīḥ Allāh Ṣafā in his authoritative work on Persian literature, the *Taʾrīkh-i adabiyyāt dar Īrān*, where he asserts further, on the basis of some verses of the poet, that he came from a well-established aristocratic Ismaili family in Quhistān.[13] The case for Nizārī's noble ancestry is also supported by Maẓāhir Muṣaffā in his lengthy introduction to the first critical edition of the poet's *Dīwān*, produced by ʿAlī Riḍā Mujtahid Zāda in 1992.[14] The publication of this edition, together with Muṣaffā's detailed analysis of Nizārī's life, poetry and thought, has done much to revive interest in his poetry in Iran as well as the Western world.

The first Western scholar to take notice of Nizārī Quhistānī was the Austrian orientalist Joseph von Hammer-Purgstall who, in a short survey of Persian literature published in 1818, disagreed with Dawlatshāh's conclusion that the poet was an Ismaili.[15] In 1854, A. Sprenger discovered a manuscript of Nizārī's *Dīwān* in the Indian principality of Oudh and was, for the first time, able to give a concise description of this work, together with some biographical data about the poet. Like Amīn Aḥmad Rāzī, he too drew attention to Nizārī's poetic talents and maintained that one should not be concerned with his religious affiliations.[16] The next contribution to this debate was made by E.G. Browne, the author of the first comprehensive history in English of Persian literature, who was sufficiently impressed by a manuscript of Nizārī's poems in the British Museum to call him 'a genius comparable to the one great Isma'ili poet hitherto known, Nāṣir-i Khusraw.' He observed:

> That Nizārī of Quhistān belonged to the Ismā'īlī sect is not merely suggested by his pen-name and place of origin, but is asserted or hinted at by most of the biographers ... It was from him [Nizār], no doubt, that the poet took his *nom de guerre*, for the other suggestion, that it was derived from the Persian adjective *nizār* ('thin,' 'weak') is quite untenable.[17]

The most significant contributions to the study of Nizārī Quhistānī in Western scholarship have been made by scholars from the former Soviet Union in the early part of the 20th century, probably inspired in part by the poet's pointed criticism of the aristocratic and land-owning classes of his time. While these Russian studies on Nizārī have been by far the most substantial, they too addressed the issues of the poet's name and faith. Y.E. Bertel's, in the introduction to his 1926 edition of Nizārī's *Dastūr-nāma*, gives examples of the various views on his pen-name. He cites Nizārī's original name as Na'īm al-Dīn b. Jamāl al-Dīn,[18] which is incorrect since the poet refers to himself in the *Kulliyyāt* as Sa'd al-Dīn b. Shams al-Dīn b. Muḥammad.[19] On the poet's religious outlook, he says that while some verses appear to challenge Sunni orthodoxy, Nizārī was very cautious in expressing his beliefs so that his words could be related with equal ease to an Ismaili *dā'ī* or a Sufi *pīr*. Although Bertel's was convinced that Nizārī was neither one nor the other, he was unable to prove his point since he did not have access to the poet's other works. His judgement was sharply contradicted by Ivanow who, in his review of the *Dastūr-nāma*, dismissed the views of the 'young editor' by stating: 'Only someone uninformed about Ismaili studies could even consider that the *Dastūr-nāma* was not written by a follower of Ismailism.'[20] In his bibliographical work on Ismaili literature, Ivanow was to comment further:

> Works of Nizārī are very interesting for the student of Nizārī

> Ismailism because they come from the period from which we have almost no information. Therefore they well deserve a careful study by a properly equipped person. Unfortunately, so far they attracted only inexperienced beginners who knew nothing of Ismailism generally and Nizārī literature in particular.[21]

Ivanow's trenchant remarks may also have been directed at the Central Asian scholar, Chengiz G. Baradin, who offered several theories, old and new, to account for Nizārī's name. According to him, the poet may have acquired the name either from his family, or his connection with the Ismaili Imam, or it was a pseudonym given to him by his Kart patrons in Harāt because of his slender build. He also suggests, on the basis of some verses in Nizārī's *Kulliyyāt*, that there may have been a cousin of Nizārī with the same name in the Kart court where he enjoyed a high position with the title of Saʿd Akbar.[22] While this is confirmed by Muṣaffā, we find no other source with a reference to this individual.

The first major scholarly study of Nizārī Quhistānī and his writings was undertaken by the Central Asian scholar, Chengiz G. Baiburdi, whose book on the life and works of Nizārī is a foundation for any work on the poet.[23] After elucidating the views of various authors on Nizārī's religious beliefs, he concludes that it would be impossible to deny or overlook the poet's Ismaili tendencies. He too joined Bertel's and Ivanow in calling for a thorough investigation and analysis of Nizārī's poetry before any conclusions on this issue could be drawn.[24]

Another modern scholar to have given attention to Nizārī is Jan Rypka, the eminent Czech specialist on Persian literature, who describes him as 'one of the most remarkable Persian poets of the 13th and 14th centuries.' Rypka does not dwell on the poet's name but alludes to his interpretations of Qur'anic verses and what he terms 'external observances' which seem to indicate to him that the poet had definite leanings towards Ismailism.[25]

It may appear curious that the name and religious convictions of Nizārī Quhistānī have been the focus of so much discussion among medieval and modern scholars. But, as we shall note later, this was a matter of intense speculation even among the poet's contemporaries, to which he alludes in these lines:

Whatever everyone says about me,
  it is not about me but about themselves;
Nobody knows who I am,
  nobody knows where I am from,
Nobody knows where am I and who I am.[26]

To some extent, as Ivanow argued, this controversy about Nizārī's identity is a result of partial or superficial readings of his poetical works which did not become fully accessible to scholars until recent times. But the debate also reflects a genuine confusion on their part arising from the seeming contrariness and disparity of his poetic compositions. On the one hand, there are many lyrics in Nizārī's *Dīwān* which give the impression of a poet given to the celebration of wine, women and song in the conventional style of Persian court poetry. A number of the poet's *mathnawīs*, on the other hand, are characterised by their strong religious and mystical outlook, expressed through themes and motifs associated with Sufi poetry in the Sunni tradition. But there are other *mathnawīs* too where Nizārī's pro-Shiʿi sentiments comes through in their most pronounced form, such as the *Safar-nāma*, regarded as his most explicitly Ismaili poem, and the *Munāẓara'i shab wa rūz* which could have been written by a Twelver Shiʿi as much as an Ismaili poet. Another factor that has contributed to the mystery surrounding Nizārī's personality is the ambiguity and equivocality of his poetic style, which makes it very difficult to pin down his religious allegiance in a specifically denominational mould. It is possible, nonetheless, to perceive Nizārī's polymorphic writings fall within a clearly discernible pattern, determined by key events of his life and conditioned to a large extent by his attempts to survive in the cruel and chaotic world of the Mongol era.

Nizārī's Early Life and Education

In addition to the few biographical notices on Nizārī Quhistānī in Persian sources which are mainly concerned with the question of his religious persuasion, the only other source of information about the poet is his own corpus of writings where he makes occasional references about himself. By abstracting these bits and pieces of data and relating them to the political and social context of Nizārī's time, a broad, fairly credible profile of his life and poetic career may be constructed.

One of the few things we are more or less certain about Nizārī is that he was born in 645/1247 in the town of Bīrjand in Quhistān, a fact that is confirmed by Ḥamd Allāh Mustawfī, in a work finished in Qazwīn in 741/1340, some twenty years after the poet's death.[27] Prior to the Mongol invasion, Bīrjand was a minor commercial centre on the routes linking Nīshāpūr to the north, Harāt to the north-east, Kirmān to the south-west and Sīstān to the south-east; according to Yāqūt, it was the most beautiful city of Quhistān.[28] Bīrjand was also an important centre of Ismaili population at this time, with a large number of their fortresses in the surrounding area, including the major strongholds of Mu'mināBād, Qā'in and Tūn.

Rypka reports that Nizārī came of an old but impoverished family of the landed aristocracy,[29] but his childhood was by no means poverty-stricken as he admits in this verse recalling his early years:

> I had a small good and fresh garden;
> I thought that there was no (other) garden to compare.
> On its lawn there was a cypress tree, flowers
>   and a redbud (*arghawān*) tree.
> The slope on the banks of the flowing water
> Was high, with mulberries, grapes and fruit,
> With quince, plums, apples and pomegranates.
> Besides that there was a field and farm
> Which was my right by inheritance.
> (It consisted of) a view, balcony and cloistered hallway,
>   a private room, bathroom and other such places.[30]

As noted in the previous chapter, when the Mongols advanced into Persia in the middle of the 7th/13th century, they had already conquered Transoxania and devastated large parts of Khurāsān and Sīstān. Hülegü, the commander of the invading force, concentrated his assault initially upon the Ismailis of Quhistān and Rūdbār in Daylam, seizing their towns and fortresses, slaughtering their inhabitants and laying waste to their lands.

Within a few months, a large number of Ismailis lost their lives or were forced to migrate and the Ismaili Imam, Rukn al-Dīn Khurshāh, was murdered by the Mongols. Nizārī's family were among those Ismailis who survived the invasion, probably because their estate lay outside the town of Bīrjand, but not without losing much of their land and property in the upheaval. This is alluded to by Nizārī in the following lines written after his father's death in which he also mentions his sibling, a brother about whom we have no further information.[31]

I have one brother; I am one, he another;
I say in life he is poor like me,
He does not have any income,
He has no savings, not even one dinār.[32]

All these events must have left an indelible mark in the mind of the young Nizārī, who was around six or seven years old when the first Mongol incursions in Quhistān took place in 651/1253; but for reasons we can only guess, he makes few references to this period of his life. What can be gleaned from his writings are a few scattered details about his upbringing and education, much of which could only have happened after the waves of Mongol invasions had subsided and some semblance of order and security had been restored in Quhistān. Nizārī's father sent him to the local *maktab* (school) in Bīrjand where he probably also learnt some Arabic and memorised parts of the Qur'an. It was apparently at this time that Nizārī's poetic talents began to be displayed in an unusual manner, sometimes appearing as fully-formed verses in his dreams. The persistence of these dreams appears to have persuaded both father and son to believe that he was destined to be a famous poet, a premonition that was subsequently confirmed by a local soothsayer and diviner of dreams:

I remember (my father) telling me when I was young that
  I had one question which I put to the learned one:
'O *khwāja*, if you know the secret of the dream,
  please tell me the answer.
I compose so much poetry during my dreams,
  but when I wake up I cannot repeat it.'
The learned teacher said: 'If you listen to me,

I will give you some good news, news of pure success.
Your son will become a famous poet in the world.
Pearls will come out of his breast like a bunch of grapes.'
This poetry is not acquired; when I was born
I brought it with me.
This heavy treasure was generated in my ruined body.[33]

It is evident from Nizārī's verses that he was especially attached to his father, Shams al-Dīn, a man of wide learning and lover of poetry, who had the greatest influence on his son's intellectual and religious formation. The poet acknowledges this fact and expresses gratitude to his father in the following words:

O God, grant my father a long and happy life,
Whose generosity has done so much for me.
What is a greater right than following the Prophet's
family (*ahl al-bayt*)?
My father convinced me of the proof of Imamate.
If my father had not made me witness this,
What kind of *qiyāma* would have occurred if I had not
recognised (this) before my death!
Even if I could not fulfil my obligations towards my father,
He fulfilled all the obligations of fatherhood.[34]

Determined to provide his son with a sound education, Nizārī's father later sent him to a local *madrasa*, but the poet does not mention the name of this college nor the *madhhab* to which it belonged. Since there is no evidence of a prominent *madrasa* in Bīrjand at this time, it is possible that he attended the one in the nearby town of Qā'in.[35] We can assume from Nizārī's recollection of his experience that it was a Sunni establishment for which the young man had little affection:

My time was lost in the wind
With a troop of ignorant people,
In whom at no time did I find
A least bit of manliness or humanity:
One group devoid of reason (*'aql*) and wisdom (*khirad*),
Another group that lied like foolish folk.
All are enemies of the family of the Chosen (Prophet).
Sometimes they claimed to be Muslims.

I repented (slapped my wrists) and shouted out:
'Woe is me, how excellent is repentance!'[36]

These observations indicate that Nizārī's early schooling could not have been the source of his knowledge of the religious and intellectual sciences which he was later to demonstrate in his works (on account of which he earned the sobriquet of *ḥakīm*, 'the sage' or 'the scholar'). It was probably a few years later, under the personal guidance of his father or through a private tutor, that he became familiar with the classics of Persian and Arabic literature.[37] He became well acquainted with the poetry of Firdawsī (d.411/1020), 'Umar-i Khayyām (d. ca. 517/1123) and Niẓāmī (d. ca. 600/1203), and his works are scattered with aphorisms of Sufi saints and poets like Sanā'ī (d. ca. 525/1131) and Farīd al-Dīn 'Aṭṭār (d. 627/1230). According to Muṣaffā, the poet who had the greatest influence on Nizārī was Sa'dī (d. 691/1292).[38] Baradin says that Nizārī also learnt some Turkish during this time, although he was apparently not fond of that language.[39] In addition to the poets, he took great interest in the various schools of Islamic law and theology, and studied the works of Muslim philosophers such as al-Fārābī (d. 339/950) and Ibn Sīnā (d. 428/1037).[40] Referring to the diversity of views and interpretations he encountered in his study of the scholars, he was later to comment:

One group has taken the way of philosophers,
Another group the *madhhab* of the Mu'tazila.
All in all, each one has their own *madhhab*,
They have put a division between each other,
Their deficiencies have resulted in extreme separation,
They have gone beyond what is the due
administration of justice.[41]

There is little doubt that Nizārī's extensive knowledge of Ismaili thought and literature was also acquired in the years before he reached his maturity. According to Bertel's, the poet undertook detailed studies of Ismaili thinkers such as Abū Ya'qūb al-Sijistānī, Ḥamīd al-Dīn al-Kirmānī and Nāṣir-i Khusraw as well as Naṣīr al-Dīn al-Ṭūsī.[42] This is quite evident from Nizārī's verses where there are many allusions to the writings of these *dāʿīs*, especially the Persian works of the last two. Nizārī's father was almost certainly instrumental in encouraging his son to read the Ismaili texts, but the young man is more likely to have received a part of this education from one or more of the Ismaili *dāʿīs* who survived the Mongol debacle. It is possible that a rudimentary form of the *daʿwa* continued to exist in Quhistān as it did in Rūdbār for several years under Mongol rule, and was attempting to rehabilitate itself through secret teaching and recruitment; in these circumstances, the young Nizārī could very well have been initiated into Ismaili doctrines by the *daʿwa*. Indeed, the poet alludes to this phase of his education by referring to himself as a *mustajīb*, that is, a 'respondent' or believer who has heard the 'call' of the *daʿwa*:

> My teacher is he who teaches the book of love;
> In vain they blamed the instructor.
> Submit (*taslīm*) to love like Nizārī; do not be
> (one of those) who opposes.
> Breaking faith with the teacher is not for a *mustajīb*.[43]

Nizārī's Career in Harāt

The poetic career of Nizārī Quhistānī was shaped to a large extent by the political and economic circumstances of north-eastern Persia in the second half of the 7th/13th century. There are many aspects of Nizārī's life and poetry whose significance become clear only in relation to the politics of the of the Īl-Khānid government in Persia, and in particular the struggle between the local rulers (*maliks*), the Karts of Khurāsān and the Mihrabānids of Sīstān for political dominance in Quhistān.

From the time of the Arab occupation of Persia, the term 'Khurāsān' was applied to a large, ill-defined, Persian-speaking region stretching from Transoxania in Central Asia, across the north-western part of present-day Afghanistan, to Quhistān and Sīstān in eastern Persia. Prior to the Mongol irruption, Khurāsān was one of the most prosperous agricultural regions of Persia. Its cities of Bukhārā, Samarqand, Nīshāpūr, Balkh and Harāt were among the major commercial and cultural centres of the medieval

Islamic world. Being the first Persian region to be conquered by Chingiz Khān and Hülegü, Khurāsān felt the full force of the Mongol onslaught. The ferocity and destruction of these incursions brought about the social and economic ruin of the entire region, many parts of which have never recovered to this day the level of prosperity they had attained earlier. Al-Harawī, citing eyewitness accounts of these times a century later, relates that there was 'neither people, nor corn, nor food, nor clothing' to be found in many places, and that the few survivors of the Mongol siege of Harāt were reduced to eating animal and human corpses.[44] Quhistān, in particular, lost its regional importance and was henceforth little documented by Persian authors for several centuries.[45]

After Chingiz Khān's death in 625/1227, serious rifts appeared among various members of the ruling Mongol family, especially regarding the distribution of *ulus* (appendages) in the conquered territories. These differences became pronounced under Hülegü's descendants, resulting in a division of their empire into a number of khanates or fiefdoms. The first Mongol state to emerge in Muslim territories was the Chaghatay Khanate in the Syr and Oxus region of Central Asia. The Īl-Khānids ruled over much of Persia and Iraq with their capital at Marāghah and later in Tabrīz in Ādharbāyjān, while the 'Golden Horde' dominated Russia and the Volga basin. These states owed their allegiance to the Great Khans in Mongolia and China, but in the course of time they became rivals of each other. The Mongols generally governed their territories through local rulers who were granted a *yarligh* or decree, which allowed them much autonomy in the areas under their jurisdiction, as long as they acknowledged the authority of the Mongols and paid tribute to them. In the Persian domains of the Īl-Khānids, this policy usually favoured their Mongol-Turkish military elite, together with the local feudal aristocracy of Persian landlords who collaborated with them. This coalition became a powerful ruling class who dominated political and cultural life in many parts of Persia, and some of them went on to found their own semi-independent dynasties under the hegemony of the Mongols.

It was in these circumstances that in 643/1245 a local feudal baron of Afghan origin by the name of Shams al-Dīn Kart (643–676/1245–1277)[46] first emerged as the Malik of Harāt. In 649/1251, he joined forces with Möngke at the height of the latter's struggle for power to succeed Chingiz Khān.[47] In reward for his service, the Great Khan granted a *yarligh* to Shams al-Dīn Kart, with sovereignty over Harāt, Balkh and the country lying between these areas and the Indian frontier, together with a grant of 60,000 dinars.[48] Möngke later extended Shams al-Dīn Kart's authority in Khurāsān to include Sīstān, replacing the local ruler Shams al-Dīn ʿAlī b. Masʿūd of the Mihrabānid dynasty.[49] The Kart ruler then spent the next few decades attempting to secure his power in Khurāsān and waging war against his rivals, especially the Mihrabānid Naṣīr al-Dīn Muḥammad b. Abū Fatḥ Masʿūd (653–718/1255–1318), also known as Naṣīr al-Dīn Sijistānī, who was a nephew of Shams al-Dīn ʿAlī. Although Naṣīr al-Dīn latter succeeded in persuading Hülegü to restore Sīstān to his family, the bitter struggle between the two dynasties continued unabated, with each side seeking supremacy over the other.

On the whole, Shams al-Dīn Kart's reign was characterised by his efforts to assert and extend his authority in Khurāsān on the one hand, and to avoid becoming entangled in the constant internal quarrels of the ruling Mongols on the other. But this proved impossible in the conflict between Hülegü's son and successor, Abaqa Khān, and Baraq, the ruler of the Chaghatay Khanate, who had encroached on Īl-Khānid territory.[50] Shams al-Dīn Kart was placed in the difficult position of choosing between the two powerful Mongol overlords, neither of whom he could afford to offend. According to Howorth, Shams al-Dīn's enemies at the court conspired against him, making Abaqa suspicious of his loyalties.[51] It was possibly as a result of these political intrigues that Shams al-Dīn met his end in 676/1278 after eating a poisoned watermelon given to him at court.[52] When Abaqa went to Harāt in the following year, he appointed Shams al-Dīn's son Rukn al-Dīn as the next *malik*. Rukn al-Dīn (also known as Shams al-Dīn II), who was then in the Īl-Khānid army stationed at Darband in Ādharbāyjān, took office in Harāt briefly; but in 1282/1865 he retired to Khaysār leaving his son ʿAlāʾ al-Dīn in Harāt. When he too left the city, Rukn al-Dīn was persuaded by Amīr Nawrūz, commander-in-chief of the Īl-Khānid ruler Ghāzān, to concede control to another son, Fakhr al-Dīn, who took over the Kart leadership in 695/1295.

Nizārī Quhistānī arrived in Harāt probably around 669/1270, when he was in his early twenties, to serve in the administration of Shams al-Dīn Kart. The destitute state to which Nizārī's family was reduced after the Mongol conquest is very likely to have been one of the factors that led him to this move; moreover, the young man's education and learning were sufficiently advanced to qualify him for government service. At the time when Nizārī arrived in Harāt, the city was being rebuilt, its crafts and industry revived, and it was once again becoming a centre of culture, attracting poets and scholars from surrounding areas. This environment presented a good opportunity to the young Ismaili poet from Quhistān to advance his education and career. Although the Kart rulers were Sunni, they were not averse to employing educated Shiʿi men in their administration. Moreover, if Nizārī had a cousin called Saʿd Akbar with a high position in the Kart court, as suggested by Baradin, he might have been helpful to the poet in procuring his position in government service.

But it is quite possible that had the circumstances of Nizārī's life and times been different, he would have preferred to devote his knowledge and skills in the service of the Ismaili cause. As noted above, Nizārī had grown up with a strong attachment to Ismaili Shiʿism and was already recruited into the Ismaili *daʿwa.* Historically, the Ismaili *daʿwa* was never confined to missionary activities alone, but also served as an educational institution providing young and talented Ismailis with the opportunity to study and attain a high level of intellectual accomplishment. The normal case for Nizārī would have been to follow the example of his illustrious forebear from Khurāsān, Nāṣir-i Khusraw, by developing his intellectual and poetic skills through the aegis of the Ismaili *daʿwa.* But this course of action was rendered difficult, if not impossible, with the Mongol destruction of Ismaili power in Persia.

According to Baiburdi, Nizārī was initially employed in the service of the Mongol military ruler of Quhistān, Toghan (Tuga

Khān),[53] but Baradin maintains that he enlisted in the administration of Shams al-Dīn Kart while still in his youth. He mentions further that Nizārī's original intention was to go into the army, but the Shah would not allow it.[54] Under Īl-Khānid rule, the military establishment was dominated by Turks, whereas the fiscal administration was commonly composed of local people proficient in the Persian language.[55] Nizārī therefore served as a official in the *dīwān-i istifā-i mamālik*, the department responsible for tax collection and financial affairs. Rypka suggests that Nizārī was recruited by the Shah in two capacities, that of a tax collector (*muḥaṣṣil*) as well as a court poet.[56] This may have been the case, since it was not uncommon in medieval Persia for aspiring poets to work for local rulers in an administrative capacity while at the same time eulogising their patrons. On the other hand, as far as we know, when Nizārī arrived in Harāt he had no literary reputation to boast of which could have warranted his appointment as the Shah's panegyrist. Although there are many *qaṣīda*s, *ghazal*s and other shorter poems in Nizārī's *Dīwān*[57] which can be traced to his Harāt period, it cannot be denied that all his major compositions, including the *mathnawī*s, were composed after 680/1281 when he ceased to work for the Karts and returned to Bīrjand.

Thus, it appears that Nizārī's initial appointment in Harāt was that of a bureaucrat in the Kart chancellery and his entry into the courtly circles of Harāt is likely to have materialised only after several years of poetic experimentation, during which he perfected his style and acquired some fame in the city. In common with many contemporary poets who turned to the local Turkish-Mongol dynasties for patronage, Nizārī must have seen his access to the Kart court as an ideal opportunity for promoting his poetic career and material prosperity. Needless to say, the poet could not have gained entry into the Sunni-dominated court of the Karts without successfully concealing his Ismaili identity and associating himself with the luxurious and self-indulgent life-style of the ruling class in Harāt. Among other things, he was obliged to compose *qaṣīda*s in praise of his patron, the Malik Shams al-Dīn Kart. Many of Nizārī's *ghazal*s in celebration of wine, women and song which are found in his *Dīwān* may have originated during this period, but there also others in the collection with a distinctive mystical outlook, suggesting the poet's increasing interest in the spiritual life at the same time.

In the course of his administrative duties, Nizārī was required to travel frequently in Quhistān, Sīstān, Rayy and other parts of Khurāsān, in the course of which he became acutely aware of the disastrous effects of the taxation regime imposed by the Mongols upon the people in rural areas. He reports seeing many deserted villages and estates abandoned by their inhabitants because of their inability to meet the demands of the tax-collectors or landlords. In a typical event, he describes how a village elder, unable to pay his tax because of the ruin of his village, received two hundred blows with a stick until he surrendered his wine jars to the tax collector.[58] Nizārī's testimony has been corroborated by a number of recent studies on the Persian economy under Mongol rule. According to Petrushevsky, the fiscal policy of the Īl-Khāns was 'a monstrous and self-contradictory combination of methods,' characterised by the imposition of heavy taxes, arbitrary exactions and widespread malpractices, including forced labour or confiscation of property for those unable to pay.[59] These iniquities were exacerbated by gross abuse of the of the tax-farming system (*iqṭāʿ*) which permitted the Turkish military aristocracy, local Persian landlords and government officials to demand extortionate rents for state-owned lands in their possession. The burden of these taxes and rents fell largely upon the *raʿiyyat*, the taxable population of peasants and town-dwellers whose lives, already impoverished by war and famine, became so intolerable that there was a regular mass exodus of people fleeing their homes and lands in fear of the tax-collectors.

From the evidence of Nizārī's writings, it is clear that he faced many moments when his moral conscience rebelled against this harsh and punitive system of fiscal administration, and his own culpability in sustaining it on behalf of the Karts and their Mongol masters. There can be little doubt that Nizārī's first-hand witness to the immense suffering of ordinary people was instrumental in the formation of his critical social outlook, which he was later to express in his poetry, as well his increasing alienation from the Kart dynasty. Nizārī's discontent was aggravated further by the sharp contrast between the misery of people in the rural areas and the luxury and frivolity of his own life in Harāt. 'O God,' he complains at one point during his travels, 'how long will You make me run around the world for subsistence?'[60]

It was against this growing sense of moral disquiet and self-disgust that Nizārī undertook his most prolonged journey from Quhistān to the Caucasus region in the year 679/1280. Although the poet has recorded his experience of this two-year journey in his versified *Safar-nāma*, the precise nature of his activities and the significance of the events he narrates in this *mathnawī* are by no means clear. In Chapter 7 we shall examine Nizārī's journey in some detail and seek to understand what the poet was intending to communicate or to conceal in the *Safar-nāma*. For the present, it is sufficient to note that this journey was pivotal in his life, so much so that either before or just after the journey, he resigned from his position in Harāt (or was possibly dismissed) and later retired to his hometown of Bīrjand.

Nizārī's Poetic Career in Bīrjand

There is little information on Nizārī's activities in the ten years following his return to Bīrjand. He would undoubtedly have given much attention to the writing of the *Safar-nāma*, while the memories of his journey to the Caucasus were still fresh in the mind. The composition of this first major *mathnawī* of Nizārī may have been facilitated to some extent by his freedom from the responsibilities of office, wife and children, as he admits in these lines:

> Where are we, where the love of children
>   and the affection of wife?
> We are free of children and free of wife.
> In affection for the light of the sun, love is a small part;
> From place, position, corner and home, we are free.[61]

However, it appears that not long afterwards, Nizārī married and eventually had three sons, Nuṣrat, Shāhanshāh and Muḥammad, the last of whom died in infancy:

God, the giver of religion and justice,
Gave me two of the best sons it is possible to give,
Shāhanshāh and Nuṣrat, with the good fortune of youth,
Both precious and worthy of affection.
There were three, but one of them was by fate
taken from the transient to the everlasting abode.[62]

Whatever the joys and comforts of Nizārī's domestic life, his world was rudely shaken once again by a renewed period of political and social turbulence which swept across Quhistān. In 688/1289, a division of troops led by Tarshīr, brother of Toghan, the commander of Mongol forces in the area, invaded the region and attacked the town of Nīh, driving out its governor. These events alarmed the Mihrabānid ruler of neighbouring Sīstān, the Malik Naṣīr al-Dīn Muḥammad, who sent his nephew, Shams al-Dīn ʿAlī, more commonly known as ʿAlī Shāh or Shāh ʿAlī, to repel the invaders. After recapturing Nīh and occupying Khūsf, he set up his encampment at Bīrjand where he declared himself the new ruler of Quhistān, before proceeding to extend his control to other towns of the province by 694/1294. In the following years, ʿAlī Shāh was confronted by more incursions, among which the most serious was led by Amīr Bek Tudakan at the head of 10,000 horsemen. The Mihrabānid prince fell back to Sīstān from where, with the help of reinforcements from his father, he returned once again to expel the invaders from Quhistān.[63]

The reign of ʿAlī Shāh was much troubled by the expansionist policy of the grandson of Shams al-Dīn Kart, Fakhr al-Dīn, who ruled in Harāt and coveted the territories of Quhistān and Sīstān. In pursuit of this goal, Fakhr al-Dīn decided to use the Nīkūdarīs, a rebellious force of Mongol-Turks based in the southern part of Afghanistan, who did not recognise the authority of the Īl-Khāns and had for many years raided and pillaged across eastern Persia. The Kart ruler supplied them with clothing and horses to attack the Mihrabānid forces in Quhistān.[64] A few years later, Nawrūz, the military commander in Khurāsān, sent an expedition of his own led by his brother Amīr Ḥājjī, which caused much destruction in the region before being driven out by the Mihrabānids. In order to consolidate and legitimise his authority in Quhistān, ʿAlī

Shāh maintained good relations with the Īl-Khānid ruler Ghāzān, who eventually granted him an official *yarligh* and flag, confirming his rule in the territory. After ruling for sixteen years, in 706/1306 ʿAlī Shāh was killed in battle and succeeded by his son Tāj al-Dīn.

It was probably in 694/1294, after ʿAlī Shāh had set up his headquarters in Bīrjand, that he met Nizārī Quhistānī and was sufficiently impressed by his poetic skills to recruit him as his court poet. As in the case of Nizārī's previous association with the Kart *malik* of Harāt, he was motivated in part by his need for regular income in the chaotic conditions of the time. At the same time, the breadth of Nizārī's education, his intimate knowledge of courtly and administrative matters, together with his antipathy for the Karts and their policies, must also have commended him to ʿAlī Shāh. Another factor that could have cemented their relationship was the Mihrabānid's inclination towards Shiʿism. Nizārī must have found this the most attractive aspect of ʿAlī Shāh's personality, since it imposed less inhibitions on his expressions of Shiʿi sentiments in verse. According to Baradin, there was genuine affection between ʿAlī Shāh and Nizārī. But in order to retain ʿAlī Shāh's favours, Nizārī was certainly obliged to conceal from him his own attachment to Ismailism, which was disapproved by the Twelver Shiʿis as much as it was detested by the Sunnis. Nonetheless, Nizārī may have harboured the hope of one day secretly converting the ruler to his own path of Shiʿi Islam, somewhat in the fashion of the Ismaili *dāʿīs* of the past, such as Muḥammad al-Nasafī, Abū Ḥātim al-Rāzī and al-Mu'ayyad fi'l-Dīn al-Shīrāzī.

Over the next two years, when ʿAlī Shāh was often away to secure his position as ruler of Quhistān, the poet composed several *qaṣīdas* in praise of the ruler. But much of his time was taken up by the composition of his *Adab-nāma* (*Book of Good Manners*), a lengthy moralistic poem in twelve chapters written in anecdotal style. In this work, completed in 697/1297, Nizārī presents a historical account and social critique of his time, together with advise on how best to rule a people. Already we can see in this *mathnawī* produced under the patronage of ʿAlī Shāh, the poet's expression of a strong interest in social conditions and good governance.

Nizārī's discussion of the deficiencies of government and his censure of the ruling classes for neglecting the needs of ordinary people were themes that were to exercise him greatly in the following years. In this verse, for instance, the poet condemns landlords for hoarding wheat and expresses deep empathy for their hungry victims:

When will the price of wheat be equal
  again to that of clay and soap (*ushnān*),[65]
So that the tears of grief can be removed
  from the purchase of a wheat-bag?[66]
My heart is wounded at the thought of no bread,
  at that wheat which leaves me destitute.
There is no bread or faith in people's mouths.
They (the landlords) sell wheat but (the people)
  cannot place faith in wheat,
In such times when wheat is hoarded in storage,
(I say) that they are oppressors.
The problem is that without gold, gems and silver,
  they will not sell wheat to the poor.
Even if wheat was to rain from the clouds,
They would not allow a single seed to go to the needy.
It is possible to overcome this calamity
  and conquer this misfortune
Only by regarding your soul cheaper than wheat...
Even if Nizārī were on his deathbed a hundred times,
Those who are to blame would not offer him any wheat.[67]

Although Nizārī was skilful in his use of allegory to conceal some of his views, it seems that he became increasingly more direct and outspoken in his criticism, sometimes accusing the Shah's leading courtiers of abusing their power and implicating them, as wealthy landlords and administrators, of being directly involved in the corruption and injustices of the time. This attitude could not but arouse the deepest hostility of the senior officials who were already envious of the poet's close relationship with ʿAlī Shāh. Some indication of the intensity of arguments in which the poet became engaged is conveyed in these lines, which also reflect the poet's weariness with such ongoing confrontations:

O woe to those who cannot distinguish
the jewel from the rubbish, like people born blind!
One of them is without shame and the other ignorant.
How long can I bear the pain of these people?
By challenging and disputing with them,
By confronting these base people,
I become like one without God.[68]

In addition to the aristocratic and land-owning classes, Nizārī also directed his criticism at the religious scholars (*ʿulamāʾ*), many of whom were dependent on the ruling aristocracy for their own survival and prestige. One of the major sources of corruption under the Mongols was the *waqf* system of religious endowments, from which a large number of jurists, theologians and Sufi *shaykh*s derived their incomes. The Īl-Khāns retained this practice inherited from the Saljūqs and continued the tax immunity traditionally enjoyed by the clergy charged with the upkeep of endowed property, but under their rule the system degenerated into a widespread mechanism for the exploitation of land and peasants.[69] In many poems Nizārī accuses the clergy of turning away from the true principles of faith and of being concerned only with their own material gain.

This world is being ruined because
of the scholar desiring *waqf*,
Go Nizārī and clothe yourself only
in clothes of ignorance.
Do not depend on marshland in
these sprouting fields of the world.
What attention can the intellect pay
to the hypocrite's sermon?
How is it possible for a doctor of the intellect
to give poppy to the insensible?
The corruption and ignobility of the people of virtue
has reached such a point
That it has become necessary to praise
and congratulate scoundrels.
What did they learn from jurisprudence
except hypocrisy?
From knowledge and learning,

what did they acquire except dispute ...?
From the spindle of widows they get fine robes,
From the evening supper of orphans
they get their own means of life.[70]

In another verse typical of Nizārī's denunciation of the clergy's accumulation of wealth and the sermons by which they exploited the credulity of the masses, he remarks:

The jurists say useless things
and the religious *shaykhs* say indecent things.
They are all thieves of stipends (*idrār*)
and desirous of income (*waqf*).
Be straightforward and stable,
and give harmonious counselling;
Don't sometimes put on a bandage
and at other times inflict a wound.[71]

As was to be expected, Nizārī came under severe attack from the Sunni *ʿulamāʾ* who resented his constant outcries against them. Inevitably, he was accused by the clergy of being a drunkard, an adherent of Ismailism, and therefore in their view a 'heretic'. However, these charges do not seem to have discouraged the poet in the least, as demonstrated in these lines where he expresses fearless contempt for his accusers:

It does not worry me if all the mullahs
of the world declared in their edicts
That among the chosen and the common
the drunken Nizārī is worst of them all.
I have no fear of being killed by them,
nor the vexations of burning flesh;
I care not what wounds they inflict on me,
because they are all liars and hypocrites![72]

In the verse below, Nizārī argues that if he was judged a heretic by religious scholars who were themselves dishonourable and corrupt, then there could be no true Muslim in the land!

If I am a non-believer, then who
and where are the Muslims?

Alas, if this one who fails in his duty (*muqaṣṣir*)
is not exaggerating in his judgement.[73]

There are many aspects of Nizārī's role in the court of ʿAlī Shāh which remain obscure to us. What cannot be doubted from the verses cited above is Nizārī's genuine sense of moral outrage at the social and economic impoverishment of Quhistān, for which he held the ruling classes responsible. Nizārī was not the only poet of his generation to express such criticism, but his views were probably the most outspoken. Clearly they were the result of an increasingly bitter political controversy in the Shah's government, in the course of which he used all the power and venom of his pen to attack his enemies inside and outside the court. It is unlikely that the poet would have been able to engage in this polemic without the implicit support and protection of ʿAlī Shāh who seemed to have tolerated his radical views for some time. A crucial factor in the Shah's attitude was probably his Shiʿi sympathies which may have encouraged him to share Nizārī's opposition to a powerful, Sunni-dominated aristocracy and ʿ*ulamā*ʾ. It is also possible that this conflict was part of the larger political struggle between the Mihrabānid and Kart dynasties for dominance in Quhistān and that the Shah suspected the loyalty of some of his courtiers. A clear picture of Nizārī's role in these events is only likely to emerge from further studies of the politics of north-eastern Persia at the turn of the 7th–8th/13th–14th centuries.

In 696/1296, Nizārī's fortunes changed drastically for the worse when he apparently criticised the Shah for having condemned a friend of his to death. We do not know the offence or crime of this person, but he was obviously close to the poet and perhaps an important ally against his enemies at court. The anger of ʿAlī Shāh at Nizārī's perceived insolence was exacerbated further by public accusations that the poet was a secret adherent of Ismailism. Thus, a few years after joining the service of ʿAlī Shāh, when the ruler returned to Bīrjand from one of his military campaigns, Nizārī was charged with treason and summarily dismissed from his position. The immediate cause of Nizārī's downfall may have been a few ill-chosen words of his which wounded the Mihrabānid prince's pride and self-esteem, but basically it was caused by his criticism of the ruling classes and suspicions of being an Ismaili.

Nizārī's Final Years

Nizārī Quhistānī was about fifty years old when he was exiled from the court of ʿAlī Shāh with a small plot of land in Bīrjand in compensation for his service. The poet was deeply hurt and disappointed by the way he was treated, referring to himself as 'a slave oppressed, prohibited from the carpet of the great lord,'[74] and he resented the difficult conditions under which he was made to live:

> I remained penniless, in need and poor.
> Poverty is a punishment and I stayed impoverished …
> In this garden which was prepared for me,
> There is nothing, neither argument nor arrangement.
> All I received in compensation (for my service)
> was a dilapidated garden
> With one hundred twists and turns.[75]

In spite of Nizārī's sense of injustice, he continued to entertain the hope of regaining the favours of ʿAlī Shāh. In 700/1300, he composed one of his major *mathnawīs* with the title of *Munāẓara-i shab wa rūz* (*The Debate of Night and Day*). This poem of about 550 couplets is an allegorical portrayal of a debate between the powers of night and day, representing the two main branches of Islam, Sunnism and Shiʿism, in which the latter is vindicated. The *Munāẓara* appears to have been an attempt by Nizārī to redeem himself by demonstrating his allegiance to Shiʿi Islam and, as such, supports the view that the poet's relationship with ʿAlī Shāh was founded on a common religious outlook. According to Baradin, in this work the poet tried to keep both his Ismaili beliefs and social criticism well concealed.[76] One way he attempted to do this and ingratiate himself with the ruler was by presenting himself as a follower of the early Shiʿi Imam Jaʿfar al-Ṣādiq and associating the light of the sun with 'Shams al-Dīn,' the sobriquet of the Shah. Apparently, the Shah was mollified by the poet's work and restored him briefly to favour before dismissing him again.

In the following year, Nizārī made another attempt to regain the good opinion of ʿAlī Shāh by dedicating to him his next *mathnawī*, the *Azhar wa mazhar* (*Revelation and Manifestation*). In this work of about 10,000 lines written in the style of Niẓāmī's *Khusraw wa Shīrīn* and Farīd al-Dīn ʿAṭṭār's *Khusraw-nāma*, Nizārī depicts the struggle against an Arabian background between Mazhar, a heroic figure embodying the values of justice and honesty, and the tyrannical Khalīl who represents injustice and oppression. Baiburdi is correct in observing that in contrast to Nizārī's other writings, the *Azhar wa mazhar* is more overt in its exposition of Ismaili beliefs, such as the principle of Imamate and the concepts of *ẓāhir* and *bāṭin*, and that it appears to him as 'the embodiment of the high ideals of the Ismaili Nizārī.'[77] In a sense, both the *Munāẓara* and the *Azhar wa mazhar* may be seen as Nizārī's recapitulations in allegorical narrative of his own bitter struggles against his enemies in the court of ʿAlī Shāh. Unfortunately for the poet, neither of these works was well received by the courtiers, nor did they succeed in appeasing the Shāh.

We have very little information on the last years of Nizārī's life. In 706/1306, when he was about sixty, his wife died, and his eldest son, Nuṣrat, was released from prison. The exact circumstances of Nuṣrat's incarceration are not known to us except that he was charged with propagating Ismaili beliefs and apparently released through the intervention of one Ḥājjī ʿAlāʾ al-Dīn Hindū, a representative of the Īl-Khānid ruler Öljeytü.[78] The last major work of Nizārī, composed in 710/1310, was the *Dastūr-nāma* (*Book of Rules*), which consists of about 300 couplets on the correct etiquette for wine-drinking, interspersed with moral advice. His remaining years were spent mostly on his farm where:

> I go to a corner and sit in seclusion like a treasure;
> now my duty towards service is just prayer.[79]

Nizārī Quhistānī passed away in 720/1320 and was buried in the east cemetery of Bīrjand, besides his wife and son Muḥammad who had died in youth. Daftary reports that Nizārī's grave was demolished in 1925 when the cemetery was transformed into a park, but that since then a new mausoleum has been erected in memory of this poet of Bīrjand.[80]

In this chapter, an attempt has been made to reconstruct the main events of Nizārī's life on the basis of the limited information available in the sources and his writings, within the socio-historical context of his time. It does not in any way represent an exploration of his poetry which is substantial, multifaceted and of a high literary quality, deserving a separate study of its own. Quite apart from their versatility and diversity, the works of Nizārī are of interest too for the anecdotal information they provide about social and economic conditions in Khurāsān and Quhistān under Mongol rule. In this respect at least, Nizārī stands out among the Persian poets of his generation for the uncompromising honesty and courage with which he denounced the corruption and injustices of his time, and for championing the cause of those people who suffered most from these conditions.

Chapter 6

Ismailism, Sufism and Nizārī Quhistānī

We have observed that the question of Nizārī Quhistānī's religious identity is no longer a matter of scholarly dispute as it is now accepted that the poet was indeed an Ismaili. The earlier debates about his religious identity appear to have arisen largely because much of Nizārī's writings is characterised by a spiritual temperament and vocabulary that has come to be associated with Persian Sufism. Nizārī's relationship with Sufism is one aspect of his poetry which, in spite of the confirmation of his Ismaili allegiance, continues to remain a matter of much curiosity and obscurity. In recent years, however, there has been significant new research on Persian religious and cultural history during the Mongol period, on the basis of which it may be possible for us to re-evaluate Nizārī's connections with Sufism with a greater degree of clarity.

Persian Religion and Culture under the Mongols

When the Mongols conquered Persia, they brought with them their religious beliefs and practices, consisting of a mixture of Shamanism and Buddhism, together with their legal code, the Yasa. Although Hülegü, the founder of the Mongol Īl-Khānid dynasty, and his immediate successors retained Buddhism as the official creed of their courts, they were not interested in converting the Muslims to their beliefs, since the Mongol incursions were from the beginning driven by economic and military considerations. Unlike their Saljūq predecessors who had sought to impose a standardised Ashʿarī-Shāfiʿī form of Sunnism on the populace, the Īl-Khānids were not inclined to support the Sunnis against the Shiʿis or to favour one Sunni *madhhab* over others. Although at the time of the Mongol conquest of Persia, the Ismailis were subjected to wholesale persecution, this policy was dictated mainly by political factors, based on their perception of the Ismailis as a continuing military threat to their rule. With this exception, the Mongol rulers were largely indifferent to the religious beliefs of their subjects, a policy which amounted to religious tolerance or freedom of worship. The Īl-Khānid capital of Tabrīz in Ādharbāyjān was frequented by representatives of major faiths – Muslim, Christian, Jewish and Buddhist – and in the course of time there emerged powerful religious factions who vied for the Khān's support, until 694/1295 when Ghāzān took the throne, became a Muslim and re-established Islam as the official religion of Persia.[1]

A major and far-reaching consequence of the Mongol policy of religious diversity was the gradual erosion of some of the tensions that had previously divided various religions and sects under the Saljūqs. Besides strengthening the indigenous non-Muslim communities, it resulted in a marked reduction in the traditional animosity between the Sunnis, Shiʿis and Sufis. Although the Sunnis remained the majority in Persia and continued to dominate its major urban centres for several more centuries, there was a gradual resurgence of Twelver Shiʿism which was allowed, for the first time, to organise and express itself openly without the fear of persecution. An important outcome of this development was the tendency of Sunni and Twelver Shiʿi scholars to share a common framework of religious piety based on the *sharīʿa* and a tolerance of each other's ideas and practices. At the same time, there is evidence of a general movement away from Sunnism to Shiʿism during the Mongol period. According to Bausani, these people sought refuge in Shiʿism 'because they were disgusted with the squabbles among the different Sunni schools, and especially as regards Iran, between the Shafi'ites and the Hanafites.'[2]

The revival of Twelver Shiʿism in the 7th/13th century can be perceived as a direct consequence of the destruction by the Mongols of its two main rivals, the Sunni caliphate of Baghdad and the Ismaili state of Alamūt. It is interesting that the foremost Shiʿi theologian of this time, Naṣīr al-Dīn al-Ṭusī, who switched his loyalties from the Ismailis to the Mongols after the fall of Alamūt in 654/1256 was also present at the sack of Baghdad as senior adviser to Hülegü. Beginning with al-Ṭusī, the Twelver Shiʿis exercised much influence in the Mongol court, as did other men of religion. The Īl-Khānid ruler Ghāzān (694–703/1295–1304), who converted from Christianity to Buddhism before embracing Islam, developed much reverence for the Shiʿi Imams and was a benefactor of the major Shiʿi sanctuaries of Iraq. His brother and successor Öljeytü (703–716/1304–1316) experimented with both Ḥanafī and Shāfiʿī Sunnism before going over to Twelver Shiʿism. The growth of Shiʿism was a gradual process and it was not until the 10th/16th century that it became the dominant faith of Persia under the Ṣafawid dynasty.

A concurrent but much more pronounced feature of Persian society was the transformation of Sufism into a mass popular movement. Sufism began to exercise strong influence in the Muslim world well before the advent of the Mongols, and by the 6th/12th century it was already a well-established feature of Persian intellectual and religious life. The trend towards mysticism was further accelerated under the Īl-Khāns, encouraged in part by their greater tolerance of Sufism, but also as a psychological response of the people to the immense human suffering caused by the Mongol conquerors.[3] In fact, for the next three centuries Sufism came to dominate the religious and cultural life of all communities and classes in Persia. The Sufi movement of this era was characterised by the establishment of spiritual orders (*ṭarīqas*), headed by *shaykhs* or *pīrs* who usually resided in *khānaqāhs* and presided over regular sessions of *dhikr* (remembrance of God), often with devotional singing and music (*samāʿ*). The multiplication of *khānaqāhs* throughout Persia attracted large numbers of people; they became centres of social integration, offering hospitality to wandering Sufis, refuge for the homeless and the outcast, as well as room and board for ordinary travellers. Unlike the traditional mosques, which continued to be controlled by the *ʿulamāʾ* and received support from the state, the *khānaqāh*s were private from the beginning, depending on the endowments (*waqf*) of generous patrons. It seems that for many Persian Muslims, the *khānaqāh* came to supplant the mosque as the main centre of their religious devotions, just as the interiorised, ecstatic religion of the Sufis became more important than the legalistic *sharīʿa*-based piety of the *ʿulamāʾ*.[4]

The social and cultural impact of Sufism was not confined to the religious domain, for its influence permeated every aspect of Persian culture, including its language and literature. The Persian language in its modernised form first arose in Transoxania and Khurāsān, especially under the patronage of the Sāmānid rulers in the 3rd/9th century. But it was under the liberating vision of Islamic mysticism that the creative imagination of the Persian soul began to bloom, resulting in an enormous output of poetry in a variety of traditional and new verse-forms – especially the quatrain (*rubāʿī*), the love-lyric (*ghazal*), the panegyric ode (*qaṣīda*) and the epic poem (*mathnawī*). The transformation of Persian poetry into a distinctive Sufi mould appears to have begun from the 5th/11th century, with poets such as Abū Saʿīd b. Abi'l-Khayr.[5] As more and more poets became attracted to the mystical life, there was an increasing flow of Sufi vocabulary into the new Persian language. An important aspect of Sufi poetry was its dependence on metaphoric and symbolic allusions to disguise the poet's real intentions or conceal his esoteric message. To this end, the Sufi poets developed a complex system of themes and motifs, often associated with human love and wine-drinking, appropriated from the courtly and folk traditions of Khurāsān and Arabic poetic literature.[6] By the time of the Mongol invasions, Sufi ideas and imagery had already come to infuse all of Persian literature, to the point that even the more secular-minded poets were obliged to use the same mystical idiom. Thus arose one of the world's finest traditions of mystical poetry which is best exemplified in the works of Farīd al-Dīn ʿAṭṭār, Jalāl al-Dīn Rūmī and Ḥāfiẓ. The popular appeal of their verses was an integral part of the process leading to the pre-eminent position of Sufism in medieval Persian culture.

A number of explanations have been offered for the spectacular rise of Sufism in this age, such as al-Ghazālī's accommodation of Sufism with Sunnism; the capacity of Sufis for transcending sectarian differences by accommodating a variety of beliefs and practices; the opportunities they offered for the expression of spiritual development, etc. A number of scholars have noted a striking similarity between the doctrinal formulations of Sufism and Shiʿism, such as the ideas of *walāya* (sainthood), *bāṭin* (esoteric knowledge) and *ta'wīl* (allegorical interpretation); the *silsila* (chain of spiritual transmission) from the Prophet and the elevation of the *nūr Muḥammadī* (light of the Prophet Muḥammad) to a metaphysical principle; the organisation of Sufi orders around the *murshid-murīd* (master-disciple) relationship and a hierarchical progression of instruction – all these characteristic expressions of Sufism are known to have developed in Shiʿism well in advance of the emergence of organised Sufism.

There is also a growing recognition in modern scholarship of the seminal contributions of early Shiʿi Islam to the development of Sufism, but no in-depth, comparative analysis of this relationship has been undertaken to date.[7] One way of examining this phenomenon is in the context of an Islamic esoteric tradition, that is, as a distinctive gnostic and mystical vision of Islam that arose as an alternative to the dogmatic and legalistic interpretation of the faith that gained prominence under the Abbasids and the Saljūqs. This development was a complex phenomenon which took many forms – philosophical, spiritual and poetic – in Muslim societies. While the roots of Islamic esotericism are to be found in the Qur'anic revelation, its principles first appeared in Shiʿi Islam and were elaborated most distinctly among the early Ismailis.[8] However, it was under the aegis of organised Sufism that the spiritual vision of Islam later acquired mass popular appeal and a certain degree of legitimacy in Sunni and Shiʿi Islam.

Shiʿism and Sufism under the Mongols

A notable outcome of the Mongol policy of tolerating different religions was a closer interaction between Shiʿism and Sufism throughout the Persian-speaking world. This trend was expressed by the Sufis in many ways, but most specifically through their increased reverence and devotion for the first Shiʿi Imam ʿAlī b. Abī Ṭālib. The Sufis have always held ʿAlī with high regard as the fount of esoteric wisdom, but it was during the Mongol era that they began to formulate systematic chains of initiatory transmission (*silsila*) going back to ʿAlī and Muḥammad. On this development in Persian Sufism, Marshall Hodgson has observed:

> Many Ṣūfīs seem to have welcomed some of the conceptions that had been developed on the esoteric side of ʿAlid loyalism, and most specially the notion that ʿAlī had received secret teachings from Muḥammad for which most of the first Muslims were not qualified; but the Ṣūfīs identified those secret teachings with their own traditions. In this way they provided a Jamāʿī-Sunnī context for some elements of ʿAlid-loyalist esotericism ... and at the same time provided a means of explaining how their own teachings could be traced back to the Prophet.[9]

Among the earliest Sufi *ṭarīqa*s to exhibit strong Shiʿi tendencies was the Central Asian order of Kubrāwiyya, founded by Najm al-Dīn Kubrā of Khwārazm (killed by the Mongols in 618/1221), who was a Shāfiʿī-Sunni with Shiʿi sympathies. Under his successors, Majd al-Dīn Baghdādī (d.616/1219) and Rukn al-Dīn ʿAlāʾ al-Dawla al-Simnānī (d.736/1336), the Kubrāwiyya became even more Shiʿi in their devotions and pietism. Other Sufi orders which became progressively permeated with Shiʿism were the Dhahabiyya, Nūrbakhshiyya and Niʿmatullāhiyya in Persia, as well as the Khalwatiyya and Bektāshiyya of Anatolia.[10] A similar process of 'Shiʿitisation' was evident among the chivalric orders of the *futūwwa* and *jawānmardī*, which had a large following in urban areas among merchants, craftsmen and guilds.[11] There was a further advance of Shiʿism under the post-Mongol era of the Tīmūrids with the emergence of Sufi-Shiʿi movements of political and social reform such as the Shaykhiyya who, in the mid–8th/14th century, joined forces with the Sarbadārids to create a mini-Shiʿi state at Sabzavār in western Khurāsān. The most powerful of these Sufi-Shiʿi orders to emerge was the Ṣafawiyya, who originated in Ādharbāyjān as a Sunni *ṭarīqa* but later became transformed into a militant Shiʿi movement. It was largely due to the strong ʿAlid loyalism and messianism of their supporters that the Ṣafawids were able to conquer Persia from the Tīmurids. However, in their zeal to impose Shiʿism on the entire country, the Ṣafawids endeavoured to wipe out almost all forms of organised Sufism which had flourished in Persia for several centuries.

It is important to note that the growing alliance between Sufism and Shiʿism that gathered pace from the 7th/13th centuries was a reciprocal process whereby Shiʿism too assimilated many aspects of Sufi theory and practice. The interpenetration of Shiʿi and Sufi ideas was not confined to the Persians but extended into the Arab world, a phenomenon that was quite apparent to the well-known 8th/14th century historian Ibn Khaldūn who observed that 'each group came to be imbued with the dogmas of the other. Their theories and beliefs merged and were assimilated.'[12] The integration of Sufi theory into Shiʿi theology was spearheaded by a number of eminent theologians led by Naṣīr al-Dīn al-Ṭūsī (d. 672/1274), Ṣadr al-Dīn Ibrāhīm (d. 722/1322), ʿAllāma-i Ḥillī (d. 726/1326) and Ḥaydar Āmulī (d. after 787/1385). The intellectual efforts of these scholars prepared the ground for the flowering in the Ṣafawid period of the rich tradition of Shiʿi gnostic philosophy (*ʿirfān*) expounded by a number of outstanding mystics and theosophers such as Mīr Dāmād (d.1040/1630) and Mullā Ṣadrā (d.1050/1640).[13]

The rapprochement of Shiʿism and Sufism was actually prefigured more than a century earlier by the Nizārī Ismailis of Alamūt who were probably the first Shiʿi community in Persia to express their doctrines in a distinctively Sufi idiom. This movement may have been encouraged, in part, by the substitution of Persian for Arabic as the principal language of the Ismaili religious literature, beginning from the 4th/10th century with the Fatimid *dāʿī* of Khurāsān, Nāṣir-i Khusraw, who composed all his philosophical and poetic works in Persian,[14] and subsequently followed by

Ḥasan-i Ṣabbāḥ, the founder of the Ismaili state of Alamūt. This process appears to have accelerated further with the reassertion of the esoteric and spiritual ideals of Ismailism by the Imam Ḥasan ʿAlā Dhikhrih'l-Salām through his declaration of the *qiyāma* in 559/1164.

Although the Ismailis held fast to their central doctrine of the Imamate and continued to interpret their doctrines in terms of classical Shiʿi Islam, the literature they produced in the last decades of the Alamūt state became increasingly exposed to Sufi vocabulary and categories of thought. This is clearly evident in the Ismaili works of Naṣīr al-Dīn al-Ṭūsī which were composed during his long association with the community. Al-Ṭūsī's use of the terms associated with Sufism, such as *ḥaqīqa* (truth) and *maʿrifa* (gnosis), are always adapted to the Ismaili understanding of the spiritual path and subsumed under the doctrines of *imāma* and *qiyāma*.[15] Furthermore, it would be incorrect to state that the Ismailis appropriated these terms from the Sufis, since their spiritual significance was first articulated by the Shiʿi Imam Jaʿfar al-Ṣādiq in the 2nd/8th century and they occur frequently in Ismaili literature of the Fatimid period.

At the same time, there was an opposite, more diffused, movement of some Ismaili ideas entering into Persian Sufism, as is evident, for instance, in the works of the mystical philosopher ʿAyn al-Quḍāt al-Hamadānī, who was executed in 525/1131 by the Saljūqs for Ismaili sympathies among other things,[16] and one of the classics of Persian Sufism, the *Gulshan-i rāz* (*Rose-garden of Mystery*) by Maḥmūd Shabistarī (d. after 740/1339) who was a contemporary of Nizārī Quhistānī and on whose work an Ismaili author later wrote a valuable commentary.[17] There is also a close similarity of thought to be found between Ismaili doctrines and the poetry of Sufi luminaries such as Jalāl al-Dīn Rūmī and Farīd al-Dīn ʿAṭṭār. In fact, Ivanow was so struck by this parallelism that he commented:

> The reason why such [Ismaili] influences can be traced in Sufic literature cannot be explained by the fact of universality and indefiniteness of Sufic doctrine, which would find room for almost every spiritual movement in Islam. ... It seems that even if there

> were real cases of 'leaking' of Ismaili ideas into general Persian literature, these were few, and there was no need for 'direct contact' for producing the impression of a very close affinity between the two doctrines. The causes of such connection lie most probably much deeper than this, especially as far as Persia is concerned.[18]

Henry Corbin reached the same conclusion regarding the penetration of Ismaili ideas in Sufi thought and literature:

> [The effect of Ismailism] on Sufism and Iranian spirituality in general presupposes some fundamental affinities which throw new light on the problem of the meaning and even the origins of Sufism. ... One hesitates at times in deciding whether a text is written by a Sufi steeped in Ismailism, or by an Ismaili steeped in Sufism.[19]

It is for the reason of this spiritual affinity that the Ismailis of Persia and Central Asia have regarded the foremost Sufi poets of their lands (Sanāʾī, Rūmī, ʿAṭṭār, Shabistarī, Ḥāfiẓ, Qāsim al-Anwār, ʿAzīz al-Dīn Nasafī and others) as their co-religionists, whose verses continue to be recited in their religious devotions to this day.[20] The same phenomenon of Ismaili ideas percolating into Sufism is observable in the popular, rural-based *darwīsh* movements that began to emerge in the frontier regions of Persia and Anatolia from the 8th/14th century, such as the Ahl-i Ḥaqq, Ḥurūfis and Nuqṭawīs, whose literature exhibits a remarkable infusion of Shiʿi and specifically Ismaili ideas.[21]

The relations between Ismailism and Sufism appears to have become even more intensified during the 10th/16th century when, under the pro-Shiʿi government of the Ṣafawids, the Ismaili Imams re-emerged in Persia with their residence in Anjudān.[22] While they adopted Sufi names, appeared in public as Sufi *shaykhs* or *pīrs*, and developed close relations with the leadership of the Niʿmatullāhī order through marriage ties, there is no firm evidence that they established formal affiliations with Sufi *ṭarīqas*.[23] On the contrary, they were careful to preserve their authority as Ismaili Imams among their followers and supervised a significant expansion of the Nizārī *daʿwa* in Persia, India and the Badakhshān region of Central Asia. The restoration of communication between the Ismaili Imams and their followers also inspired a revival of Ismaili literature in Persian which was strongly coloured by Sufi ideas and constructions (as illustrated in the works of the *dāʿīs* Abū Isḥāq Quhistānī, Khayrkhwāh-i Harātī and Khākī Khurāsānī); the same is a notable feature of the devotional and mystical poetry of Nizārī Ismailis in the Indian subcontinent.[24]

Nizārī's relations with Sufism

The foregoing discussion of the far-reaching changes in the intellectual and spiritual fabric of Persian Islam in the 6th–7th/12th–13th centuries is pertinent not only for locating the poetic career of Nizārī Quhistānī in the historical and cultural context of his time, but also for the key it provides for unlocking certain aspects of his writings, especially its ambiguous admixture of Ismailism and Sufism. Although the poet's Ismaili affiliation is now an established fact, it would be a mistake to regard his writings exclusively through the prism of Ismaili ideas, because he was very much a product of his age, and his poetry documents many of the social, cultural and political currents of his time.

It is apparent from even a cursory examination of Nizārī's writings that they are couched predominantly in the metaphoric language of Sufi mystical poetry. Throughout his works, Nizārī deploys the full repertory of Sufi themes, motifs and symbolism, including the interlacing imagery of lover and beloved, separation and union, wine-drinking and spiritual ecstasy, etc. In this respect, Nizārī Quhistānī has the singular status of being the first Ismaili writer to depart radically from the poetic styles and conventions of the earlier Ismaili literary tradition of the Fatimid period, as typified in the devotional verses of al-Mu'ayyad fi'l-Dīn al-Shīrāzī in Arabic and Nāṣir-i Khusraw in Persian. This contrast is equally apparent when Nizārī's poems are compared with the verses of his immediate Ismaili predecessors of the Alamūt period, the poets Ra'is Ḥasan and Ḥasan Maḥmūd who lived in the early decades of the 7th/13th century just prior to the Mongol conquest.[25]

The extensive scope of Nizārī's Sufi discourse and the dexterity with which he employs its idiom suggests that his acquaintance with Sufism was not merely literary, acquired through his education in Bīrjand and Harāt. There can be little doubt that the poet's intimate knowledge of Sufi doctrines and practices could only have been acquired through previous association with Sufi *ṭarīqas* in his homeland of Khurāsān. Since the early centuries of Islam, Khurāsān has been one of the cradles of Sufism, being associated generally with the so-called school of 'intoxication' (*sukr*), in contrast to the Iraqi school of 'sobriety' (*saḥw*), as well as the Malāmatiyya tradition of eclectic mysticism.[26] This province has been the birthplace of many renowned mystics, including Ibrāhīm b. Adham, Bāyazīd Bisṭāmī, Ḥakīm al-Tirmidhī, ʿAbū Saʿīd b. Abi'l-Khayr, ʿAbd Allāh Anṣārī, ʿAbd al-Qādir Gīlānī, Farīd al-Dīn ʿAṭṭār and Jalāl al-Dīn Rūmī. The institutionalisation of Sufism with its *ṭarīqas*, *khānaqāhs* and *samāʿ* ceremonies first began to take shape in Khurāsān before spreading to other parts of Persia. It was among the Sufis of Khurāsān too that there arose a new kind of mystical poetry combining the profane with the sacred, which came to dominate Persian literature. Since Khurāsān retained its pre-eminent position in Persian Sufism during the Mongol period, it is likely that, in common with many of his Sunni and Shiʿi contemporaries, Nizārī may have had close contact with one of the region's Sufi *ṭarīqas*, such as the Khalwatiyya or the Suhrawardiyya who were especially active in and around the city of Harāt during his time.

Whatever may have been the sources of Nizārī's deep familiarity with Sufi theory and practice, this aspect of his poetry has presented scholars of both Persian literature and Ismaili studies with much difficulty in demarcating the poet's Sufism from his Ismailism. It will be worthwhile, therefore, at this point to review briefly how Nizārī defines his own position vis-à-vis the Sufis and other religious communities among whom he lived. It will be convenient further to use as our point of reference the poet's allusions to the fundamental issue of the Imamate or, to be more precise, the concept of spiritual authority (*walāya*), about which there is a divergence of views in Islam between Sunnism, Twelver Shiʿism and Sufism.

There is no single equivalent in English of the Arabic term *walāya,* which conveys a variety of meanings such as friendship, protection, authority and power, and is applicable generally to the initiatory functions of a spiritual guide.[27] This significance of the term was first formulated in Shiʿi Islam, where it is used exclusively for the Imams descended from the Prophet's family (*ahl al-bayt*); subsequently it was adopted by the Sufis to denote the authority of their spiritual masters. In Ismaili theology, the principle of *walāya* is regarded as the first pillar of faith.[28] There are many verses in Nizārī's works which clearly attest to his adherence to this Shiʿi doctrine, which the poet espoused openly without concealing it from his patrons in Harāt or Bīrjand. In contradistinction to the Sunni view that the leadership of the Muslims after the Prophet passed to the caliphs chosen by the community, Nizārī asserts his unequivocal adherence to the Shiʿi belief that the Prophet's temporal and spiritual authority was inherited by his progeny and that it is only by allegiance to these Imams that salvation is possible for the faithful.

If you follow the Book of God
 and the progeny of Muḥammad,
You will be saved, otherwise you will
 be drowned in a whirlpool.[29]

The principle of direct hereditary descent of the Shiʿi Imams from the Prophet is championed by Nizārī in many verses, often with the support of the Qurʾanic verse 3:33–34: 'Allāh did choose Adam and Noah, the family of Abraham, and the family of ʿImrān above all people – offspring, one of the other, and Allāh knows and hears all things.'

We search for a union with the family
 of the Chosen (Prophet Muḥammad).
We search for the truth (*ḥaqq*) of son after son.
We are totally obedient to his 'offspring, one of the other.'
There is no other thing we can add to this but itself.
We endeavour (in our faith) so that we do not
 turn out to be faithless.[30]

It will be recalled that during his two-year service at the court of the Mihrabānid prince ʿAlī Shāh in Bīrjand, Nizārī became embroiled in a bitter dispute with leading courtiers and *ʿulamāʾ* whom he held responsible for the oppressive conditions of the poor in Quhistān. These arguments were possibly part of a larger struggle for ascendancy between the Shiʿi and Sunni factions in the court of ʿAlī Shāh, a Sunni with definite Shiʿi sympathies. This accounts for Nizārī's polemical arguments with Sunni theologians and jurists, on which a few verses were cited in the previous chapter. In the following lines, the poet criticises the *ʿulamāʾ* for accepting *qiyās* (analogical reasoning) and *raʾy* (subjective opinion) as a basis for interpreting the faith. For him this is tantamount to idolatry since it subordinates the divine message to the vagaries of human opinion; he defends the standard Shiʿi precept that true knowledge of God can only be derived from His true representative on earth:

> Don't be a follower of your own opinion
> and analogical reasoning,
> Prevent yourself from idolatry.
> Recognise Him (God) through him (the Imam) who is peace;
> His Face is only (found) through the face
> of another (the Imam).[31]

In addition to defending the Shiʿi principle of Imamate, Nizārī clearly expresses in the following verse his distinctively Ismaili perspective that the Imam must always be physically present in the world at any given time as a permanent vehicle of divine grace to humanity. In doing so, he also makes a sharp distinction between the Shiʿi understanding of the Imamate as a unique status on the one hand, and the more general application of the term 'imam' in Sunni Islam for a prayer-leader or religious scholar.

> Whenever you see anyone stand before you
> wearing a turban, you stand behind him,
> As if he your imam – not for a moment
> is the world without the Imam of the time![32]

> Do not be annoyed if you find this
> offensive –what else can I do?
> It is based on the Prophet's designation (*naṣṣ*)

(of ʿAlī as his successor).

If you do not know the Imam of the time
with certitude, then know for sure that
Your wife, your wealth and even the head
upon your shoulders are unlawful to you.[33]

I will sell your imam for the sweetmeats
of drunkards who have drained their cups,
Because the turban that sits on his head
is worth only a pledge of wine and goblet.[34]

The same notion of the 'Imam of the time' (*imām-al-waqt*) as the source of human salvation, who succeeds his predecessor in hereditary descent and is thus accessible to human beings in every generation, is underscored by the poet in another verse:

Salvation is to be found in the Imam of the time.
I found the essence of faith in obedience to
the command of his representative.
I have given up everything except that contained in
the (Qurʾanic verse) 'offspring, one of the other.'
Ever since I found the Imamate
permanently in human form …
I have known no other guide than
the living, everlasting Imam,
For in his command (*amr*) I have found
peace in both the worlds.[35]

One of the arguments often put forward by Ismaili authors on the necessity of a living Imam is the human need for divine guidance in every age according to the changing needs and circumstances of people. Nizārī echoes this view in the following lines:

My lover appears always in different forms,
Because for each period there comes a new guidance (*ḥukm*);
'One after the other,' there follows another *qāʾim*
Abū Turāb (Imam ʿAlī);
The permanent connection (with him)
can never be broken.[36]

For the opponents of Nizārī, his assertion of a continuing line of Imams was probably sufficient evidence of his connection with the Ismailis rather than the Twelver Shiʿis whose twelfth Imam disappeared in 260/873–4. It is precisely on the basis of Nizārī's insistence on this principle that we can also infer that, while he was intensely interested in Sufi mysticism and had close connections with Sufi *ṭarīqa*s in Khurāsān, he always retained his core Ismaili beliefs. The poet clarifies this issue in the verse below by pointing out that whereas there are many Sufi *shaykh*s and *pīr*s among whom the individual may choose his spiritual master, the Ismaili Imam is unique in the world, for he is not subject to choice or election by his followers, but inherits his position exclusively by means of the *naṣṣ* (designation) of his predecessor:

> The Sufis agree with us (on the necessity of a guide),
> but we have an alternative view.
> We believe in the *naṣṣ* of the Imam,
> but they believe in their own choice.
> I don't have to share more of this secret (with you).
> Fortunate indeed is the one who obtains
> certainty from my warning.
> Listen to the warnings of Nizārī
> so that you may be in security.
> Seek (the Imam's) teachings (*taʿlīm*)
> and submit (*taslīm*) to (him) bravely.[37]

Nizārī makes a further, more crucial, distinction between the Sufi *shaykh* and the Ismaili Imam by asserting the Shiʿi belief that every Imam is a bearer of the Light (*nūr*) of God, and that it is only by virtue of this Divine Light that God can be recognised and salvation attained:

> It is well that you should follow the Imamate
> For the Light of God is in his pure heart.
> Through that Light you will be freed from darkness.
> Follow that Light and may peace be with you.[38]

In addition to the verses cited above where Nizārī expounds his Shiʿi and Ismaili views on the Imamate, there are many others where he refers to the Ismaili principles of *ẓāhir* and *bāṭin*, *taʿlīm*, *ta'wīl*, etc., articulated earlier by Fatimid thinkers, as well as the notions of *qā'im* and *qiyāma* associated particularly with the Nizārī Ismailism of Alamūt.[39] The significant point to note here is that the allusions which Nizārī makes to Ismaili principles and ideas are often expressed through the vocabulary of Sufi mysticism. This is well as illustrated in the following poem about Alexander's vain search for the fountain of life, in which the figure of Khiḍr, the travelling companion and guide of Moses mentioned in the Qur'an (28:60–82) stands for the Ismaili Imam.

When Alexander became renowned for his pomp and naivete,
 he went to the east while his object was hidden in the west.

The fountain of the water of life did not come close to him,
 because he was in the stage of ignorance and darkness.

His Aristotle was unaware of the secret of that fountain,
 and its symbol was hidden from the precepts of the Greek.

Had it been so easy to reach that famous fountainhead,
 Moses would not have returned from Khiḍr in bewilderment.

Think of yourself as Alexander: what is that you seek?
 Tell me, what do you mean by this water and that fountain?

What do you know of the fountain except that it has a name?
 And what is Khiḍr to you except for an imaginary being? [40]

The few verses cited above are sufficient to demonstrate conclusively not only the fact of Nizārī Quhistānī's adherence to Ismailism, but also his disagreement with the Sufis on the question of the spiritual guide. The poet rejects the notion that the Ismaili Imam can be compared or equated with the Sufi masters. He upholds the argument often presented by Ismaili thinkers and most forcefully by Ḥasan-i Ṣabbāḥ in his doctrine of *ta'līm*, that among all the different interpreters of faith with their divergent views, there has to be one authoritative teacher, a supreme preceptor who can only be recognised by his own assertion of the truth. This person, according to the poet, is none other than the 'Imam of the time' whose knowledge and authority is based not on election or choice by humans but is derived from divine appointment. Nizārī defends this principle vigorously throughout his works and, as such, it can be regarded as a clear statement of his position on Ismailism vis-à-vis Sufism.[41]

Nizārī and the Limits of *Taqiyya*

Apart from the poetic contribution of Nizārī Quhistānī, there is little recorded evidence of Ismaili intellectual and cultural activity in Persia during the Mongol era, a fact that may be accounted for by the enormous upheaval caused in the community by the Mongol conquest. In the following decades, however, the Ismaili *daʿwa* began to reorganise itself and a sizeable community of Ismailis continued to exist in Quhistān throughout this period. In view of the inveterate hostility of the Mongols and the Sunni *ʿulamāʾ* towards the Ismailis, their lives must have been difficult at the best of times. Anyone suspected of being an Ismaili was liable to be ostracised as a 'heretic' or persecuted as a 'subversive'. In these circumstances, according to Daftary, it became necessary for many Persian Ismailis to adopt Sufi, Twelver Shiʿi or Sunni disguises as a form of *taqiyya*, the traditional Shiʿi practice of concealing one's belief as a precautionary measure against persecution.[42]

The life and poetic career of Nizārī Quhistānī cannot be understood without taking note of this unremitting climate of suspicion and fear in which most Ismailis lived, and their concomitant need to observe *taqiyya* in the initial period of Mongol rule at least. The principal instrument employed by the poet to promote his ambitions in this hostile environment was to conceal his Ismaili identity from his Sunni patrons, the *malik*s Shams al-Dīn Kart of Khurāsān and ʿAlī Shāh of Quhistān. Nizārī's professional advancement under them would not have been possible without the poet disassociating himself in public from the Ismailis. Nonetheless, the poet seems to have encountered serious problems in adhering to this practice from time to time, resulting eventually in his dismissal from court under accusations of being an Ismaili. In view of the centrality of this issue in the life and career of Nizārī, it will be worthwhile to explore the matter further in the context of the Ismaili doctrine of *taqiyya*.

The Arabic term *taqiyya*, or its Persian equivalent *kitmān*, means 'prudence', 'fear' or 'protection,' and refers to the act of covering, concealment or dissimulation of one's religious beliefs when there is a possibility of danger or harm.[43] The Qur'an allows this practice for those acting under compulsion and in certain circumstances of everyday life (3:27, 5:3, 6:119, 16:106). For obvious reasons, this question did not become a major doctrinal issue for the Sunni Muslims, but it acquired special significance for the minority Shiʿis from an early period of their history.

The requirement of *taqiyya* is said to have been introduced in Shiʿi Islam by the Imam Muḥammad al-Bāqir among his followers and was made into an article of faith by his successor Jaʿfar al-Ṣādiq;[43] it was subsequently adopted by both Twelver and Ismaili Shiʿis as a religiously sanctioned means of protection in hostile environments. Basically, it permitted the Shiʿis in times of persecution to conceal their religious beliefs and adopt the outward observance of the Sunni *sharīʿa*. Among the Ismailis in particular, this principle of *taqiyya* was extended to include the obligation of those initiated in the *daʿwa* to preserve the secrecy of its esoteric doctrines from unauthorised people, an undertaking that became an essential part of the vow of allegiance (*ʿahd* or *mīthāq*) administered to converts.[44] The practice of *taqiyya* also came to be associated in Ismaili thought with the periods of *satr* (concealment) when the faithful were duty-bound to observe it, in contrast to the periods of *kashf* or *ẓuhūr* (manifestation) when it was no longer required.

In the light of these doctrinal perspectives, Nizārī Quhistānī's attempts to conceal his Ismaili allegiance may be seen as a form of *taqiyya* in its original sense of precautionary dissimulation. The poet's response in this respect was probably typical of most Persian Ismailis in the post-Alamūt period, who are likely to have resorted to similar acts of dissembling as much out of pragmatic considerations as out of a sense of religious duty or conviction. The imperative of *taqiyya* arose simply out of their desperate need to survive in a political and religious milieu that was inimical to their existence as a community; it was a necessary part of their efforts to reconstruct their lives and adapt to the harsh realities of

Mongol rule. It is also important to note that this behaviour was not peculiar to the Ismailis, but expressed by other sections of society too; there are many cases of prominent poets and Sufis who were similarly obliged to conceal their beliefs or intentions from the political and religious authorities of their time for a variety of reasons.

In any event, Nizārī's observance of *taqiyya* appears to have become increasingly problematic because he chose to make a living in the midst of political establishments in Khurāsān that were dominated by a Mongol-Turkish aristocracy with the support of the Sunni *ʿulamāʾ*. We do not know for sure what religious identities Nizārī assumed in order to attain the influential positions he did under the Karts and the Mihrabānids. Since both the dynasties were favourably inclined towards the Sufis and not averse to employing Shiʿis other than Ismailis, it is likely that in both cases Nizārī posed as a Twelver Shiʿi with a strong inclination towards Sufism. For an educated man like Nizārī, thoroughly familiar with the theology of Islamic schools and steeped in Sufi literature, this form of dissembling would have presented little difficulty. The common doctrinal basis of Ismaili and Twelver Shiʿism on the one hand, and the spiritual affinity between Ismailism and Sufism on the other, would have made it relatively easy for Nizārī to retain the integrity of his Ismaili allegiance. Nonetheless, the observance of such practice required the poet to be constantly vigilant against any overt admission of his Ismaili beliefs or associations, and it seems that he was fairly successful in maintaining this form of subterfuge for several years, first in Harāt and then in Bīrjand.

Nizārī's policy of dissimulation may have been relatively easy to maintain in his early years as a tax administrator in Harāt. The poems he composed eulogising Shams al-Dīn Kart indicate that the young man thrived in the fame and luxury which came with his admission to the Shah's court. But as noted, after a few years he become disenchanted with the extortionate tax policies of the Karts and disgusted by his own culpability in maintaining this system. The poet could no longer live with the conflicting demands of his social and moral selves, nor continue his service for a Sunni dynasty requiring the suppression of his Ismaili beliefs. This situation appears to have contributed to the spiritual crisis that overtook him around 679/1280 when he resigned from his position and embarked on his journey to the Transcaucasus.

Likewise, when Nizārī returned from his journey and won the favours of the Mihrabānid prince ʿAlī Shāh in Bīrjand, the two of them seem to have struck up a strong friendship based on their common ʿAlid sympathies and mutual loathing for the Karts. This shared interest may have been a major factor in encouraging the poet to challenge the land-owning aristocracy in the Shah's court. Whether Nizārī's outspoken attacks on them was part of a secret agreement with ʿAlī Shāh to rid him of his Sunni opponents it is impossible to say. Whatever the nature of their relationship, as we have seen, the Shah was ultimately unable to protect the poet from charges of being an Ismaili, on account of which he was summarily dismissed and exiled from the court.

Clearly, one of the central dilemmas of Nizārī's life and a focal point of tension in his poetic career was how to ensure his political survival while at the same time maintaining his own integrity as an Ismaili. If Nizārī's attempts to conceal his Ismaili identity from his benefactors is perceived as an expression of *taqiyya*, he used this policy primarily as an instrument for promoting his personal career and not necessarily for the purpose of protecting his life and limb, nor for preserving the sanctity of any esoteric doctrines. Nonetheless, there was a decisive turning point in Nizārī's life when he cut his links with the Kart dynasty and decided to go on a journey of his own. By thus renouncing the ideology of the ruling classes he was also reasserting the principles of his faith and the moral integrity of his being. The poet recognised a danger inherent in the long-term practice of *taqiyya* – one that many other Ismailis of his generation are also likely to have faced sooner or later in their lives – that it can lead, through a series of compromises and accommodations over the years, to a catastrophic collapse of one's faith and complete assimilation within the host community.

Given Nizārī's persistent efforts to conceal his Ismaili identity from his Sunni patrons, it is inevitable that his *taqiyya* should be reflected, in one way or another, in all his works. Thus, Nizārī's expressions of Ismaili ideas are conveyed covertly or implicitly, usually in the more general semantic context of Shiʿi Imamism and Sufi mysticism. He uses a variety of narrative devices (metaphorical, allegorical and symbolical) to allude to ideas whose Ismaili provenance would be apparent only to the more careful readers familiar with Ismaili doctrines. The use of such symbolic and anagogic language was, of course, commonplace among Sufi and many other poets to conceal the true purport of their verses and protect themselves from criticism of the orthodox-minded *ʿulamāʾ*. In the mystical poetry of Rūmī and Ḥāfiẓ especially, this technique was developed into a highly sophisticated and subtle system of allusions and hidden meanings which Hodgson calls 'the esoteric style in literature.'[46] Needless to say, this mode of writing has been employed universally by writers working in an environment of censorship and persecution. As pointed out by Leo Strauss in his essay on this subject:

> Persecution, then, gives rise to a peculiar technique of writing, and therewith to a peculiar type of literature, in which the truth about all crucial things is presented exclusively between the lines. The literature is addressed, not to all readers, but to trustworthy and intelligent readers only. It has all the advantages of private communication without having its greatest disadvantage – that it reaches only the writer's acquaintances. It has all the advantages of public communication without having its greatest disadvantage – capital punishment for the author ... an author who wishes to address only thoughtful men has but to write in such a way that only a very careful reader can detect the meaning of his book.[47]

The preponderance of Sufi ideas in Nizārī's poetry has sometimes been cited as a form of *taqiyya* by which the poet endeavoured to conceal his Ismaili faith.[48] The underlying assumption of this theory, first propounded by Ivanow, is that Ismailism and Sufism represent two fundamentally different schools of thought, with alternative spiritual visions of Islam. According to this view, any Ismaili thinker or writer espousing Sufi ideas could only do so out of the necessity of exercising precautionary prudence. The validity of this theory needs to be questioned in the light of the far-reaching social and cultural changes in Persia discussed earlier in this chapter. The penetration of Sufism into Persian language and literature was so all-pervasive during Nizārī's time that no community, class or group, least of all the poets, could be impervious to its influence. By using the Sufi idiom, Nizārī was in fact conforming to the conventional poetic medium of his time, in much the same way that the Fatimids thinkers of the 4th/10th century employed the philosophical language of Neoplatonism to articulate their doctrines. At the same time, Nizārī was giving expression to a growing interface between Ismailism and Sufism that began to emerge in Persia during the Mongol period. Nizārī's works represent the earliest documentation of a kind of 'Sufi Ismailism' that was to become more pronounced in the following centuries in Persia, Central Asia and the Indian subcontinent.

Nizārī's Connections with the Ismaili *Daʿwa*

As already noted, Nizārī was introduced to the Ismaili *daʿwa* in his early youth and obtained his education in Ismaili theology and philosophy from his father and the guidance of one or more *dāʿīs*. We do not know exactly when he was first admitted into the *daʿwa*, but since all Ismailis were required to take an oath of allegiance to the Ismaili Imam, this ceremony is likely to have taken place at an early stage of his life, well before his departure for Harāt. There are several verses, some of which have been cited before, in which Nizār refers to himself as a *mustajīb* (novitiate), *maʾdhūn* (licentiate) and *dāʿī* (summoner), revealing that he set off on the path of the organizational hierarchy of the Ismaili *daʿwa*.

Nizārī does not clearly detail the various stages of his progression in the Ismaili *daʿwa*, but it is possible to conclude from his testimony that the number of ranks in the organisation was reduced, as was the case during the Alamūt period. It is also interesting to note that Nizārī reverts to the terminology used during the Fatimid period. The most plausible explanation of this is that in the first decades after the collapse of the Alamūt state, the organisation of the *daʿwa* entered a period of rapid structural change. This process is corroborated in fact, by the Persian Ismaili *dāʿī* Abū Isḥāq Quhistānī in his treatise, *Haft bāb-i Bū Isḥāq*, written three centuries later in the 10th/16th-century, where he describes the *daʿwa* hierarchy of his time in a nomenclature strikingly similar to that of the Fatimid system, but also reflecting some of the organisational reforms introduced at Alamūt:

> When the new initiate (*mustajīb*) perfects his skill in teaching (*taʿlīm*) and his ability to prove (*ḥujjat*) is so developed that he is able to guide others and bring them out of confusion, he is appointed as *ma'dhūn*. Then, by permission of the *muʿallim* who has the rank of the 'senior' *ma'dhūn*, he receives the rank of junior *ma'dhūn* and starts preaching the *daʿwa* amongst the people for which his teacher gives him permission. When he is successful in discharging his duties of his rank, he claims promotion, he receives from the *ḥujja* the rank of senior preacher, *mad'hūn akbar*, and this rank implies absolute discretion to anyone to whom it he thinks it is desirable to do so. And when he receives still further promotion, he attains the rank of teacher, *muʿallim*, and the great *ḥujja* appoints him into a locality (*jazīra*). ... After this comes the rank of the *dāʿī*. A *dāʿī* receives absolute permission to carry on the *daʿwa* and he is not restricted to any *jazīra*.[49]

According to Baiburdi, Nizārī attained the rank of *dāʿī* when he was thirty-three years old,[50] that is to say around the time of his journey to the Caucasus in 679/1280. If this is the case, then Nizārī's journey represents a critical turning-point in his efforts to integrate himself more actively within the Ismaili community. It is reasonable to suppose that the poet's association with Ismaili *dāʿīs* intensified during his final years in Harāt when he had become disillusioned with the Kart dynasty and was seeking to recover the moral and spiritual integrity of his life. It follows too that Nizārī was already a fully-fledged Ismaili *dāʿī'* when he returned to Bīrjand and entered the service of the Mihrabānids, a fact which he admits openly in the works he wrote during this period:

> Listen to the advice of a *dāʿī*,
> Don't be a follower of your analogy and opinion.[51]
>
> Every *ẓāhir* you see cannot be without a *bāṭin*.
> Listen to the call of the *daʿwa* from an authorised *dāʿī* (*dāʿī muṣaddaq*).[52]

If you listen to the advice of a *dāʿī*,
you will become the accepted one (*muqbil*),
You will become alive and your heart will be enlightened.[53]

In addition to such overt declarations which may have confirmed the suspicions of Nizārī's enemies about his Ismaili allegiance, there is other circumstantial evidence – for instance, the arrest and imprisonment of his son Nuṣrat for preaching Ismailism – to indicate that after his return from the Caucasus and decisive break with the Kart dynasty, Nizārī was indeed an active member of the Ismaili *daʿwa* with the rank of a *dāʿī*. However, it is only through a close examination of his *Safar-nāma*, in which the poet narrates his journey from Quhistān to Ādharbāyjān and his interactions with other Ismailis he meets in various places, that we hope to be able to formulate a more informed opinion about his role as a *dāʿī* and the character of the Ismaili *daʿwa* during the period of Mongol domination.

Chapter 7

Nizārī's Safar-nāma: *The Journey of a* Dāʿī

On the first day of Shawwāl 678/4th February 1280, when Nizārī Quhistānī was 33 or 34 years old, he embarked on a long journey in the company of Tāj al-Dīn ʿĀmīd, an official of the Mongol government. They travelled west from Tūn in Quhistān through central Persia via Iṣfahān to Ādharbāyjān, Arrān, Armenia and Georgia, as far as Baku on the shores of the Caspian Sea. Shortly before Nizārī's departure or soon after his return in 681/1282, he resigned from his administrative position in Harāt and returned permanently to Bīrjand. The poet devoted himself here to his first major composition, the *Safar-nāma* (*Travelogue*), a versified *mathnawī* of about 1200 verses, in which he describes his journey, making observations of each place he visited and the people he met. Nizārī's travelogue, which gives the impression of having been based on notes made during the journey, was almost certainly completed before his appointment as court poet to the Mihrabānid governor of Quhistān, ʿAlī Shāh, in 694/1294.

The Enigma of Nizārī's *Safar-nāma*

The *Safar-nāma* stands out among Nizārī Quhistānī's works for several reasons. It is characterised, first of all, by its highly autobiographical content, and it therefore constitutes an important source of information on his life and activities. Secondly, this *mathnawī* is arguably the poet's most 'Ismaili' work with numerous allusions to Ismaili doctrines and ideas scattered throughout the text, thus providing a good profile of the poet's religious views and identity.

In spite of its 'confessional' nature, the *Safar-nāma* is also perhaps the most complex and enigmatic of Nizārī's *mathnawīs*. The difficulties of the text arise partly from the errors and ellipses introduced by the scribes at many points of the surviving manuscripts, which make it difficult to decipher the meaning of some passages.[1] But more importantly, it is caused by the poet's deliberate reticence or silence about significant details of his journey. There is a marked reluctance of the author to give the reader anything more than the barest information about the key events and personalities he encounters in various places. As a result of such evasiveness, Nizārī's entire journey appears to be shrouded in a veil of mystery and secrecy. This aspect of the *Safar-nāma* strongly suggests that when the poet sat down to compose this work, he was observing the principle of *taqiyya* in order to conceal the true nature of his journey from all but a few of his readers, the exception being those Ismailis able to 'read between the lines' and understand the real significance of his narrative.

The problem of interpreting Nizārī's travelogue is further compounded by the fact that his Ismaili ideas are expressed principally through the medium of Sufi poetic language, so that the entire narrative is coloured with Sufi imagery, themes and motifs. Leonard Lewisohn has observed that 'of all Nizārī's poetry, it is the *mathnawī* poem *Safar-nāma* that is the most pervasively Sufi in tenor in terms of doctrinal teaching and morality.'[2] As discussed earlier, this aspect of Nizārī's poetry cannot be regarded *ipso facto* as an expression of the poet's *taqiyya*, since he was merely observing the most popular poetic idiom of his time. Nonetheless, the extensive scope of Nizārī's Sufi vocabulary can lead some readers, especially those not familiar with Ismaili thought, to believe that the text was written by a Sufi poet. Such confusion is likely, for instance, with the various individuals whom Nizārī mentions having met during his journey and with whom he spends some time in spiritual converse or mystical concerts called *samāʿ*. Since the poet is extremely discreet about these people, giving little or no information about them other than that they were his close 'friends' (*rafīqān*, sing. *rafīq*), these figures may appear to some readers as 'Sufi' *shaykhs* or *pīrs*. However, given Nizārī's Ismaili background and his self-professed rank of an Ismaili *dāʿī*, there are indications in the *Safar-nāma* which lead us to assume that these dignitaries may have been his Ismaili co-religionists, and that one of them was possibly the Ismaili Imam of the time, Shams al-Dīn Muḥammad. If this is indeed the case, Nizārī's travelogue provides valuable documentation of the continuing existence in of an organised Ismaili community in the post-Alamūt period, as well as the remarkably close connections that had already arisen between the Ismailis and the Sufis in Persia within a few decades of the Mongol conquest.

Finally but not least, Nizārī's *Safar-nāma* is interesting for the anecdotal information he presents regarding the social, political and ethnographical conditions of the areas through which he passed in Ādharbāyjān, Armenia and Georgia, including his impressions of the preparations being made by the Īl-Khānid government for a coalition of military forces from these countries for an offensive against Syria.[3]

In many ways, Nizārī Quhistānī's *Safar-nāma* bears a close resemblance to the prose work of the same name by his more illustrious Ismaili forbearer of the 5th/11th century, the Fatimid poet, theologian, philosopher and chief *dāʿī* of Khurāsān, Nāṣir-i Khusraw. In his prose *Safar-nāma*, Nāṣir-i Khusraw describes his seven-years journey which took him from Marw in 437/1045 across northern Persia, Ādharbāyjān, Armenia, Anatolia, Syria and Palestine to Egypt (where he remained for three years and undertook several pilgrimages to Mecca and Medina), before his return via Baḥrayn and Iraq to Balkh in 444/1052. Nāṣir-i Khusraw's *Safar-nāma* occupies a special place in Persian literature, not only for the author's meticulous recording of the topography and ethnography of the various towns and cities he visited, but also for the simplicity and lucidity of his style of writing. In view of Nizārī's close familiarity with Ismaili literature, there is every reason to believe that his *Safar-nāma* was inspired by, and to a certain extent modelled upon, the more famous travelogue of the great Ismaili scholar.[4]

The Context of Nizārī's Journey

In the light of Nizārī Quhistānī's secretive and evasive style of writing in the *Safar-nāma*, it should come as no surprise to readers that at no point does he offer a clear, unequivocal statement of his motives for the journey, and whether he undertook it in his capacity as a government official or for some other, religious or private reasons of his own. The poet's silence on this matter is obviously deliberate rather than an oversight; the only hint of his intentions comes at the beginning of the *mathnawī*, where he tells us that his purpose in composing the poem was not just to tell an interesting story but to record important events and meetings with friends he met in the course of the journey:

> To remember the good and bad at every stage,
> To record those who were present and absent...
> I did not intend to make just a simple fable of this journey,
> Nor to describe or explain buildings and bath-houses,
> (But) to remember appointments with my friends;
> To remember them is my aim from (writing) this.[5]

There is no reason for us to doubt the poet's declaration of intent for writing the *Safar-nāma* and his dedication of the work to the memory of his friends. A good portion of the *Safar-nāma* is indeed devoted to Nizārī's meeting and conversing with these individuals, even though he is not forthcoming about his precise relations with them. Still, the question remains as to why he should have taken the trouble of going on such a long journey if his purpose was merely to keep 'appointments' with his friends. To undertake a journey of several hundred miles in the medieval world was an arduous and difficult task, which one did not normally do without a clearly-defined goal such as a pilgrimage, to search for knowledge, or for reasons of trade, government duty or some such specific need or assignation, etc.[6]

It is significant that Nizārī took the journey with Tāj al-Dīn ʿĀmīd who was, according to Baradin, an agent (*maʾmūr*) of the Īl-Khānid *dīwān* (treasury), responsible for tax collection in Ādharbāyjān and Arrān regions.[7] Baiburdi does not specify Tāj al-Dīn's position other than that he was a state official, but mentions that it was he who appointed or invited Nizārī to accompany him on the journey.[8] This is confirmed by Muṣaffā who also adds that Tāj al-Dīn may have been the son of the Mihrabānid prince Shams al-Dīn ʿAlī, the future patron of Nizārī after his return from the journey.[9]

In any case, upon reaching Tabrīz, the capital of Ādharbāyjān, the two travellers joined the official entourage of the chief minister (*wazīr*) of the Īl-Khānid ruler Abaqa Khān by the name of Shams al-Dīn Juwaynī (brother of the famous historian, ʿAlāʾ al-Dīn ʿAṭā-Mālik), and travelled with him to various military bases in the Caucasian region. But Nizārī does not explain why they accompanied the *wazīr*, leaving it to his readers to reach the appropriate conclusions, nor does he mention any personal encounters with the minister himself.[10] In fact, throughout the *Safar-nāma*, Nizārī offers little information on Tāj al-Dīn's activities as a tax-collector, thus suggesting that he took no active part in this aspect of their journey and was accompanying Tāj al-Dīn for purely personal reasons. The most likely explanation for Nizārī's journey, therefore, is that its itinerary was determined by a dual agenda based on the Tāj al-Dīn's official duties and Nizārī's own interest in meeting up with his 'friends'.

There are many remarks which the poet makes in the *Safar-nāma* about Tāj al-Dīn which suggest that their relationship was based on something more than a mutual interest in fiduciary matters. Nizārī took much pleasure in travelling with Tāj al-Dīn, and throughout the work he always refers to him with the greatest respect as his guide and constant companion in public and private. But in some verses Nizārī's depicts Tāj al-Dīn in a much more spiritual light, eulogising him with the honorific title of 'Khwāja,' calling him 'the light of my awakening heart,' the one who was 'on the same path' as himself,[11] and that together they were 'setting out on the path of unity (*ṭarīqat-i ittiḥād*), with one heart and one belief.'[12] The special character of their relationship is revealed further in these lines:

In ease and adversity, I was always beside him,
I was always obedient to his righteous thinking,
I was devoted to him in good or ill, in benefit or harm.
I was always his companion on the journey or at home.
I was indeed among his most special friends (*khāṣṣ al-khāṣṣ*)
In the dust of the path of sincere devotion to him.[13]

The expression *khāṣṣ al-khāṣṣ* used here by Nizārī is significant because, as mentioned in Chapter 5, it was applied by the Ismailis of the Alamūt period to the 'super-elite' (*khawāṣṣ al-khāṣṣ*) class of their *daʿwa* who had attained a high degree of spiritual development. A similar term, *mardān-i khāṣṣ*, is found in the poet's *Dastūr-nāma*: 'I came to the teaching (*taʿlīm*) of a friend who had the rank of an angel. When he saved me from painful torment, he became my guide to the unique people (*mardān-i khāṣṣ*).'[14]

These references to Tāj al-Dīn, besides intimating that he and Nizārī shared a common spiritual fellowship as Ismailis, suggest that there may have been another purpose behind their journey superseding whatever professional connections they had. Bearing in mind Nizārī's newly acquired position as an Ismaili *dāʿī*, there is a distinct possibility that he set out on his journey with the intention of meeting other members of the *daʿwa*, as hinted by the poet in the following lines:

To travel around the world is a happy state,
But only if you have the companionship of an intimate friend.
On the journey there is no stopping without a bend,
Especially if the traveller has no desire in mind.
Even if someone travels for pleasure alone,
he must set out with the *daʿwa* at every interval.
Then when he makes a choice, it will be a good one for him;
Travelling on the journey (*marḥal*) and the stopping place
(*manzil*) will be in his hands.
If the traveller is able to make such a journey,
Then he will succeed in attaining his heart's desire.
But if not, other than grief and anxiety,
There will be no accomplishment in his journey.[15]

We can assume from this discussion that in all probability Tāj al-Dīn ʿĀmīd too was an Ismaili adept who had succeeded in attaining an important position in the Īl-Khānid government, in the same way as Nizārī had done at the local level in Harāt, that is, by resorting to *taqiyya* in order to conceal their Ismaili identities. Baiburdi mentions in this connection that since many Ismaili *dāʿīs* of the Alamūt period were well-qualified individuals, it is quite likely that after the Mongol conquest some of them managed to find employment in the government.[16]

Understanding Nizārī's Journey

As in most traditions of religion and mythology, the Ismailis have understood the notion of a journey (*safar kardan*) symbolically as the quest for true knowledge. In early Ismaili thought, this journey is usually depicted in terms of an interiorised movement, proceeding from the *ẓāhir* (exoteric) to the *bāṭin* (esoteric), from one's perceptions of the outer world of physical phenomena to an intuitive grasp of their hidden, spiritual meanings, which in turn leads to a third level where one discovers the innermost secrets (*bāṭin al-bāṭin*) of existence.[17] As we have seen, among Persian Ismailis of the Alamūt and post-Alamūt periods, this threefold progression became equated with the stages of *ṭarīqa* (path), *maʿrifa* (gnosis) and *ḥaqīqa* (truth) common to Sufism.

For Nizārī Quhistānī, it seems that the journey was part of his own spiritual odyssey to raise his level of spiritual of knowledge within the structured scheme of *taʿlīm* (instruction) offered to him by the Ismaili *daʿwa*. 'To journey away from one's beloved home is a *qiyāma*,'[18] he says, thus connecting the journey with the Ismaili understanding of 'resurrection,' the transforming moment of spiritual awakening when one's life enters upon a new pattern of existence. According to the 4th/10th-century Ismaili *dāʿī* and author Abū Yaʿqūb al-Sijistānī, all entities are characterised by a series of *qiyāmāt*, of beginnings and ends, creation and annihilation, in which their existential constitution becomes remoulded.[19] The same view was expressed three centuries later in Alamūt by Naṣīr al-Dīn al-Ṭūsī who conceived the evolution of all beings, from mineral, plant and animal to the human and angelic, in terms of a *qiyāma*.[20] In a like manner, he says human existence consists of a number of cumulative phases when one cycle reaches its zenith to be replaced by another of a higher and greater potency. The Ismaili thinkers associated these stages of spiritual maturity with the progressive movement of a *dāʿī* through the ranks of the *daʿwa* hierarchy. Henry Corbin has aptly described this process in terms of an 'alchemy of Resurrection':

> In the Ismaili schematisation of the world, the sum of the degrees of the esoteric hierarchy appears to the adept as a cycle of *resurrections*, each one of which must be transcended, as a succession of Paradises which must be surmounted on pain of falling back into a Hell. Each rank or spiritual degree is a resurrection (*qiyāmāt*) whereby the adept becomes conjoined with new immaterial forms which appear on his horizon.[21]

There can be little doubt that Nizārī Quhistānī was familiar with this interpretation of the *qiyāma*, for that is how he understood, remembered and recorded his own journey in the *Safar-nāma*, and the same idea recurs in several other places of his *Kulliyyāt*. Throughout the narrative, the poet presents his journey both as a physical excursion as well as a spiritual experience for him, wherein each significant encounter is presented as a 'paradise.' Baiburdi recognised the spiritual dimension of the poet's journey when he compared it to those undertaken by searching Ismailis, Sufi ascetics and wandering *darwīsh*es.[22]

There is some resemblance between Nizārī's conception of the journey and Nāṣir-i Khusraw's description of his conversion and search for truth as given in the first few pages of his prose *Safar-nāma*, as well as in his famous autobiographical *qaṣīda* addressed to the Fatimid chief *dāʿī* al-Mu'ayyad fi'l-Dīn al-Shīrāzī.[23] The travelogues of both Ismaili poets may be seen outwardly as a record of their impressions of different places and people they visited. But there was also an underlying Ismaili dimensions of their journeys, which were undertaken within the initiatory structure of the *daʿwa*. According to W. Thackston, Nāṣir-i Khusraw described in his *Safar-nāma* every important Ismaili centre west of Transoxania, and the only places upon which he expended favourable comment were those ruled by Ismailis. He concludes from this: 'If [Nāṣir-i Khusraw] was not being sent from one Ismaili stronghold to another, there is little to justify his eccentric skirting of the central Islamic world.'[24] The same observation can be applied to Nizārī Quhistānī's travelogue if it is understood as a memoir dedicated to the Ismaili *rafiqān* he met in the course of his journey.

In the Islamic tradition, the pilgrimage (*ḥajj*) to Mecca is regarded as the journey *par excellence* which all Muslims are obliged to observe at least once in their lifetime. Traditionally, it required a great deal of personal effort and sacrifice, often involving months of arduous travel over difficult terrain and through strange places before the faithful were able to arrive at their destination and perform the required rituals around the Kaʿba. When Nāṣir-i Khusraw departed from Khurāsān on his journey to the west, his ostensible reason was to undertake this pilgrimage, but his real destination was the headquarters of the Ismaili Imam in Cairo, and it was only later that he was able to don the garb of a pilgrim and visit the Kaʿba. For both Nāṣir-i Khusraw and Nizārī Quhistānī, as indeed for most Ismaili authors, the physical pilgrimage to Mecca has its counterpart in one's spiritual journey towards the Imam of the time who represents, in the esoteric sense, the true Kaʿba of the heart, the *miḥrāb* (niche) and *qibla* (direction) of one's devotions. In a passage reminiscent of Nāṣir-i Khusraw's famous poem on the inner meaning of the rites and rituals of pilgrimage,[25] Nizārī writes in his *Safar-nāma*:

I don't know of any *qibla* except the face
  of my Beloved,
And wherever he is, that is my *qibla*.
East or West is one place (for me);
I am certain of that, even if you doubt it.
Your face is towards the *miḥrāb*, but your heart
  is in another place,
While you are busy doing some work in the bazaar.
The Kaʿba of the heart should be kept pure.
When you sow the seed of obedience, it must be
  sown with purity (of purpose);
If your intentions are impure and imperfect,
Then whatever direction you take, your *qibla* (is useless).

If a man is in the Kaʿba of truthfulness and purity,
Whatever direction he takes, his *qibla* is permissible.
For a man of truth, East and West are the same.
I am certain about it, even if you doubt it.
I do not have any path (*madhhab*) other than this.
O my Friend, keep me (steadfast) on this path.
Take me as one of your servants,
So that I can make your face my *qibla*.[26]

Notwithstanding these similarities of sentiment between Nāṣir-i Khusraw and Nizārī, there are major differences arising from the individual talents and temperaments of the two Ismaili poets, as well as the special circumstances of their respective journeys. In the major portion of his travelogue, Nāṣir refrains scrupulously from religious teachings and confines himself to an objective description of the physical and social terrain through which he travelled. By contrast, Nizārī's work is a highly devotional and didactic narrative in which his main purpose is to describe his encounters with his 'friends' and to propagate certain religious and ethical ideas. The poet often makes long digressions to present anecdotes, tales and maxims from the classics of Persian poetry and mysticism to support the principles of his teachings. Much of this Sufi-like discourse is usually in support of Ismaili doctrines, such as the necessity of an Imam, the importance of following his instructions (*taʿlīm*) and submission (*taslīm*) to his commands, together with implicit references to authors and arguments typical of Ismaili literature in general and in keeping with the pedagogic function of a *dāʿī*.

A good illustration of the Ismaili underpinnings of Nizārī's homilectic style is the instance where he recalls his father's advice to be careful in love and choose one's beloved wisely. The moral which the poet draws out of this is that one cannot undertake a spiritual journey without the guidance of the 'truthful person' (*mard-i mard*). The poet is probably alluding here to the third proposition of Ḥasan-i Ṣabbāḥ's doctrine of *taʿlīm*, according to which there can be only one authoritative and truthful teacher (*muʿallim-i ṣādiq*) in the world.[27]

Without a friend (*rafīq*) no one can find his own way,

Otherwise everyone would be in solitude.
The one who goes alone will be left in confusion.
No one can find the path by himself.
Only the one who subdues his own self can have
access to the guide.
Do not assume that the path is self-illuminated.
Its light comes from the enlightened friend.
If the moon had not followed the sun,
How do you think it became illumined (at night)?
You should appeal to the adept of the truthful (*mard-i mard*),
Because without such a companion, one is left
(unprotected) like a widow.
Your guide must be a truthful person,
(Because) not everyone can be a true guide.
Much illusion is on your way unless you enter through
the door of submission (*taslīm*).
No, brother, no, this is not the work of a delicate-hearted person.
Unless a disciple (*murīd*) dispenses with unbelief and faith,
How can he enter the path of submission?[28]

In another story, Nizārī describes an army commander who despatched a volunteer with a message for the *qāḍī* of Gīlān. However, when he arrived hot and tired before the judge he realised that he had failed to understand the message accurately. After questioning the man for a while, the *qāḍī* came to the conclusion that what the commander wanted was a huge stone and so the messenger set off with this burden on his back. The commander was angered to see the man return with a stone he had not requested and ordered him back to get a different kind of stone. The poor man dragged himself all the way back to the *qāḍī* to exchange one stone for another which he finally delivered to the commander. Nizārī draws a number of lessons from this amusing tale to stress the importance of a correct relationship between the spiritual guide and his disciple, which has to be based on right instruction on the one hand and absolute obedience on the other.

If the (relations) of the commander and the commanded
are not based on a true foundation,
Although they are there, they do not exist in principle.
The absolute commander of all is the lord (*khudāwand*),

and that is that:
There is no command above this to be abided to.

Nizārī's allegory will remind those familiar with the Ismaili writings of Naṣīr al-Dīn al-Ṭūsī's discussion of the 'commander' and the 'commanded' in his autobiographical treatise the *Sayr wa sulūk*, where he distinguishes between the followers of the command (*farmān*) as revealed in the holy books and those who attend to the commander (*farmāndih*) appointed by God. 'It is in terms of this distinction,' says Ṭūsī, 'that hypocrites are separated from the faithful, the exotericists from the esotericists, the people of legal prescriptions (*sharīʿāt*) from the people of resurrection (*qiyāmat*), the people of plurality from the people of unity.'[29]

The intermingling of the narrative and the didactic in Nizārī's *Safar-nāma* is particularly reflected in his account of a friend who fell in love with a beautiful woman. This man became totally obsessed with her, spending years in pursuit of her friendship, until she finally agreed to meet him; but when the time came for him to meet her, the unlucky lover fell asleep and missed the appointment. The poet uses this story to convey his own allegorical message that all seekers after truth must seek and know the Imam of the time. For Nizārī, as for all Ismaili thinkers, it is not sufficient to recognise the name and physical person of the Imam but to seek his inner, mystical reality, the 'light' (*nūr*) which dwells in him. Here too the poet alludes to the well-known Qur'anic parable of divine light (24:35–36), also much quoted in Ismaili literature through the centuries:

As you become aware of yourself,
You will remove the veil from yourself.
Then the truth should be recognised by the truth.
You must recognise him through himself.
Through him means 'the light of his light' (*nūrun ʿalā nūrin*),
His *nūr* – that is to say, by following his commandment.[30]

From the few examples given above, there can be little doubt not only of the Ismaili orientation of Nizārī's *Safar-nāma* but also the fact that he composed this *mathnawī* specifically for the instruction and edification of his Ismaili readers and fellow *dāʿīs*, as expressed clearly in this homily:

> If you listen to the advice of a *dāʿī*,
> You will become accepted (*muqbil*),
> You will become alive
> And your heart will become enlightened.[31]

Springtime in Iṣfahān

As mentioned, Nizārī and Tāj al-Dīn commenced their journey in the spring of 678/1280, from the town of Tūn in eastern Quhistān. It is interesting that the travellers started their journey from Tūn which used to be one of the major Ismaili strongholds of Quhistān where, it will be recalled, a large number of Ismailis were massacred by Hülegü's forces in 650/1252 and again in 654/1256. But the community was not entirely wiped out since it could still be found in the province towards the end of the century in Nizārī's time. Since Tūn was located not far from the poet's hometown of Bīrjand, he must have known many people in this town, but makes no mention of it in the *Safar-nāma*. Tūn was also a convenient starting-point for the caravan route west through the great desert of Persia to the city of Iṣfahān. The fact that the two travellers did not take the shorter, northern route to Ādharbāyjān via Nīshāpūr, Simnān and Rayy, which Nāṣir-i Khusraw had taken two centuries earlier on the first leg of his journey from Balkh, suggests that Tāj al-Dīn and Nizārī had a special reason for visiting Iṣfahān, either for the purpose of tax collection or to meet certain individuals.

The travellers arrived in Iṣfahān in the first month of spring when the city was bathed in bright sunlight and the fruit trees growing in the orchards. The strategic location of Iṣfahān, at the crossroads of caravan routes from eastern and western parts of the Muslim world, made it an important and prosperous city of medieval Persia. It became the capital of the Saljūqs and subsequently of the Ṣafawid dynasty in the 10th/16th century. When Nāṣir-i Khusraw visited the city in 444/1052, he reported that 'of all the Persian-speaking cities, I never saw a finer, more commodious, or more flourishing city than Iṣfahān.'[32] According to the historian Rashīd al-Dīn, Iṣfahān was completely destroyed by the Mongols twenty-five years earlier, its inhabitants massacred and the cultivated land reduced to waste,[33] although it appears to have escaped complete destruction.[34] The speedy recovery of the city has been be attributed to the stringent measures taken by Khwāja Bahā' al-Dīn (d. 678/1279), son of Shams al-Dīn Juwaynī, the *wazīr* of the Īl-Khānids, who was placed in charge of Persian and Arab Iraq ('Irāq-i 'Ajam) by Hülegü after his Persian conquests. The governor is reported to have been extremely rigorous in his rule of this area by eliminating theft and crime, and building many palaces, buildings and pleasure grounds.[35]

Thus, when Nizārī arrived in Iṣfahān, he found it to be a thriving and prosperous metropolis once again and the land restored to cultivation. So captivated was the poet by the beauty and charm of this place that he compares it to paradise:

> Iṣfahān is like paradise, fresh and blooming;
> Her beauty is a hundred times better than
> the sound of her description;
> The life of her river is sweeter than
> the running streams of Paradise.
> Every side was full of trees and sown fields,
> with roses blooming in every garden,
> (And) my heart rose up like a nightingale.[36]

Nizārī tells us nothing about any administrative functions that Tāj al-Dīn may have had to observe in Iṣfahān, but he does state quite explicitly that the purpose of their visit to the city was to meet a certain friend called Īrānshāh. There was apparently a close religious bond between the two for the poet refers to him as 'a pious man and true in his allegiance (*'ahd-i nīkū*),' the 'keeper of my secret (*rāz*) and my companion night and day.' Baiburdi is of the opinion that this person was an Ismaili, since the names 'Īrānshāh' and 'Khurshāh' were typical among Ismailis at this time.[37] Muṣaffā also considers Īrānshāh to have been an Ismaili, adding further that he may have come from the family of the last Ismaili Imam of the Alamūt period, Rukn al-Dīn Khurshāh, murdered by the Mongols in 655/1257.[38] Nizārī informs us that he and Īrānshāh spent many happy hours together, listening to the music of harp (*nay*) and lute (*chang*) and drinking wine (*nūsh*).

The poet continues that after putting aside the wine and music, both he and Īrānshāh were invested with a *khirqa* by a *pīr* whom he does not identify by name. The term *khirqa* is commonly used in Sufism for the patched frock or cloak given by a *shaykh* or *pīr* to his *murīd* (disciple) at the time of his initiation and pledge of allegiance. According to Seyyed Hossein Nasr, the *khirqa* ceremony has a Shiʿi origin from the tradition that the Imam ʿAlī once clothed al-Ḥasan al-Baṣrī with such a cloak when he initiated him into the mystic path.[39] The bestowal of the *khirqa*, usually coloured blue, green, white or black, signified the establishment of a permanent spiritual bond between the master and his pupil. There were different orders of *khirqa* in Sufism according to the spiritual development of the aspirant; it was believed sometimes to transmit a master's spiritual power (*baraka*) directly to his chosen successor or other favoured disciples.[40]

In spite of Nizārī's receipt of a *khirqa* in Iṣfahān, he is critical of the obsession of many Sufis to acquire this dress from a variety of masters. He narrates in this connection the tale of a young man who went to his *pīr* to beg for a *khirqa*, but the *pīr* sends him away with the instruction to first cleanse himself of worldly desires and learn to forget his lower, acquisitive self.[41] Elsewhere in the *Safarnāma*, Nizārī explains that the possession of a *khirqa* is not a genuine indicator of one's spirituality. What matters is not one's outer appearance but the inner state of the soul:

How can a *faqīr* (*darwīsh*) become accepted
If he is entrapped in a dispute about right and wrong?
If being a Sufi is to possess something blue and green,
Then every person who wears a ragged cloth
  would be a Khiḍr of his time
Quietly follow the Khiḍr and leave aside all these objections
  of your disobedient soul.
(Don't indulge) in discussion of whether it's black or white.
If you dispute between what is outside and inside,
Then you bring into yourself the effect of this separation.
As long as the *darwīsh* is not pure in his esoteric knowledge,
He cannot fight successfully in the army of the King.[42]

Nizārī supplies us with few other details about his stay in Iṣfahān other than to say that he stayed in the city for a while and took the opportunity to meet Īrānshāh for a second time because they were such good friends. It was Īrānshāh, in fact, who suggested to Nizārī that he should write a memoir of his journey. Some readers may see Nizārī's encounters with Īrānshāh and others in Iṣfahān taking place within a purely Sufi context, but given the poet's Ismaili background and the teachings he expounds in the *Safar-nāma*, it is equally likely to have been a gathering of Ismailis.

Iṣfahān had been a centre of the Ismaili *daʿwa* since the 4th/10th century when it was introduced into the region by the early *dāʿī* Abū Ḥātim al-Rāzī. Later it became the centre of the *daʿwa*'s activities in Persia under ʿAbd al-Malik b. ʿAṭṭāsh, before its headquarters was moved to Alamūt by his successor, Ḥasan-i Ṣabbāḥ. In 494/1100, the Ismailis of Iṣfahān, under the leadership of ʿAbd al-Malik's son Aḥmad captured the nearby fortress of Shāhdiz. This caused considerable concern to the Saljūqs who instigated several massacres of the community in the city and mounted a military offensive against Shāhdiz which fell in 500/1107 after a prolonged siege. Thereafter, the Ismaili presence was much reduced in Iṣfahān, although a small number appears to have survived there in the following centuries, probably living clandestinely as Twelver Shiʿis or Sufis.[43]

If the assembly which Nizārī Quhistānī attended in Iṣfahān was indeed among a group of his Ismaili co-religionists, it is reasonable to assume that the *pīr* he met on this occasion was a senior Ismaili *dāʿī*, and that by being invested with a *khirqa*, both Nizārī and Īrānshāh were being initiated formally into a higher rank of the Ismaili *daʿwa*. Be that as it may, the most significant aspect of this scenario is its reflection of the remarkable transformation of the Nizārī Ismaili community of Persia into an organisation very similar to that of the Sufi *ṭarīqa*s, and that this process was already well advanced in the latter part of the 7th/13th century, more than a century earlier than the time when, during the Ṣafawid period, the Ismaili Imams and their *daʿwa* organisation emerged in the public domain under the mantle of Sufism.

Meetings with Friends in Tabrīz

It was in the middle of Dhu'l-Qa'da (mid-March) that Nizārī Quhistānī and Tāj al-Dīn set off from Iṣfahān for Ādharbāyjān, arriving in Naṭanz, a town situated to the north of Iṣfahān and west of Ardistān.[44] This part of their journey is likely to have taken no more than two weeks, since he describes the time of their arrival as the 'season of flowers,' presumably early summer. As in Iṣfahān, Nizārī was captivated by the beauty of the place, comparing it to heaven, which made him feel happy and joyful. Here too the poet reports having met some of his 'friends' and 'drinking wine' in a spiritual assembly.

On the third day they set off for Tabrīz, the capital of Ādharbāyjān some thirty miles from the lake of Urmiyya. Nāṣir-i Khusraw found Tabrīz in to be a flourishing city when he visited it 437/1046,[45] and Yāqūt notes that it was a major manufacturing centre in the early part of the 7th/13th century.[46] After the death of Hülegü in 663/1265, his son and successor Abaqa Khān transferred the Īl-Khānid capital from Marāghah to Tabrīz. According to Barthold, the Mongols favoured Tabrīz because of its strategic location in the north of the country and its open, natural environment which was more attractive to nomadic people.[47]

At the time when Nizārī and Tāj al-Dīn arrived in the city, on the first day of the month of Dhu'l-Ḥijja, 679/1280,[48] Abaqa was gathering a large army for an invasion of Syria. The reign of Abaqa (663–680/1265–1282) was largely determined by his efforts to prevent encroachment of his Persian empire from the predatory designs of rival Mongol powers, the Golden Horde based in the steppes of southern Russia and the Chaghatayids of Transoxania, as well as his own ambition to extend his empire into Syria which was then ruled by the Mamlūk sultans of Egypt. In pursuit of his goals, Abaqa attempted to create a grand alliance with the Christian powers of Europe and the Saljūqs of Anatolia against the Mamlūks who, in turn, cultivated diplomatic and trade relations with the Golden Horde.[49] According to Rashīd al-Dīn, the immediate cause of Abaqa's plans for attacking Syria was to seek revenge for a Mamlūk incursion into Anatolia which was part of his fiefdom.[50] The invading force consisted of between 40,000 and

50,000 Mongol-Turkish troops, including sizeable contingents of Saljūqs, Armenians, Georgians and Franks, under the nominal leadership of Abaqa's younger brother Mengü Timür.[51]

When Nizārī composed the *Safar-nāma* upon his return to Quhistān, he was undoubtedly aware of the political and military circumstances of the Mongol invasion of Syria, but he makes no direct reference to this event in his travelogue, in spite of having stayed in the city for three months. Instead of describing his impressions of Mongol power and prestige in which he, as a civil servant, would have taken a keen interest, the poet prefers at first to write about the exceptional merits of the capital city, praising it in even more glowing terms than Iṣfahān as a paradisical place inhabited by a hospitable and beautiful people:

> We found a place full of food and hospitality,
> Like a paradise it was, full of handsome youths
> And angelic maidens (*ḥūr*) all around me,
> A place where my heart (rejoiced) within me.[52]

As we follow Nizārī's *Safar-nāma*, a certain pattern emerges in which he likens some places he visits to paradise or heaven, in contrast to others for which he expresses his distaste clearly. The frequency of the paradise image in the *Safar-nāma* suggests that Nizārī is using the term not as a rhetorical device but symbolically in the spirit of the Ismaili *ta'wīl* (allegorical interpretation) of the Qur'anic descriptions of Paradise (Arabic, *janna*; Persian, *bihisht*) consisting of heavenly gardens, rivers of pure water, milk, honey and wine, palaces with beautiful youth and maidens, etc. According to Naṣīr al-Dīn al-Ṭūsī's *Rawḍat al-taslīm* (*Paradise of Submission*):

> Both Paradise and Hell are products of man's mental conceptions and such conceptions are of no more than three categories: sensory (*ḥissī*), psychical (*nafsī*) and intellectual (*'aqlī*) conceptions. If his mental conception started out [at the level] of sensory perception and proceeds no further, then such a conception makes of itself a sensible hell for him in his soul, his soul being in his very own hell. If his mental conception begins on a psychical level and proceeds no further, that conception will effect a glimpse of paradise within his soul, his soul sensing the effects of his inner heaven. If his mental conception proceeds from

> intellectual knowledge and remains at that level, that conception will become a real paradise within the soul for him, his soul being in its very own paradise.[53]

For al-Ṭūsī, paradise is the perpetual state of the genuine seeker after the truth. Whoever is on the spiritual path, actively seeking and finding the inner meaning of the words of scripture is already 'a denizen of Paradise.' As one progresses steadily through various spiritual stages, he encounters a series of paradises, one after the other, which al-Ṭūsī calls 'paradises of relative perfections,' until the soul attains its ideal perfected condition which is its 'real Paradise'. He describes this ultimate state in terms of 'the attainment of God in all His aspects,' 'the upright (*mustaqīm*) intellect united with the divine volition (*amr*),' 'the gnosis of pure intellect,' and 'total freedom of the will (*ikhtiyār-i maḥḍ*).'[54]

Since Nizārī makes multiple references to paradise in his *Safarnāma* with some of the meanings conveyed by al-Ṭūsī's discussion, it is likely that he was familiar with the great philosopher's text. It is interesting, moreover, that the places which Nizārī praises so extravagantly as paradisical are those where he encounters his spiritual 'friends' and joins them in private audiences of mystical conversations, music and wine-drinking. The poet's use of the term 'paradise' in this context can therefore be interpreted in al-Ṭūsī's sense of a 'relative paradise,' that is of an occasion when he was able to make a specific advance in his spiritual understanding, or as a progression from one stage to another on his journey through the hierarchical structure of the Ismaili *daʿwa*.

Of all the places Nizārī visited in the course of his journey, he found Tabrīz the most heavenly and spiritually rewarding because during the three months he stayed in the city the poet was able to interact with a number of like-minded individuals on the spiritual path. It is noteworthy that Tāj al-Dīn is conspicuously absent from these activities, suggesting that he was probably occupied most of this time with his official duties as tax-collector. Nizārī's extended stay in Tabrīz would have certainly given him plenty of opportunity to make contact with other people of similar interests in poetry and spirituality. But as in the case of Nizārī's friends in Iṣfahān and Naṭanz, he gives us no information about these personalities and we are never sure of their precise standing or relationship with him. One of the people Nizārī met in Tabrīz was someone called Khwāja Fakhr al-Dīn, about whom he writes:

We struck the canopy of our pleasure on the Pleiades,
We shared a cup of wine with Khwāja Fakhr al-Dīn.
Day turned to night and night into day,
listening (*samā*ʿ) to the harp (*chang*) amidst lovely faces.[55]

Nizārī had a similar session with another man of whom he says:

May a friend sacrifice himself for Sayf Kāshānī!
May he benefit from the fruit of the tree of life!
Day and night continuously he spent with us.
He was in our company enduring both pain and pleasure.
When I was with him, I was unaware of the cup of drink.
For a time I was free of the pain
And the mind was taken away from desire.[56]

As noted before, this precautionary style is a characteristic feature of the *Safar-nāma* and an expression of poet's observance of *taqiyya*, which he sometimes carries to the point of obscurity, leaving it to the readers to figure out the circumstances of his meetings according to their own capabilities. Some readers would prefer to see these activities taking place in an entirely Sufi setting, but an Ismaili reading of the text would suggest strongly that these 'friends' of Nizārī may have been his co-religionists resident in Tabrīz who had adopted some of the customary practices of Sufi or *darwīsh* orders in Ādharbāyjān when he visited the region.

The Ismaili presence in Ādharbāyjān and the adjacent areas of the Caspian Sea has been recorded since the early part of the 4th/10th century, when their *dāʿīs* succeeded in converting the local ruler of the Musāfirid dynasty, Marzūban b. Muḥammad (d. 346/957).[57] As a result, the Ismaili faith began to be disseminated openly and established a strong presence in Tabrīz and other areas (which was probably one reason why Nāṣir-i Khusraw visited the city in 437/1046). Although they subsequently came under severe persecution when the Saljūqs took control of the region, a good number of Ismailis seem to have survived in Ādharbāyjān well into the Mongol period, possibly developing links with a number of Perso-Turkish *darwīsh* orders in the region with a strong Shiʿi colouring and particular reverence for the Imam ʿAlī.[58]

One of the practices which Nizārī reports having participated with his friends is the *samāʿ* ceremony, the musical sessions which became popular among certain Sufi orders in the Persian world. The *samāʿ* typically involves the performance of poetry, music and sometimes dance with the chanting of *dhikr* for the purpose of inducing religious ecstasy (*wajd*). This practice appears to have been first introduced into Sufism by the Khurāsānian poet and mystic Abū Saʿīd b. Abi'l-Khayr in 5th/11th century,[59] after which it was adopted by many Sufi *ṭarīqa*s. The lawfulness of music and dance provoked much debate among Sufis and theologians. Some Sufi orders such as the Chishtiyya permitted *samāʿ* as a legitimate outlet for religious devotion, whereas others such as the Naqshbandiyya rejected it as against the religious law. The most widely known example of this practice today is the whirling dances of the Mevlevi order founded by the successors of Jalāl al-Dīn Rūmī.[60]

In the various references which Nizārī makes to such musical sessions in the *Safar-nāma*, there is no specific mention of dancing, but he refers frequently to wine-drinking. As discussed in the previous chapter, the imagery of wine and wine-drinking, together with the associated motifs of lover and beloved, is one of the most distinctive aspects of Sufi literature, a poetic idiom which the Sufis derived from earlier Arabic and Persian traditions of a more secular kind. In fact, the love and wine vocabulary of the Sufis became so popular that it was adopted by virtually all poets and became part of the common linguistic stock of Persian-speaking peoples everywhere. The Sufi poets deployed these terms symbolically to express a whole range of spiritual meanings – thus, wine represented the extremity of love (*ʿishq*), intoxication (*sukr*) as the experience of ecstasy (*wajd*), and the cup-bearer (*sāqī*) as the image of the divine Beloved.[61] It is arguable that much of the power and beauty of Persian mystical poetry, exemplified in the verses of Rūmī and Ḥāfiẓ, arise from their use of this symbolism in such a skilfully ambiguous way that the boundaries between the profane and the sacred, the human and the divine, are never clearly delineated.

As in the case of these Sufi poets, Nizārī's allusions to wine-drinking are infused with ambiguities and equivocations, so that it is often difficult to decipher whether he is referring to wine in the literal sense as an intoxicating beverage or in the metaphoric sense of love for the Divine. The drinking of wine was a common practice in medieval Persia, especially in the courts and among the ruling classes, and the glorification of wine was one of the major themes of early Persian poetry. It is possible that Nizārī first acquired this habit during his career with the Kart dynasty in Harāt, which is reflected in the numerous references he makes to wine-drinking in the *qaṣīda*s composed in this period, some of which may be understood in the literal sense. It is possible, further, that the spiritual crisis which overtook Nizārī in his final year in Harāt was connected, in one way or another, with his aversion to the epicurean pattern of his life there. It seems, however, that like his mentor Nāṣir-i Khusraw who renounced wine-drinking on the eve of his journey to Cairo, Nizārī too may have abandoned this habit upon his departure from Harāt, as hinted in the following lines from the *Safar-nāma*:

> You did not give thanks for all you had before.
> You were caught up in the chains of bad fortune.
> You are in the sleep of negligence – wake up,
> At last be wise about drinking the wrong drink.
> Kill the thief of the cheerful self,
> Go towards the truth and seek forgiveness.[62]

What is certain is that in his old age, the poet developed a more critical attitude to the inebriating drink as indicated in one of his later *mathnawī*s, the *Dastūr-nāma*, a didactic poem which he composed for his sons on the subject on wine-drinking. In addition to admitting its forbidden nature (*ḥarām*) and criticising the excessive drinking of wine as the cause of human strife, the poet has a highly revealing passage about the metaphorical character of his own language of wine-drinking and his addiction to a different kind of drink – the wine of spiritual ecstasy:

Now I will say for whom it is permitted.
Wine is food for the body and strength for the soul.
How can I describe it since it is more than this?
For forty years I have composed words in praise of it,
Still I do not praise it out of necessity.
Night and day I have praised and boasted about it,
But not because of habit or custom.
I have nurtured it like the soul in its body,
So that with every breath I take, the intoxication
Of it lifts up my soul to its greatness.
Sometimes I call it 'my sweet soul' because
The cup of Jamshīd is the cup of my ancestors.
Sometimes I call it 'the remembrance of the Messiah,'
But I may be wrong in taking the example of Jesus.
Sometimes I say its mother is Maryam (Mary) since
The son of Maryam was blessed with the (divine) breath.
Sometimes I give it the name of the 'the second spirit,'
Since it sets fire to the water of the grapevine.
If I am to describe the peculiar nature of it,
I do not know how can do justice to it.
Although I have made a thousand descriptions of it,
I have been unable to give single (true) description of it.[63]

In these verses Nizārī is alluding that, at some point in his poetic career, there was a transformation of signification associated with wine. Whereas in some of his early poetry wine may have referred quite literally to the grape, it later came to symbolise for him an internal state of mystical intoxication generated in a contemplative state. The poet compares this experience with the magical goblet of Jamshīd (*jām-i jam*) wherein the legendary king of ancient Persia perceived the knowledge of all things, and the miraculous breath of Jesus by which he revived the dead to life. The point of transition, when the spiritual meaning began to predominate decisively over the profane in Nizārī's poetry, may have occurred around the time when he embarked on the journey narrated in the *Safar-nāma*, the poet's most spiritually-orientated work, where he expresses a similar hermeneutical outlook:

There is another sun for the sky of the learned ones.
For our Adam there is another mix of earth and water.

For those intoxicated by sitting in seclusion
  there is another drink.
For the throat of al-Ḥallāj (when he said) 'I am the Truth,'
  there is another rope.[64]

It is reasonable to suppose from these verse that in many places of the *Safar-nāma* where Nizārī refers to 'sharing a cup of wine' or 'becoming intoxicated' with his friends, he is most likely to be alluding to devotional practices involving mystical ecstasy and the transmission of gnosis. Nonetheless, the metaphorical ambivalence of Nizārī's wine symbolism remains potent in all his works, which is precisely what the poet probably intended. It is this quality of Nizārī's poetry which seems to have much impressed Ḥāfiẓ and influenced the development of his own inimitable poetic style in the next century.[65]

Another person Nizārī met in Tabrīz was 'a close, young friend' whom he typically does not name except to say that they spent much time together. In the course of their conversations, the young man gradually disclosed to Nizārī the story of his life and finally described meeting a handsome young man of exceptional spiritual authority with a large following in the city:

Once someone stole my heart away.
There were others like me who had lost
  their hearts to him.
No one could get enough of him.
The feet of many were willing to walk
  on swords (for his sake).
His beauty was immeasurable and the marketplace
  was inflamed by him,
While he was always fleeing from the tumult
  of the common folk.[66]

The young man continued that because of his love for this person and the difficulties of meeting him, he suffered terribly until he discovered that his beloved was in the habit of visiting a place called the *dār al-shifā'* (literally, a 'house of healing') where the mad and the mentally distraught were looked after, and that whoever wanted to 'circle him' (*ṭawāf kardan*) would have to go there. So he pretended to behave like a madman and was admitted to the *dār al-shifā'* where he was able to meet the beloved. The young man completes his story by advising Nizārī that should he wish to see this beloved he would have to use the same approach. For reasons which Nizārī does not explain, he too develops an intense desire to see this person and, following his friend's example, he begins to feign lunacy, as a result of which a group of people he calls the Ikhwān al-Ṣafā' take pity on him and escort him to the *dār al-shifā'*. Here he meets the beloved, whom Nizārī refers to as 'the intoxicated one,' and confides to him the secret of his love. However, the beloved is not amused and reprimands Nizārī for coming all the way from Khurāsān to meet him. He tells the poet that the lover and the beloved are in reality never apart: 'When was Qays ever without the face of Layla?' he asks.[67]

Nizārī's account of this unusual sequence of events in Tabrīz constitutes one of the most complex and obscure passages in the *Safar-nāma*. The difficulty of the text is caused partly by the convoluted way in which Nizārī presents it, making it difficult to distinguish one character from the other; but it is also due to the poet's unwillingness to identify the mysterious person who is the object of his devotion or to shed any more light on the incident – no doubt out of his zeal for maintaining *taqiyya*. Perhaps the key to unlocking this puzzle lies in the psychological connection between passionate love (*'ishq*) and 'lunacy' (*dīwānagī*) which in Sufism denotes the distracted, bewildered or intoxicated state of the lover. The reference to Qays and Layla is significant for it tells us that Nizārī's experience in the *dār al-shifā'* was of an intensely spiritual rather than a pathological character. It will be recalled by those familiar with Niẓāmī's Persian rendition of the old Arabic romance that Qays is the love-sick hero who is so grief-stricken when denied access to his beloved Layla that he behaves like a *majnūn* (madman), until he comes to recognise the divine nature of his passion.[68]

There is also a certain resonance between Nizārī's account of this experience and the relationship of the great Persian poet and mystic Jalāl al-Dīn Rūmī with the wandering *darwīsh* Shams-i Tabrīz. As is well-known, Rūmī was completely enraptured by this man when they met in Konya in 642/1244 and to whom he became devoted as his spiritual guide and personification of the divine beloved. For the next two years, Rūmī spent much of his time with Shams, conferring in private, listening to music (*samā'*) and dancing. This caused much resentment among Rūmī's sons and disciples, whose hostility caused Shams to flee on several occasions and resulted in his murder around 645/1247. Shams-i Tabrīz, who was reportedly born in an Ismaili family, had a pivotal bearing in Rūmī's life, transforming his personality and inspiring in him an outpouring of magnificent lyrical poetry. It was in memory of Shams that Rūmī composed the mystical odes collected in the *Dīwān-i Shams-i Tabrīzī* and introduced among his followers the Mevlevi dance with its reed flute and drum accompaniments.[69]

It is not possible for us to examine here the manifold dimensions of mystical love in its human and divine expressions, but given the highly spiritual flavour of Nizārī's description, his meeting with the mysterious beloved in Tabrīz can only be understood within the spiritual context of a master-disciple relationship. Moreover there is strong possibility that this event took place within an Ismaili setting. Also, according to the *Shāfiya*, a 9th/15th-century treatise in Arabic on Ismaili doctrines attributed to the Syrian *dā'ī* Abū Firās b. al-Qāḍī Naṣr b. Jawshan al-Maynaqī,[70] the name Ikhwān al-Ṣafā' (Brethren of Purity) was used by the Ismailis of Ādharbāyjān to designate themselves during the Mongol period.[71] This appellation was obviously derived from the famous group of Ismaili-inspired scholars of the 4th/10th century who composed the encyclopaedic work of philosophical and scientific thought, the *Rasā'il Ikhwān al-Ṣafā'*.

The same Syrian author also confirms Persian sources that the Ismaili Imam of the time, Shams al-Dīn Muḥammad, was living in this region at a place called Quṣūr, which is now a little village six kilometres north of Riḍā'iyya, just outside of Tabrīz. Muṣṭafā Ghālib mentions that the Imam lived in the town of Zardūz and was therefore referred to as Muḥammad Zardūzī, but according to Daftary this nickname could also have been derived from his outward trade in embroidery.[72] We know very little about the activities of this Imam, apart from the report that he arrived in Ādharbāyjān when he was four or five years old, having been despatched there by his father Rukn al-Dīn Khurshāh, the last Ismaili Imam of the Alamūt period, just before the fall of Alamūt to the Mongols in 654/1256.

Furthermore, there is a curious tradition of the Indian Ismailis associating the Imam Shams al-Dīn with Shams-i Tabrīz, the spiritual mentor of Rūmī.[73] According to this legend, this Imam went to India in 710/1310 under the name of Shams-i Tabrīz where he studied Sanskrit and other languages and performed many miracles. There is even a mausoleum dedicated to the memory of this Shams-i Tabrīz in Multan and maintained to this day by the local Sunni community. The same tomb is, however, also venerated by the Indian Ismailis as the tomb of the Nizārī Ismaili *dāʿī* and preacher Pīr Shams who propagated the faith in Sind, Kashmir and Punjab, and is credited with the same miracles attributed to Shams-i Tabrīz. The threefold identification of Shams al-Dīn, Shams-i Tabrīz and Pīr Shams is obviously spurious since the Ismaili Imam was born about 650/1252, five years before the murder of Rūmī's mentor, and the Ismaili *pīr* flourished in the first half of the next century.[74] The confusion seems to have arisen partly from the allegedly Ismaili parenthood of Shams-i Tabrīz and the fact that the Ismaili Imam acquired the same title (meaning 'the Sun of Tabrīz') on account of his handsome appearance.

In any case, what appears to be certain from Persian and Syrian Ismaili sources is that the Imam Shams al-Dīn was living somewhere in the vicinity of Tabrīz at the time when Nizārī Quhistānī visited the city in the summer of 679/1280. He would have been about thirty-three years old at this time, which is more or less the same age as the poet himself. We also know that there was an Ismaili community in Ādharbāyjān who called themselves the Ikhwān al-Ṣafāʾ. These facts point to the possibility that the Ikhwān al-Ṣafāʾ of Tabrīz who befriended Nizārī there were a group of Ismailis. It can further be deduced that the *dār al-shifāʾ* was their religious centre since Nizārī uses this term in his *Dastūr-nāma* to refer to a place where one may be healed of the sickness of ignorance through the teachings (*taʿlīm*) of the Imam.[75] Such a reading of the text is supported by the only other reference to the Ikhwān al-Ṣafāʾ towards the end of the *Safar-nāma* where, among the various friends and companions whom the poet singles out for praise, he invokes the memory of 'Abd al-Malik, whom he is very likely to have met in Tabrīz:

The pride of the Prophet's family was 'Abd al-Malik.
He was the candle of the Ikhwān al-Ṣafā',
Without equal in his time with regards to speech;
His writings in verse was the envy of all the poets.
A friend of the *Sāḥib-i 'ahd,* in happiness and grief,
On the path of friendship he was very firm.
In his enlightening *majlis,* by the morning
we were totally intoxicated.[76]

Besides conveying to us the religious character of the Ikhwān al-Ṣafā' and the high status of 'Abd al-Malik in the organisation, this verse is significant for its mention of the *Sāḥib-i 'ahd,* an expression which literally means 'the Master to whom allegiance is given' and in the terminology of Persian Ismailism is synonymous with 'the Imam of the time'. There is thus a strong probability that it was through the intervention of this 'Abd al-Malik that Nizārī was able to obtain access to the *dār al-shifā',* and that the handsome, young man to whom Nizārī confided his secret there was a very important dignitary of the Ismaili *da'wa,* probably the Imam Shams al-Dīn himself. It is impossible to establish the identity of this person conclusively, but such appears to have been the considered judgement of Ivanow, the foremost authority on Persian Ismaili literature, who asserted that the purpose of Nizārī's journey was in fact to offer *dīdār* (homage) to the Imam of the time.[77]

With the Mongol Army in the Caucasus

We have noted several times that Nizārī Quhistānī's narrative of his journey in the *Safar-nāma* is interspersed throughout with religious teachings and moralistic tales of an inspirational kind. Apart from these didactic passages, the poet has been concerned so far mainly with recording his meetings with certain '*rafiqān*'. It is only after his departure from Tabrīz that Nizārī begins to describe the social and political environment in which he was moving and to convey a sense of the official or governmental aspect of his journey with Tāj al-Dīn. On the morning of the 5th day of Ṣafar 679,

18 June 1280, Nizārī says that they left Tabrīz in a large party of government officials in the entourage (*nawkarān*, literally 'servants') of the chief minister of the Īl-Khānid government, Shams al-Dīn Juwaynī. The poet refers to this *wazīr* by several honorific titles such as *Ṣāḥib-i ṣāḥib qirān, Ṣāḥib-i dīwān ʿālam* and *Shāh rā dastūr-i aʿẓam* (approximating the English expressions 'minister of finance,' 'chief minister' and 'prime minister' respectively).[78]

It is important to note that precisely at the time when Nizārī set off from Tabrīz, the chief minister was involved in an intense power struggle in the court of Abaqa Khān. According to Rashīd al-Dīn,[79] the *wazīr*'s position had become extremely tenuous because of accusations of conspiring with the Mamlūks while, at the same time, his brother the historian ʿAlāʾ al-Dīn ʿAṭā Malik, who occupied the governorship of Baghdad, was under investigation for misappropriating state funds. These charges were brought against the Juwaynī brothers repeatedly over several years by a certain Majd al-Mulk with the support of Abaqa's son Prince Arghun.[80] The Khān was so alarmed by these allegations that he had ʿAlāʾ al-Dīn arrested, put on trial and executed in 679/1280; and he also appointed Majd al-Mulk as joint *wazīr* with Shams al-Dīn, thus placing him in the invidious position of having to work with his own accuser. Although Shams al-Dīn survived the remaining two years of Abaqa's reign, he too was later executed by Arghun for having supported Hülegü's son, Tegüdar (Aḥmad), in the succession dispute that followed Abaqa's death in 680/1282.

Nizārī makes no mention of the precarious political position of Shams al-Dīn in his *Safar-nāma*, nor does he tell us explicitly the purpose of the *wazīr*'s tour, or why he and Tāj al-Dīn accompanied him. But from the poet's account of the various military bases and encampments they visited subsequently, it was evidently connected with the organisation of a large army of Mongol, Turkish, Armenian and Georgian troops who were then assembling in the frontier areas of northern Ādharbāyjān for an imminent invasion of Syria.[81] It is very likely that one of the *wazīr*'s objectives was to ensure that the military campaign was adequately organised and funded; this may explain why his first destination was Telah, an island in the middle of Lake Urmiyya, a large expanse of salt-water located approximately thirty miles to the west of Tabrīz.

That Telah was bewitching, strange and subdued.
In the middle of it was built a fortress,
the place of the treasure of the powerful king.
At its head thirty dragons protected it.[82]

Nizārī's description of Telah is essentially correct, for according to Le Strange, this island was the storage house of the treasure collected by Hülegü Khān during his conquest of Persia, as well as his burial place; to which Howorth adds that during the time of Hülegü, it was guarded by 1,000 men, with its commander changing each year.[83]

The next morning Shams al-Dīn Juwaynī's retinue proceeded to Khoy, a small town in the northern basin of the lake by a stream that flows to the Aras (or Araxes) river near the border with Armenia,[84] where a large force of Khitay Turks loyal to the Īl-Khānids had gathered. Their next stop was Alātāq in Armenia, the site of Abaqa's summer residence where the bulk of his army was based.[85] Nizārī does not refer to the presence of the Khān here because apparently he was on a hunting expedition on the banks of the Euphrates river in Iraq at this time.[86] However, he mentions that this army was under the command of 'the Shah,' by which he presumably means Abaqa's son Mengü Timür. Subsequently, this Shah gave orders for his army to decamp, and everyone, including the *wazīr* and his companions, proceeded towards Armenia, possibly with the aim of joining up with the Christian forces of Leon III who was a vassal of Abaqa Khān.[87]

For much of the next six months, Nizārī and Tāj al-Dīn appear to have either accompanied the Īl-Khānid army in its movements or occasionally travelled a few days ahead of it with Shams al-Dīn's party. The sight of a large concentration of troops including infantry, cavalry, animals, numerous slaves to carry supplies and their attendants, etc., must have been a rare and awesome sight for Nizārī (even if it was a small proportion of the total Mongol-led force of more than 50,000 men who invaded Syria in the following year). But Nizārī gives few details of the scale and logistics of this operation; in fact, throughout this part of the *Safar-nāma*, he gives the impression of being quite unconcerned with, or deliberately evasive of, the military manoeuvres taking place all around him. What Nizārī prefers to record instead at this point when he is with the army in Armenia are his observations of the Christian people of this region. In a style somewhat reminiscent of Nāṣir-i Khusraw's travelogue, he is impressed by the structure and design of the buildings which he finds strange and innovative (*badīʿ*). The poet is equally curious about the churches which he claims are used by the people for 'idol-worship'. Referring possibly to the ancient city of Anī on the Arpa-Chay tributary of the river Aras,[88] he remarks:

Built on very hard stony earth
Was the town; before it a deep river.
The ceilings, walls and beams of every place,
Were completely made of shaved stone.
The walls of stone were raised high
With strange workings and new ideas.
They built places for idol worship in such a way
That you would have been completely shocked.[89]

It took the Īl-Khānid army several days to pass through Armenia to Georgia (Gurjistān), possibly to meet up with a contingent of troops supplied by the young King Dimitri.[90] Nizārī found this part of the journey very depressing because of the cold and wet weather, for which reason he also seemed to have taken a dislike to the people of this region:

The sky was covered night and day,
The clouds laden like the cloud of my tears.
The world was warm from my heart
(But) the sun was hidden behind a veil of shame.
If I say that I saw a man in Gurjistān
That would be a lie.
People were uneducated, scarlet of face,
With yellow skin and green eyes,
Always covered from the (light of the) sun…
Their beards never saw a comb.
On top of their hats they wore a veil,
A black veil like the clothes of mourning.[91]

There is no need for us to follow in detail Nizārī's account of his travels in the Caucasus region with the *wazīr* Shams al-Dīn. After passing through the mountainous region of Kitu Karakh and resting briefly by the lake of Gukchah Tangiz in Armenia,[92] the army returned to Ādharbāyjān via the plain of Arrān, a great triangle of land lying to the west of the junction point of the rivers Kūr and Aras. In 617/1220, when the Mongols stormed this region, they destroyed many of its towns which appear to have been rebuilt since then. At the time when Nizārī passed through Arrān, it was under the governorship of the Armenian ruler Leon III.[93] Nizārī observes that the plain was so full of Turkish troops that it took nearly one month for all of them to cross the Kūr river. From Nizārī's description it appears as though all of Abaqa's invading force was converging upon Arrān for the attack on Syria.[94]

Nizārī reports that on Friday, the 8th day of Jumādā II 679/4 September 1280, Shams al-Dīn's retinue arrived in Manṣūriyya ahead of the army, where they teamed up again to go to Darband, a major port on the Caspian, known to the Arabs as the Bāb al-abwāb, where the Caucasus sinks into the sea. At this time Darband and the surrounding area was the scene of constant warfare between the Īl-Khānids and their Mongol rivals of the Golden Horde.[95] The poet narrates that after passing through Baku and Barmak,[96] as they approached the city of Darband, they came across a force of armed and hostile Turks, probably belonging to the Golden Horde, but because their numbers included many wounded troops and the heavy snowfall around them, the Turks withdrew to the north.

Subsequently, the Īl-Khānid army came upon the enemy stronghold of Anīq[97] to which they laid siege and, after a fierce battle, managed to kill all the defenders. This is the only military incident which Nizārī narrates in his *Safar-nāma*, and it appears to have upset him a great deal, especially because his sympathies lay with the people of Anīq. Leaving the army to assert its authority in and around Anīq, Shams al-Dīn and his party returned to Baku where they stayed for thirty to forty days until they received news of the victorious army.

It appears that the *wazīr* parted company with the Īl-Khānid army when he decided to leave Baku for the Kūr river. The poet was so overjoyed by this that he describes himself as a bird freed from its cage or a prisoner forgiven for his crimes. We assume that the reason for his happiness was that he had become thoroughly tired of marching with the troops for several months over difficult terrain and in freezing weather with little or no freedom to pursue his own interests. Indeed there were times during the latter part of this portion of the journey when Nizārī had felt much discomfort, even loneliness and despair. On their way to the Kūr river, the *wazīr* was requested by the Khān to go to Arrān, where the party stayed for the first twenty days of Ramaḍān. Tāj al-Dīn was then instructed by the chief minister to move to Ardabīl to help with the collection of taxes there. Ardabīl had been the capital of Ādharbāyjān before the region was conquered by the Mongols under Chingiz Khān in 617/1220 and the administration transferred to Tabrīz. Although Nizārī expresses criticism of its people for their ignorance and its governor for his tyrannical rule, the two companions appear to have been based in this place through the rest of the winter.

During this period, Tāj al-Dīn and Nizārī made several excursions to the surrounding areas as well as visits to the Arrān. Among the various places they visited were Pilsuwār (approximately 150 kilometres from Ardabīl, just south of the Aras river[98]) Manṣūriyya, Shirwiyāz (in the fertile district between Zanjān and Abhar, where the town of Sultāniyya was later built by Arghun Khān[99]), Zanjān (a small town to the west of Qazwīn[100]) and Abhar (a town in the Jibāl province, which lay to the west of Qazwīn on the road to Zanjān).[101] Needless to say, the poet offers no explanation for these trips, other than to say that Tāj al-Dīn had certain appointments to keep, presumably with the *wazīr* or other government officials.

Having recounted in summary Nizārī's six-month expedition in the retinue of Shams al-Dīn Juwaynī, a large part of which was devoted to visiting military forces gathering for the invasion of Syria, it is worthwhile revisiting the question of the purposes behind the poet's journey. The role of Tāj al-Dīn ʿAmīd requires little explanation, for as a senior official of the Īl-Khānid treasury charged with tax collection in Ādharbāyjān, it was perhaps necessary for him to be by the side of the *Ṣāḥib-i qirān*. But Nizārī's contribution to all these activities is far less clear. Not only does he give us little information about the military movements taking place all around him, but he has little to say about the chief minister himself in whose company he travelled for many months. At no point does he tell us of having been introduced personally to the *wazīr* or of assisting Tāj al-Dīn in his official duties, even though he possessed first-hand experience of tax collection in Khurāsān. Thus, the overall impression Nizārī conveys is that of being a detached observer rather than an active participant in this part of the journey, and his presence in the *wazīr*'s caravan may have been seen by others as that of a personal assistant or attendant to Tāj al-Dīn. These observations reinforce the view presented earlier that the poet was travelling with Tāj al-Dīn purely in a personal or private capacity.

In fact, it was during the time when Nizārī and Tāj al-Dīn were stationed in Ardabīl, freed of the encumbrance of following government officials and military forces all over the Caucasus, that the poet took the opportunity to seek out his spiritual friends wherever possible. Thus, during one of his trips to Arrān with Tāj al-Dīn when they spent a week near the Kūr river, he had meetings with several good friends, including Shihāb al-Dīn Futūḥ of whom he says, 'When I was with him, it was better than Paradise,' and Ṣadr al-Dīn.[102] Similarly, when Nizārī was in Barmak, close to the port of Baku in the region of Shirwān, he met Tāj-i Munshī, a person of 'incomparable knowledge,' with whom he had discussions over several days, leaving him in a state of intoxication and ecstasy. He acknowledges his gratitude to this person later in the *Safar-nāma*:

> You are a real soul, a pure soul without any stain.
> Your outside (*ẓāhir*) and inside (*bāṭin*) are both pure.
> I have become totally unaware of myself because
> you snatched me from myself.[103]

During his stay in Ardabīl, Nizārī also made special trips to visit friends in Zanjān (Zangān)[104] and Shirwiyāz (Shirūyāz). The poet provides an interesting glimpse of the polite and learned atmosphere of these meetings (*mulāqāt*) of which the poet was so fond and from which he took much pleasure:

> Shirwiyāz was pleasant like a bright heaven.
> Night and day we were a group drinking together,
> Good friends with no end, with no equal,
> With sharp understanding and speech most excellent
>   and ingenious,
> with sweet logic and experts in theology.
> We were one in both humour and seriousness.[105]

Perhaps as a result of these inspirational conversations, Nizārī reverts to his didactic style again at this point of his narrative with several uplifting stories conveying a religious teaching or a moral lesson. For instance, he recounts the anecdote of a rich and greedy man who fell into the Kūr river. Instead of grabbing a rope to save himself from drowning, the man held on to his beautiful turban which he did not want to lose. According to Nizārī, this allegory is meant to illustrate the man's stupidity for clinging to the exoteric, his turban, rather than the esoteric, his precious soul. The poet adds that in all circumstances of life one should hold on to the *ḥabl-i matīn* (strong rope), thus alluding to the Qur'anic verse, 'Hold fast to the Rope of God,' (3:103), often quoted in Ismaili literature as a symbol of the perpetual link between God and mankind preserved through the Prophet Muḥammad and his *ahl al-bayt*, the Imams.

Return to Quhistān

At the beginning of the month of Dhu'l-Ḥijja/March 1281, when Nizārī was resting in Ardabīl between his various excursions outside the city, a messenger arrived with letters for him from Quhistān. He describes his reaction to the receipt of these letters in the following words:

> One day when I had many thoughts in my head,
>   a hundred thoughts of every type inside my heart,
> A young man suddenly came to my door,
> And said there was a message from Quhistān.

I jumped up from my place like a flea
And bowed down at the feet of the messenger out of joy.
He entered and I was very overwhelmed.
I kissed the sole of his shoes forcefully
And told him: O your shoes should be the crown of my head,
One nail of your shoe is like a payment of tax for me.[106]

Nizārī does not tell us the contents of his letters, but one of them in particular encourages him to compare the messenger to the hoopoe bird sent by Sulaymān (Solomon) to Sabā (Sheba), and the message he received to the ones from Yūsuf (Joseph) to Yaʿqūb (Jacob), from Layla to Majnūn and from Shīrīn to Khusraw. It is possible that Nizārī received instructions to return home, since from this time on his mind is occupied with the happy thoughts of returning to Quhistān. The poet describes himself in lyrical language as a bird released from its cage and of a soul returning to the body with renewed life.

However, Nizārī was unable to depart immediately for home because Tāj al-Dīn had several engagements to fulfil and it was not until two months later in Rabī I/June 1281, that they set off from Abhar for Quhistān. Before his departure, Nizārī called upon his friends to request their forgiveness for his shortcomings. He also despatched a messenger to rush ahead of him with a letter addressed to his friends in Quhistān, with specific instructions for him to go by way of Turshīz, Qā'in and Bīrjand, all important centres of the Ismaili community in Quhistān, where his friends presumably lived. Nizārī explains that in this letter he gives an account of his journey, together with the names of the people he met and the discussions they shared, in the hope that it would act as a cure for all the pain and suffering people have to endure in life. He also admits that he did not reveal the full names of his friends in the letter, undoubtedly out of his customary prudence in case the letter was intercepted and compromised the people concerned.

Since Nizārī's *Safar-nāma* ends with a similar list of individuals whose memory he wished to honour, it is possible that the names in both the letter and the *mathnawī* were identical, and that the letter was perhaps an early version of the *Safar-nāma* written during the course of his journey. From the few lines of praise the poet devotes to each person, it is difficult to establish their identities, but it can be assumed that many if not all of them were Ismailis. The two dozen names or so he enumerates could even be seen as a roll-call of the Ismaili *daʿwa* operating in parts of Persia and Ādharbāyjān at the time of his journey. Nizārī begins this final section of his narrative in characteristic style:

> O wine-bearer, fill up the first glass of wine, give it to me,
> so that I drink to remember the happiest people of
> the world![107]

By thus invoking the symbolic purveyor of mystical wine in Sufism, and then recalling the wine-bearer to replenish his cup each time he mentions the name of a friend, the poet creates the impression of addressing all of them gathered before him in a grand assembly (*majlis*) of intimate comradeship and spiritual fellowship.

Among the various people Nizārī praises with a quaff of wine are the following: Sayf al-Dīn, described as a man of high religious ranking, 'without like, without similarity and without equal'; Jamāl al-Dīn Muḥammad, a person 'as rare as a cypress tree with fruit' and 'one from whose opinion light is transmitted'; ʿAbd al-Malik, 'the pride of the Prophet's family' and 'the candle of the Ikhwān al-Ṣafāʾ' whom Nizārī probably met in Tabrīz; Zayn al-Dīn ʿAlī Fakhār, a clever, witty and skilled poet, 'without like in all the gates of friendship'; Sharaf Masʿūd with whom Nizārī shared much laughter; Naṣīr al-Dīn Ḥasan, whose speech 'removed grief from sad people like me'; Jamāl, Tāj and Saʿd, 'hermits of the world' who 'made the second heaven their dwelling'; Shihāb, 'the pride of Irān' and 'leader of all his peers' with 'a high degree of authority (*ḥaqq*)'; Shams al-Dīn Muẓaffar, 'the light of my dark heart' from whom Nizārī could not bear to be separated; Majd al-Dīn Mubārak Shāh, at whose memory 'a flood of blood comes from my eyes'; Jamāl al-Dīn Raʾīs, a 'pure and exquisite jewel'; Shams and Asaʿd, both learned and pious sons of Saḍīd; Ḥasan Masʿūd, famous for his sweet music at the harp; Shihāb-i Najd, 'my closest and oldest friend, equal to me in everything'; Shams al-Dīn ʿAbd al-Rahīm, who was totally obedient to the Divine; ʿAlī Sābiq, in whose company one felt like flying through the sky; and Tāj al-Dīn Ḥasan, compared to whom the poet counts himself quite insignificant. Nizārī concludes his *Safar-nāma* by dedicating the work to a certain Amīn al-Dīn or Amīn al-Dīn al-Maʿadī. The poet's reverential eulogy of this person as the 'second Jesus' (a term that the Ismailis applied only to the *ḥujja* of the Imam)[108] and obedient to the commandments of the lord of the time (*khudāwand-i zamān*)' suggests that he was the most senior dignitary of the Ismaili community in Persia:

This testimony I am addressing to Maʿadī.
I do not do it with any ill intention but out of faith.
My secrets are known to the Supreme Master
(*shaykh al-shuyūkh*),
The essence of the Divine Light of reality (*ḥaqq*).
He whose name is Amīn al-Dīn is the second Jesus,
Before whom all the heavens prostrate in magnanimity.
The uprooter of innovation, he is the sword of the time
And the follower of the commandments of
the lord of the time (*khudāwand-i zamān*).
O Amīn al-Dīn! You are a soul unique in creation,
And like intelligence, a pure and unravelled jewel.
In my company are those whose glory is to keep the secret,
Like the Virgin Mary with Jesus in her womb.
Your magnanimity is the highest in the world.
I invoke the names of all these friends for their intercession.
If I have committed a mistake, don't chastise me.
If this (dedication) is an unforgivable mistake,
accept it from me.
I finish this memorandum in your name.
May God bless the completion of my task with good things.[109]

Concluding Remarks

The *Safar-nāma* of Nizārī Quhistānī is a unique document for the invaluable information it provides about the Ismaili community of Persia during the Mongol period which is not available in any other source. It makes clear that despite the destruction of their political power and territorial independence, a sizeable number of Ismailis survived in Quhistān and other parts of Persia. Nizārī's work also illustrates the continuing existence of the long-standing tradition of the Ismaili *daʿwa* after the fall of Alamūt. Through Nizārī's own example as a *dāʿī*, it becomes evident that the *daʿwa* must have continued to exist in some form with its characteristic functions and sense of mission within the community.

At the same time, it appears that the Ismaili *daʿwa* of the post-Alamūt period adapted some of its methods and expressions to the prevailing religio-cultural milieu dominated largely by Sufism. Among the many fascinating insights to emerge from Nizārī's work is the close association between the Ismailis and the Sufis already underway during his lifetime and which was to become more pronounced in the following centuries. This interaction is vividly reflected both in the content and the narrative style of the *Safar-nāma*, lending support to the view that the phenomenon of Sufism was much more fluid, diverse and heterogenous than has been suggested in the standard works on the subject.

Although our study of Nizārī Quhistānī's life and writings has been conducted mainly from the perspective of his relations with the Ismailis and based largely on the *Safar-nāma*, we have none the less been able to catch glimpses of the poet's complex personality – as a highly skilled and ambitious poet, a dedicated Ismaili *dāʿī* steeped in the Sufi tradition, and an outspoken social critic. We are also offered an insight into the tension between writing and persecution, between secrecy and disclosure, and between conscience and conformity, that characterises much of his poetry.

Thus, quite apart from their value for students of Persian Ismailism, Nizārī's works are of wider interest for their intrinsic poetic and literary qualities, the light they shed on the evolving nature of Sufism and their depiction of political and social conditions of Persia during the Mongol era. But since the major portion of Nizari's writings remains unedited and accessible to scholars only in manuscript form, the significance of his poetry and contribution to Persian literature in general has yet to be fully investigated and assessed. For these and other reasons, it is hoped that the present study will pave the way for further scholarship on this important Persian Ismaili poet.

Notes

Chapter 1: Introduction

1. 'Izz al-Dīn 'Alī b. Muḥammad b. al-Athīr, *al-Kāmil fi'l-ta'rīkh*, cited by E.G. Browne in his *A Literary History of Persia* (Cambridge, 1928), vol. 2, pp. 427–30.

2. Throughout the present work, the term 'Persia' is used for the Persian-speaking world of medieval Islam from Transoxania to the western part of Iraq, which constituted a single, culturally homogenous region; the term 'Iran' will only be used in connection with the area currently encompassed by the country of that name.

3. For an analysis of the principal sources on the Ismailis of this period, see Farhad Daftary, 'Persian Historiography of the Early Nizārī Ismā'īlīs,' *Iran*, 30 (1992), pp. 91–7.

4. 'Alā' al-Dīn 'Aṭā-Mālik b. Muḥammad Juwaynī, *Ta'rīkh-i jahān gushāy*, ed. M. Qazwīnī (Leiden-London, 1912–37); English tr. J.A. Boyle, *The History of the World-Conqueror* (Manchester, 1958; repr. 1997). Juwaynī's account of the Ismailis comes in the third volume of the Persian text and the second of the English translation.

5. Rashīd al-Dīn Faḍl Allāh, *Jāmi' al-tawārīkh: qismat-i Ismā'īliyān va Fāṭimiyān va Nizāriyān va dā'īyān va rafīqān*, ed. M.T. Dānishpazhūh and M. Mudarrisī Zanjānī (Tehran, 1338/1959); and *Jāmi' al-tawārīkh*, ed. A.A. Alizade (Baku, 1957), vol. 3.

6. Abu'l-Qāsim 'Abd Allāh b. 'Alī Kāshānī, *Zubdat al-tawārīkh: bakhsh-*

i Fāṭimiyān va Nizāriyān, ed. M.T. Dānishpazhūh (2nd. ed., Tehran, 1366/ 1987).

7. A modern abridgement of this work appears in *Taḥrīr-i Ta'rīkh-i Waṣṣāf*, ed. 'A. Āyātī (Tehran, n.d.).

8. 'Izz al-Dīn 'Alī b. Muḥammad b. al-Athīr, *al-Kāmil fi'l-ta'rīkh* (Beirut, 1965–7), based on the edition by C.J. Tornberg in 13 volumes (Leiden, 1851–76).

9. A.I. Silvestre de Sacy, 'Mémoire sur la dynastie des Assassins, et sur l'étymologie de leur nom,' *Mémoires de l'Institut Royal de France*, 4 (1818), pp. 1–84; English tr. 'Memoir on the Dynasty of the Assassins, and on the Etymology of their Name,' in Farhad Daftary, *The Assassin Legends: Myths of the Isma'ilis* (London, 1994), pp. 136–88.

10. J. von Hammer-Purgstall, *The History of the Assassins*, tr. O.C. Wood (London, 1835; repr. New York, 1968), pp. 1–2.

11. Wladimir Ivanow, 'Tombs of Some Persian Ismaili Imams,' *JBBRAS*, NS, 14 (1938), p. 49.

12. Marshall G.S. Hodgson, *The Order of Assassins* (The Hague, 1955); see also his 'The Ismā'īlī State,' in *The Cambridge History of Iran*, Volume 5 (Cambridge, 1968), pp. 422–82.

13. Farhad Daftary, *The Ismā'īlīs: Their History and Doctrines* (Cambridge, 1990), p. 435.

14. Muḥammad b. Khwāndshāh Mīrkhwānd, *Rawḍat al-ṣafā'* (Tehran, 1338–39/1960), vol. 4, p. 193; Ghiyāth al-Dīn Khwānd Amīr, *Ḥabīb al-siyar*, ed. J. Humā'ī (Tehran, 1333/1954), vol. 2, p. 457; Dawlatshāh b. 'Alā' al-Dawla, *Tadhkirat al-shu'arā'*, ed. E.G. Browne (London, 1901), pp. 231–4.

15. Wladimir Ivanow, *A Guide to Ismaili Literature* (London, 1933), pp. 105–6; Tch G. Baradin, 'Ḥakīm-i Nizārī Quhistānī,' *Farhang-i Īrān Zamīn*, 6 (1337/1958), pp. 178–203; J. Durri, 'Ba'ze ma'lumot dar borayi Nizori,' *Sharqi Surkh* (1958–59), pp. 140–54.

16. Jan Rypka, *History of Iranian Literature*, ed. Karl Jahn (Dordrecht, 1968), p. 256: Ivanow, *Ismaili Literature*, p. 138.

17. Chengiz G. Baiburdi, *Zhizn i tvorchestvo Nizārī-Persidskogo poeta* (Moscow, 1966). Persian tr. M. Ṣadrī, *Zindigī va āthār-i Nizārī* (Tehran, 1370/ 1991). In this work, Baiburdi cites many verses from the poet's *Kullīyāt*, some of which have been quoted in our study. See also his 'Rukopisi Proizvedeniy Nizārī,' in *Kratkie Soobsheniya Instituta Naradov Azii*, 65 (1964), pp. 13–24.

Chapter 2: The Early Ismaili and Fatimid *Da'was*

1. This historical scheme is derived partly from Wladimir Ivanow, *Brief Survey of the Evolution of Ismailism* (Leiden, 1952), pp. 28–30, and Daftary, *The Ismāʿīlīs*, pp. 29–31. For a critical discussion of these and other categorisations of Ismaili history, see Tazim R. Kassam, *Songs of Wisdom and Circles of Dance: Hymns of the Satpanth Ismāʿīlī Muslim Saint, Pīr Shams* (Albany, NY, 1995), pp. 20–2.

2. For a discussion of this subject, see Louis Massignon, 'Time in Islamic Thought,' in *Man and Time: Papers from the Eranos Yearbooks* (New York, 1957), pp. 108–14.

3. For an overview of the Qur'anic conception of history and the historical outlook of the Prophet Muḥammad, see Franz Rosenthal, *A History of Muslim Historiography* (Leiden, 1968), pp. 18–30.

4. Louis Gardet, 'Ḳiyāma,' *EI2*, vol. 5, pp. 235–8.

5. Among the few Western scholars to have examined the significance of these proto-Shiʿi discussions in Islamic intellectual history has been Henry Corbin, principally in his *History of Islamic Philosophy*, tr. P. Sherard (London, 1993), especially pp. 23–104.

6. On the Ismaili conceptions of time and history, see Henry Corbin's essays on this subject collected in *Cyclical Time and Ismaili Gnosis*, tr. R. Manheim and J.W. Morris (London, 1983); also Farhad Daftary's article 'Dawr' in *Encyclopaedia Iranica*, vol.7, pp. 151–3, and the two essays by Paul E. Walker: 'An Early Ismaili Interpretation of Man, History and Salvation,' *Ohio Journal of Religious Studies*, 3 (1975), pp. 29–35, and 'Eternal Cosmos and the Womb of History: Time in Early Ismaili Thought,' *International Journal of Middle East Studies*, 9 (1978), pp. 355–66.

7. Henry Corbin provides a detailed discussion of the cosmological, meta-historical and soteriological aspects of the doctrine in 'Divine Epiphany and Spiritual Birth in Ismailian Gnosis,' in his *Cyclical Time*, pp. 59–150.

8. Marius Canard, 'Daʿwa,' *EI2*, vol. 3, pp. 168–70.

9. On the historical and doctrinal development of early Shiʿism, see S. Husain M. Jafri, *Origins and Early Development of Shīʿa Islam* (London, 1979), Heinz Halm, *Shiism*, tr. J. Watson (Edinburgh, 1991), and Muḥammad Ḥusayn Ṭabāṭabāʾī, *Shiʿite Islam*, ed. and tr. S.H. Nasr (London, 1975).

10. The seminal contribution of al-Bāqir to Shiʿi doctrines has been investigated by Arzina R. Lalani in her *Early Shīʿī Thought: The Teachings of Imam Muḥammad al-Bāqir* (London, 2000).

11. Ibid., p. 107–13.

12. Al-Qāḍī al-Nuʿmān, *Kitāb al-Iftitāḥ al-daʿwa*, ed. F. Dachraoui (Tunis, 1975), pp. 27–9. The despatch of the two *dāʿīs* to North Africa is also recorded by Rashīd al-Dīn, *Jāmiʿ al-tawārīkh*, ed. Dānishpazhūh, p. 18.

13. For the most comprehensive account of the Ismailis, based on the original sources and modern scholarship, see Daftary, *The Ismāʿīlīs*. An overview of the same with additional information appears in his *A Short History of the Ismailis: Traditions of a Muslim Community* (Edinburgh, 1998).

14. Wilferd Madelung, 'al-Mahdī,' *EI2*, vol. 5, pp. 1230–8. See also A.A. Sachedina, *Islamic Messianism: The Idea of the Mahdi in Twelver Shiism* (Albany, NY, 1981).

15. On the complex origins of Ismailism, see: Wilferd Madelung, 'Das Imamat in der frühen ismailitischen Lehre,' *Der Islam*, 37 (1961), pp. 43–135; Farhad Daftary, 'The Earliest Ismāʿīlīs,' *Arabica*, 38 (1991), pp. 214–45, and *The Ismāʿīlīs*, pp. 91–143; as well as Ivanow's *The Alleged Founder of Ismailism* (Bombay, 1946), all of which supersede the earlier work by Bernard Lewis, *The Origins of Ismāʿīlism: A Study of the Historical Background of the Fāṭimid Caliphate* (Cambridge, 1940).

16. Some of the earliest Ismaili accounts of this formative period were collected and translated by W. Ivanow in his *Ismaili Tradition Concerning the Rise of the Fatimids* (London, etc., 1942).

17. See Abū Yaʿqūb al-Sijistānī, *Tuḥfat al-mustajībīn*, ed. ʿĀrif Tāmir, in his *Khams rasāʾil al-Ismāʿīliyya*, ed. ʿĀ. Tāmir (Salamiyya, 1956), pp. 145–56.

18. For a survey of the activities of early Ismaili *dāʿīs* in Persia, see S.M. Stern, 'The Early Ismāʿīlī Missionaries in North-West Persia and in Khurāsān and Transoxania,' *Bulletin of the School of Oriental and African Studies*, 23 (1960), pp. 56–90, and reprinted in his *Studies in Early Ismāʿīlism* (Jerusalem and Leiden, 1983), pp. 189–233.

19. Paul E. Walker, *Early Philosophical Shiism: The Ismaili Neoplatonism of Abū Yaʿqūb al-Sijistānī* (Cambridge, 1993), p. 14.

20. A critical edition of the Arabic text with English translation and annotations of the *Kitāb al-ʿĀlim wa'l-ghulām* has been recently produced by James W. Morris under the title of *The Master and the Disciple: An Early Islamic Spiritual Dialogue* (London, 2001). A part of the text was previously translated by W. Ivanow as 'The Book of the Teacher and the Pupil' in his *Studies in Early Persian Ismailism* (2nd ed., Bombay, 1955), pp. 61–68, and analysed by H. Corbin in his 'L'Initiation Ismaélienne ou l'ésoterisme et le Verbe,' *Eranos Jahrbuch*, 39 (1970), pp. 41–142; repr. in *L'Homme et son ange* (Paris, 1983), pp. 81–205.

21. See Ian R. Netton, *Muslim Neoplatonists: An Introduction to the Thought of the Brethren of Purity (Ikhwān al-Ṣafā')* (London, 1982), and S. Hossein Nasr, *An Introduction to Islamic Cosmological Doctrines* (Cambridge, Mass., 1964), pp. 44–74.

22. Madelung has collected and analysed an impressive amount of data on this controversy in his seminal article, 'Das Imamat'. See also Farhad Daftary, 'A Major Schism in the Early Ismāʿīlī Movement,' *Studia Islamica*, 77 (1993), pp. 123–39.

23. These events are narrated in a remarkable first-hand account recorded by one of the confidants of Abū 'Abd Allāh al-Shīʿī in the *Kitāb al-Munāẓarat*, ed. and tr. W. Madelung and P.E. Walker, *The Advent of the Fatimids: A Contemporary Shiʿi Witness* (London, 2000).

24. The most recent work on the Fatimids are by Heinz Halm, *The Empire of the Mahdi: The Rise of the Fatimids*, tr. M. Bonner (Leiden, 1996), and Michael Brett, *The Rise of the Fatimids: The World of the Mediterranean and the Middle East in the Fourth Century of the Hijra, Tenth Century C.E.* (Leiden, 2001), both of which deal mainly with the early North African period. For a general survey of Fatimid history, see Daftary, *The Ismāʿīlīs*, pp. 144–255.

25. For a discussion of some of the problems encountered by the Fatimids in North Africa, see Paul Walker's introduction to *The Advent of the Fatimids*, pp. 1–59.

26. Al-Qāḍī al-Nuʿmān, *Daʿā'im al-Islām*, ed. A.A.A. Fyzee (Cairo, 1951–1961); partial English tr. A.A.A. Fyzee, *The Book of Faith* (Bombay, 1974).

27. The earliest mention of these sessions is in the biography of the *dāʿī* 'Abū 'Abd Allah al-Shīʿī, who held them to provide men and women with wisdom (*ḥikma*) and admonishments (*mawāʿiẓ*). Heinz Halm, 'The Ismaʿili Oath of Allegiance (*ʿahd*) and the "Sessions of Wisdom" (*majālis al-ḥikma*) in Fatimid Times,' in Farhad Daftary, ed., *Mediaeval Ismaʿili History and Thought* (Cambridge, 1996), pp. 99–115.

28. For a discussion of some of the problems connected with the Fatimid *daʿwa* as an institution of state, see Paul E. Walker, 'The Ismaili *Daʿwa* in the Reign of the Fatimid Caliph al-Ḥākim,' *Journal of the American Center in Egypt*, 30 (1993), pp. 161–82, and also the same author's *Ḥamīd al-Dīn al-Kirmānī: Ismaili Thought in the Age of al-Ḥākim* (London, 1999).

29. Aḥmad al-Naysābīrī, *al-Risāla al-mūjaza fi shurūṭ al-daʿwa al-hādiya*, cited in Heinz Halm, *The Fatimids and their Traditions of Learning* (London, 1997), pp. 63–4. The same work by Halm provides a detailed, lucid account of the organisation of the Ismaili *daʿwa* under the Fatimids.

30. Ḥamīd al-Dīn al-Kirmānī, *Rāḥat al-ʿaql*, ed. M.K. Ḥusayn and M.M. Ḥilmī (Cairo, 1953); ed. M. Ghālib (Beirut, 1967), as cited in Corbin, 'Divine Epiphany,' *Cyclical Time*, pp. 90–4. Unlike al-Sijistānī and other Ismaili thinkers who correlated the hierarchy of the *daʿwa* to the Neoplatonic emanationist model of the cosmos (God, Intellect, Soul, etc.) al-Kirmānī uses Aristotle's system of ten Intellects, probably deriving it from the philosopher al-Fārābī. On this point, see Walker, *Ḥamīd al-Dīn al-Kirmānī*, pp. 89–98.

31. Daftary, *The Ismāʿīlīs*, pp. 231–2.

32. Stern, *Studies in Early Ismāʿīlism*, p. 249.

33. On the changing fortunes of the Ismaili *daʿwa* outside the Fatimid state, see F. Daftary, 'The Ismaili *Daʿwa* outside the Fatimid *Dawla*,' in Marianne Barrucand, ed., *L'Egypte Fatimide, son art et son histoire* (Paris, 1999), pp. 29–43.

34. See S.M. Stern, 'The Epistle of the Fatimid Caliph al-Āmir (*al-Hidāya al-Āmiriyya*) – its Date and its Purpose,' *JRAS* (1950), pp. 20–31.

Chapter 3: The Nizārī Ismaili *Daʿwa*

1.The Mustaʿlī Ismailis survive today in the form of two main offshoots, the Dāʾūdīs and the Sulaymānīs, mainly in Yemen and India. For an overview of their history, see Daftary, *A Short History*, pp. 108–14, 185–93.

2. This is the estimate of Peter Willey, the author of *The Castles of the Assassins* (London, 1963) based on his archaeological surveys of Ismaili fortresses in Persia; he is currently writing a new, more comprehensive account of his findings.

3. Farhad Daftary, 'Ḥasan-i Ṣabbāḥ and the Origins of the Nizārī Ismaʿili Movement,' in Daftary, ed., *Mediaeval Ismaʿili History and Thought*, p. 184, and his *A Short History*, p. 125.

4. Daftary, *The Assassin Legends: Myths of the Ismaʿilis.*

5. For an assessment of this method of warfare by the Ismailis, see Hodgson, *Order of Assassins*, pp. 110–15.

6. Translated by A.K. Kazi and J.G. Flynn, *Muslim Sects and Divisions* (London, 1984), pp. 167–70. Al-Shahrastānī's version of the *Fuṣūl* has also been translated into English by Hodgson in *Order of Assassins*, pp. 325–8

7. The intellectual and political significance of al-Ghazālī's major polemic against the Ismailis, the *Kitāb al-Mustaẓhirī*, has been closely scrutinised by Farouk Mitha in *Al-Ghazālī and the Ismailis: A Debate on Reason and Authority in Medieval Islam* (London, 2001). See also Henry

Corbin, 'The Ismā'īlī Response to the Polemic of Ghazālī,' in S.H. Nasr, ed., *Ismā'īlī Contributions to Islamic Culture* (Tehran, 1977), pp. 69–98.

8. Rashīd al-Dīn, *Jāmi' al-tawārīkh*, ed. M.T. Dānishpazhūh, p. 132.

9. Juwaynī reports having seen conciliatory letters from Sultan Sanjar to the Ismailis in the library of Alamūt after its surrender to the Mongols. See his *Ta'rīkh*, vol. 3, pp. 214–15; tr. Boyle, vol. 2, p. 682.

10. Muṣṭafā Ghālib, *The Ismailis of Syria* (Beirut, 1970), p. 100.

11. Azim Nanji, 'Ismā'īlism,' in S.H. Nasr, ed. *Islamic Spirituality: Foundations* (London, 1987), pp. 179–98, and his 'Assassins,' in Mircea Eliade, ed., *The Encyclopaedia of Islam* (London-New York, 1987), vol. 1, p. 470; Hodgson, *Order of Assassins*, pp. 148–84, and Henry Corbin, 'Huitième centenaire d'Alamūt,' *Mercure de France* (Feb., 1965), pp. 285–304.

12. The main Ismaili sources on the doctrine of *qiyāma* are the *Haft bāb-i Bābā Sayyidnā* by an anonymous author, ed. W. Ivanow, in his *Two Early Ismaili Treatises* (Bombay, 1933), pp. 4–44; tr. by Hodgson in *Order of Assassins*, pp. 279–324; and Naṣīr al-Dīn al-Ṭūsī, *Rawḍat at-taslīm, yā taṣawwurāt*, ed. and tr. W. Ivanow (Leiden, 1950).

13. Hodgson, *Order of Assassins*, pp. 172–4.

14. For a discussion of this episode in Abbasid-Ismaili relations, see Hodgson, *Order of Assassins*, pp. 217–25, and Daftary, *The Isma'īlīs*, pp. 405–40.

15. On the origins and spread of the Nizārī *da'wa* in South Asia, see Azim Nanji, *The Nizārī Ismā'īlī Tradition in the Indo-Pakistan Subcontinent* (Delmar, NY, 1978).

16. Naṣīr al-Dīn al-Ṭūsī, *Rawḍat al-taslīm*, text pp. 122–4, translation pp. 143–4.

17. Naṣīr al-Dīn al-Ṭūsī, *Sayr wa sulūk*, ed. and tr. J. Badakhchani as *Contemplation and Action: The Spiritual Autobiography of a Muslim Scholar* (London, 1998).

Chapter 4: The Mongol Catastrophe

1. C.E. Bosworth, 'The Political and Dynastic History of the Iranian World (A.D. 1000–1217), in *The Cambridge History of Iran*, Volume 5, p. 15.

2. On the subject of the Mongol conquests, see David Morgan, *The Mongols* (Oxford, 1986), J.J. Saunders, *The History of the Mongol Conquests* (London, 1977), Henry Howorth, *History of the Mongols* (New York, 1888), as well as Reuven Amitai-Preiss, *Mongols and Mamlūks: The Mamlūk-Īlkhānid War, 1260–1281* (Cambridge, 1995).

3. As cited in Boyle, 'The Ismāʿīlīs and the Mongol Invasion,' in Nasr, ed., *Ismāʿīlī Contributions to Islamic Culture*, p. 10.

4. Rashīd al-Dīn, *Jāmiʿ al-tawārīkh*, p. 177.

5. Boyle, 'The Ismāʿīlīs and the Mongol Invasion,' p. 8.

6. Morgan, *The Mongols*, pp. 117–18.

7. Ibid., pp. 147–8.

8. Ḥamd Allāh Mustawfī Qazwīnī, *Nuzhat al-Qulūb*, partial tr. by G. Le Strange, *The Geographical Part of the Nuzhat al-Qulūb* (Leiden and London, 1915–19), vol. 2, pp. 54–5.

9. Daftary, *The Ismāʿīlīs*, pp. 8–9.

10. Juwaynī, *Ta'rīkh*, tr. Boyle, pp. 615–6.

11. Ibid., p. 719.

12. See Hodgson, *Order of Assassins*, pp. 259–60 and his 'The Ismāʿīlī State,' in *The Cambridge History of Iran*, Volume 5, pp. 422–82, as well Daftary, *The Ismāʿīlīs*, pp. 429–30.

13. There is a useful analysis of al-Ṭūsī's complex relations with the Ismailis in J. Badakhchani's introduction to the *Sayr wa sulūk*, pp. 1–19. See also Hamid Dabashi, 'The Philosopher/Vizier: Khwāja Naṣīr al-Dīn al-Ṭūsī and the Ismaʿilis,' in Daftary, ed., *Mediaeval Ismaʿili History and Thought*, pp. 231–45.

14. Juwaynī, *Ta'rīkh*, tr. Boyle, pp. 723–5.

15. Daftary, *The Ismāʿīlīs*, p. 429.

16. Ibid., p. 616; Rashīd al-Dīn, *Jāmiʿ al-tawārīkh*, ed. Alizade, pp. 29–30.

17. Hodgson, 'The Ismāʿīlī State,' p. 482.

18. Juwaynī, *Ta'rīkh*, vol. 3, p. 275; trans. Boyle, vol. 2, p. 273.

19. Hodgson, 'The Ismaili State,' pp. 423–4.

20. Amitai-Preiss, *Mongols and Mamlūks*, pp. 39–48.

21. For an overview of the debate on Mongol impact, see Marshall G.S. Hodgson, *The Venture of Islam: Conscience and History in a World Civilization* (Chicago, 1974), vol. 2, pp. 371–91.

22. Daftary, *A Short History*, p. 160.

23. Von Hammer-Purgstall, *History of the Assassins*, p. 201. The same is confirmed by Wilferd Madelung in his 'Ismāʿīliyya,' *EI2*, vol. 4, p. 204.

24. Daftary, *The Ismāʿīlīs*, p. 434.

25. Muʿīn al-Dīn Muḥammad Isfīzārī, *Rawḍat-i jannāt fī awṣāf-i madīnat-i Harāt*, ed. M.K. Imām (Tehran, 1338/1959), [pp. 307, 368]. He notes that old women sent one-tenth of a roll of thread as a religious due to their Imam, and that there was also a special tax which was sent to the tomb of Ḥasan-i Ṣabbāḥ. See also C.E. Bosworth, 'The Ismaʿilis of

Quhistān and the Maliks of Nīmrūz or Sīstān,' in Daftary, ed., *Mediaeval Isma'ili History and Thought*, pp. 221–9.

26. On this subject, in addition to Nanji, *Nizārī Ismāʿīlī Tradition*, and Kassam, *Songs of Wisdom*, see Christopher Shackle and Zawahir Moir, *Ismaili Hymns from South Asia: An Introduction to the Ginans* (London, 1992); Ali S. Asani, *Ecstasy and Enlightenment: The Ismaili Devotional Literature of South Asia* (London, 2002).

27. On the so-called Anjudān revival of Nizārī Ismailism in general, see Daftary, *The Ismāʿīlīs*, pp. 451–2 and 467–91.

Chapter 5: The Poet Nizārī Quhistānī

1. There are three copies of Nizārī's *Kulliyyāt*, the earliest and most complete of which, copied by ʿAbd al-Rashīd b. Shaykh ʿAbd Allāh al-Khālibī in 838/1434, is at the National Library of St Petersburg (marked Dorn 415). The second, copied in 972/1564–5 by a scribe whose name is not clear, is preserved at the Institute of Language and Literature of the Academy of Sciences in Dushanbe, Tajikistan (AH Taj SSR 100). The third, least complete manuscript copied by Zayn al-ʿĀbidīn b. Muḥammad in 865/1460–1, is at the Genel Kutuphane in Corum, Turkey (1955). On this copy, see also A.M. Boldyrev et al., *Katalog Vostochnykh rukopisei, Akademii Nauk Tadzhikskoi SSSR* (507). All references to the *Kulliyyāt* hereafter are to the St Petersburg manuscript.

2. W. Ivanow, 'Hakim Nizārī Kohistani,' *Africa Ismaili*, Nairobi (Sept., 1969), pp. 6–7.

3. Kātibī Nīshāpūrī, *Dīwān*, as excerpted in Chengiz G. Baiburdi, *Zhizn i tvorchestvo Nizārī-Persidskogo poeta* (Moscow, 1966). Persian tr. M. Ṣadrī, *Zindigī va āthār-i Nizārī* (Tehran, 1370/1991), pp. 24–5.

4. Browne reports in his *Literary History*, vol. 3, p. 395, that under Bāysunghur's auspices 'forty artists were employed in copying manuscripts under the guidance of Mawlānā Jaʿfar of Tabrīz.'

5. Nūr al-Dīn ʿAbd al-Raḥmān Jāmī, *Bahāristān-i rasāʾil-i Jāmī*, ed. Aʿlā Afṣahzād, et al. (Tehran, 1379/2000), p. 791.

6. Dawlatshāh, *Tadhkirat al-shuʿarāʾ*, pp. 231–4.

7. Mīrkhwānd, *Rawḍat al-ṣafāʾ*, vol. 4, pp. 70, 193.

8. Khwānd Amīr, *Ḥabīb al-siyar*, vol. 2, p. 457.

9. Amīn Aḥmad Rāzī, *Haft iqlīm*, ed. Javād Fāḍil (Tehran, n.d.), vol. 2, pp. 322–3.

10. Luṭf ʿAlī Beg Ādhār, *Ātashkada*, ed. Ḥasan Sādāt Nāṣirī (Gīlān, 1339/1960), p. 529.

11. Mujtahid Zāda Bīrjandī, *Nasīm-i bahārī dar aḥvāl-i Ḥakīm Nizārī* (Mashhad, 1344/1926), p. 4.

12. ʿAbbās Iqbāl, *Ta'rīkh-i mufaṣṣal-i Īrān* (Tehran, 1341/1962), p. 170; ʿA.R. Mujtahid Zāda, *Ḥakim Nizārī Quhistānī* (Mashhad, 1344/1926), pp. 13–17.

13. Zabīḥ Allāh Ṣafā, *Ta'rīkh-i adabiyyāt dar Īrān* (various editions, Tehran, 1342–73/1963–1994), vol. 3, p. 736.

14. *Dīwān-i Ḥakīm Nizārī Quhistānī*, ed. ʿAlī Riḍā Mujtahid Zāda, with an introduction by Maẓāhir Muṣaffā (Tehran, 1371/1992).

15. J. von Hammer-Purgstall, *Geschichte der schönen Redekunste Persiens* (Vienna, 1818), pp. 223–4.

16. A. Sprenger, *A Catalogue of the Persian Manuscripts of the King of Oudh* (Calcutta, 1854), p. 154.

17. Browne, *Literary History*, vol. 3, p. 154–5.

18. See Bertel's' introduction to Nizārī's *Dastūr-nāma*, which appeared in *Vostochniy Sbornik*, 1 (1926), pp. 37–104; also J. Durri, 'Baʿze maʿlumot dar borayi Nizori,' p. 140, and Baradin, 'Ḥakīm Nizārī,' pp. 180–2.

19. Nizārī, *Kulliyyāt*, folio 292b.

20. W. Ivanow *Guide to Ismaili Literature*, pp. 105–6.

21. Ivanow, *Ismaili Literature: A Bibliographical Survey* (Tehran, 1963), p. 138.

22. Nizārī's words quoted by Baradin ('Ḥakīm Nizārī,' p. 180) are: 'You are Saʿd al-Dīn and I am Nizārī Saʿd.'

23. On Baiburdi's works, see note 17 of Chapter 1 above.

24. Baiburdi, *Zhizn*, p. 180.

25. Jan Rypka, 'Poets and Prose Writers of the Late Saljūq and Mongol Periods,' in *The Cambridge History of Iran*, Volume 5, pp. 604–5.

26. Cited by Baradin, 'Ḥakīm Nizārī,' p. 178.

27. Ḥamd Allāh Mustawfī, *The Geographical Part of the Nuzhat-al-Qulūb*, p. 143.

28. Shihāb al-Dīn Abū ʿAbd Allāh Yāqūt al-Ḥamawī, *Muʿjam al-buldān*, ed. F. Wüstenfeld (Leipzig, 1866–73), p. 783.

29. Rypka, 'Poets and Prose Writers of the Late Saljūq and Mongol Periods,' p. 604.

30. Nizārī, *Kulliyyāt*, f.372b, untitled *mathnawī*.

31. Durri mentions, in his 'Baʿze maʿlumot dar borayi Nizori,' pp. 140–54, that Nizārī's brother was called Sharaf al-Dīn Ḥasan, but this is inconclusive.

32. Cited by Baradin, 'Ḥakīm Nizārī,' p. 183; *Dīwān*, edited version,

vol. 1, p. 22. While Baradin mentions only one brother, it is unclear whether Nizārī had other siblings.

33. Nizārī, *Kulliyyāt,* f.292b, *Muqaṭṭaʿāt.*

34. Nizārī, *Kulliyyāt,* f.179b; *Dīwān,* edited version, vol. 1, p. 174.

35. According to Daftary, *The Ismāʿīlīs,* p. 445, Nizārī was educated in both Bīrjand and Qāʾin.

36. Nizārī, *Kulliyyāt,* f. 320b–321a, *Muqaṭṭaʿāt* (incorrectly referred to in Baiburdi as 309b).

37. Rypka, 'Poets and Prose Writers of the Late Saljūq and Mongol Periods,' p. 604.

38. Maẓāhir Muṣaffā, introduction to *Dīwān-i Ḥakīm Nizārī Quhistānī,* pp. 10 and 315–45. Riḍā Qulī Khān Hidāyat, *Majmāʿ al-fuṣahā,* ed. M. Muṣaffā (Tehran, 1336–40/1957–61), vol. 3, pp. 1358–9, reports that Nizārī was personally acquainted with the poet Saʿdī (d. 691/1292). That there was a correspondence between the two is evident from various verses of Nizārī and is confirmed by Muṣaffā in his introduction to the *Dīwān,* p. 321.

39. Baradin, 'Ḥakīm Nizārī,' p. 185.

40. Ibid., p.189.

41. Nizārī, *Kulliyyāt,* f.172a; *Dīwān,* edited version, vol. 1, p. 499.

42. Bertel's in *Dastūr-nāma,* pp. 44–5; see also Baradin, 'Ḥakīm Nizārī,' p. 186, and Baiburdi, *Zhizn,* p. 37.

43. Nizārī, *Kulliyyāt,* f.51b; *Dīwān,* edited version, vol. 1, p. 499.

44. As cited by I.P. Petrushevsky, 'The Socio-Economic Conditions in Iran under the Īl-Khāns,' in *The Cambridge History of Iran,* Volume 5, pp. 486–7.

45. J.H. Kramers, 'Ḳūhistān,' *EI2,* vol. 5, pp. 354–6.

46. Shams al-Dīn Kart was a descendant of the Shansabānī house of Ghūr. T.W. Haig and B. Spulet, 'Kart,' *EI2,* vol. 4, p. 272.

47. On this, see Terry Allsen, *Mongol Imperialism: The Policies of Grand Qan Mongke in China, Russia, and the Islamic Lands, 1251–1259* (Berkeley, Calif., 1987), p. 67.

48. Sayf b. Muḥammad al-Harawī, *Taʾrīkh nāma-yi Harāt,* ed. M. Zubayr al-Ṣiddīqī (Calcutta, 1944), pp. 171–2. According to al-Harawī, when Shams al-Dīn reached Tūs, the governor of Khurāsān, Argun Aga, who was also a viceroy of the Chagatay Khanate, gave him 50,000 dinars.

49. *Taʾrīkh-i Sīstān,* ed. M.T. Bahār (Tehran, 1314/1935), p. 398; English tr. M. Gold (Rome, 1976), p. 324. On the Mihrabānids in general, see C.E. Bosworth, *The History of the Saffarids of Sistan and the Maliks of*

Nimruz (247/861 to 949/1542–3), (Costa Mesa, CA, and New York, 1994), pp. 410–24, 429–40.

50. L. Potter, 'The Kart Dynasty of Harat: Religion and Politics in Medieval Iran,' (Ph.D. thesis, Columbia University, 1992), p. 42.

51. Howorth, *History of the Mongols*, Part 3, p. 251.

52. According to Kramer, 'Ḳūhistān,' Shams al-Dīn Kart died in 1285, which appears to be incorrect.

53. Baiburdi, *Zhizn*, p. 87.

54. Baradin, 'Ḥakīm Nizārī,' p. 190.

55. On the administrative structure of Īl-Khānid rule in Persia, see Howorth, *History of the Mongols*, part III, p. 220; also Hodgson, *The Venture of Islam*, vol. 2, p. 407.

56. Rypka, for instance says in 'Poets and Prose Writers,' p. 605: 'From his youth on he served at the court and in the chancellery of the Kart rulers of Herāt, and he had perforce to sing their praises in qaṣīdas.'

57. See reference to Nizārī's *Dīwān* in note 38 above

58. Cited by Petrushevsky, 'The Socio-Economic Conditions of Iran,' from Nizārī's *Kulliyyāt* and *Dastūr-nāma*, p. 527.

59. Ibid., especially pp. 529–37, where Petrushevsky also mentions recent studies on the subject.

60. Nizārī, *Kulliyyāt*, f.380b.

61. Nizārī, *Kulliyyāt*, f.186b; *Dīwān*, edited version, vol. 2, p. 167 (where the poet's reference to a wife is missing).

62. Nizārī, *Kulliyyāt*, f.384b; *Dastūr-nāma*, edited version, vol. 1, p. 263. All references to the *Dastūr-nāma* are from Mujtahid Zāda's edition of the *Dīwān*.

63. *Ta'rīkh-i Sīstān*, p. 408.

64. Harawī, *Ta'rīkh nāma-yi Harāt*, p. 432.

65. *Ushnan*, the herb *alkalī*, and the ashes made from it, was used as a washing powder. Steingass, *Persian-English Dictionary*, p. 67.

66. Literally, 'Who will remove the water of the cheek from the jewel of the wheat bag?'

67. Nizārī, *Kulliyyāt*, f.178a; *Dīwān*, edited version, vol. 1, p. 131.

68. Nizārī, *Kulliyyāt*, f. 301a, *Muqaṭṭaʿāt*; incorrectly referred to in Baiburdi as 310a.

69. Petrushevsky, 'The Socio-Economic Conditions of Iran,' p. 517.

70. Nizārī, *Kulliyyāt*, f.157a (inaccurately referred to in Baiburdi as 137a); *Dīwān*, edited version, vol. 1, p. 83.

71. Nizārī, *Dīwān*, edited version, vol. 1, p. 1271.

72. Nizārī, *Kulliyyāt*, f.201b; *Dīwān*, edited version, vol. 1, p. 675.

73. Nizārī, *Kulliyyāt*, f.157a, *Dīwān* (not found in the edited version).
74. Nizārī, *Kulliyyāt*, f.44b.
75. Nizārī, *Kulliyyāt*, f.327b.
76. Baradin, 'Ḥakīm Nizārī,' p. 197.
77. Baiburdi, *Zhizn*, p. 179.
78. The first mention of Hajji 'Alā' al-Dīn Hindū is in Harawī's *Ta'rīkh nāma-yi Harāt*, p. 570. He was the patron of the poet Amīr Maḥmūd b. Amīr Yamīn al-Dīn Tughrā'ī, also called Ibn Yamīn Faryāmādī (d. 743/1342). The Ḥājjī possibly came from the influential Faryāmādī family in Harāt. Nizārī alludes to him in one of his verses for having saved his life twice. J.T.P. de Bruijn, 'Nizārī Kuhistānī,' *EI2*, vol. 7, pp. 83–4.
79. Cited by Baradin, 'Ḥakīm Nizārī,' p. 202.
80. Daftary, *The Ismāʿīlīs*, p. 446.

Chapter 6: Ismailism, Sufism and Nizārī Quhistānī

1. A. Bausani, 'Religion under the Mongols,' in *The Cambridge History of Iran*, Volume 5, pp. 538–49.
2. Ibid., p. 544.
3. For a discussion of the rise of Sufism under the Mongols, see Leonard Lewisohn, 'Overview: Iranian Islam and Persianate Sufism,' in L. Lewisohn, ed., *The Heritage of Sufism*, vol. 2; *The Legacy of Medieval Persian Sufism (1130–1500)*, (Oxford, 1999), pp. 11–43.
4. Marshall Hodgson gives an insightful account of the popularity of Sufism in medieval Islamic culture in his *The Venture of Islam*, vol. 2, pp. 201–54. For a historical survey of Ṭarīqa Sufism, see J. Spencer Trimingham, *The Sufi Orders in Islam* (Oxford, 1971) and Annemarie Schimmel, *Mystical Dimensions of Islam* (Chapel Hill, N.C., 1975), pp. 228–58.
5. Terry Graham, 'Abū Saʿīd b. Abi'l-Khayr and the School of Khurāsān,' in L. Lewisohn, ed., *The Heritage of Sufism*, vol. 1: *Classical Persian Sufism from its Origins to Rumi (700–1300)*, pp. 83–135.
6. G. Lazard, 'The Rise of the New Persian Language,' in *The Cambridge History of Iran*, Volume 4 (Cambridge, 1975), p. 608–9.
7. On the relationship between early Shiʿism and Sufism, see Corbin, *History of Islamic Philosophy*, pp. 28–30, 188–90; S.H. Nasr, 'Shiʿism and Sufism: Their Relationship in Essence and History,' in his *Sufi Essays* (London, 1972), pp. 104–20; and Trimingham, *The Sufi Orders in Islam*, pp. 133–7.
8. The first systematic study of the contribution of early Shiʿism to the Islamic esoteric tradition is by Muhammad Ali Amir-Moezzi, *The Divine*

Guide in Early Shiʿism: The Sources of Esotericism in Islam, tr. D. Streight (Albany, NY, 1994).

9. Hodgson, *The Venture of Islam*, vol. 2, pp. 214–16.

10. Trimingham, *The Sufi Orders in Islam*, 52–6.

11. Muḥammad Jaʿfar Maḥjūb, 'Chivalry and Early Persian Sufism,' in Lewisohn, ed., *The Heritage of Sufism*, vol. 1, pp. 549–81.

12. Ibn Khaldūn, *The Muqaddimah: An Introduction to History* (New York, 1958), vol. 3, p. 92.

13. For an overview of the revival of Twelver Shiʿi theology and philosophy from the Mongol era to the 19th century, see Corbin, *History of Islamic Philosophy*, pp. 319–63.

14. Alice C. Hunsberger, *Nasir Khusraw, The Ruby of Badakhshan: A Portrait of the Persian Poet, Traveller and Philosopher* (London, 2000), is the first full-length study of the life and works of Nāṣir-i Khusraw to appear in English. See also Annemarie Schimmel, *Make a Shield from Wisdom: Selected Verses from Nāṣir-i Khusraw's Dīvān* (rev. ed., London, 2001).

15. Daftary, *The Ismāʿīlīs*, pp. 395–6.

16. Hamid Dabashi, *Truth and Narrative: The Untimely Thoughts of ʿAyn al-Quḍāt al-Hamadhānī* (London, 1999), pp. 405–8, 476.

17. This commentary, entitled *Baʿḍī az ta'wīlāt-i Gulshan-i rāz*, has been edited with a French translation by Henry Corbin in his *Trilogie Ismaélienne* (Tehran, 1961). See also W. Ivanow, 'An Ismaili Interpretation of the Gulshani Raz,' *JBBRAS*, NS, 8 (1932), pp. 68–78.

18. W. Ivanow, 'Ismailism and Sufism,' *Ismaili Bulletin*, vol. 1, no. 12 (Karachi, 1975), pp. 3–6.

19. Corbin, *History of Islamic Philosophy*, p. 95.

20. Daftary, *The Ismāʿīlīs*, p. 279.

21. See Ivanow, *Ismaili Literature*, pp. 182–90; Daftary, *The Ismāʿīlīs*, pp. 452–6, 461, ff.; Abbas Amanat, 'The Nuqṭawī Movement of Maḥmūd Pisīkhānī and his Persian Cycle of Mystical-materialism,' in Daftary, ed., *Mediaeval Ismaʿili History and Thought*, pp. 281–97; and A. Bausani, 'Ḥurūfiyya,' *EI2*, vol. 3, pp. 600–1.

22. For a discussion of Nizārī Ismailism and Sufism in Persia, see F. Daftary, 'Ismāʿīlī-Sufi Relations in early Post-Alamūt and Safavid Persia,' in Lewisohn, ed., *The Heritage of Sufism*, vol. 3, pp. 257–89.

23. N. Pourjavady and P.L. Wilson, 'Ismāʿīlīs and Niʿmatullāhīs,' *Studia Islamica*, 41 (1975), pp. 118–35; Daftary, *The Ismāʿīlīs*, pp. 498–518.

24. On Ismaili-Sufi relations in the Indian subcontinent, see Nanji, *The Ismāʿīlī Tradition*, pp. 120–30, and Ali S. Asani, *The Būjh Niranjan: An Ismaili Mystical Poem* (Cambridge, Mass., 1991), pp. 37–41.

25. Unfortunately, there have been no studies of these Ismaili poets of the Alamūt period, some of whose writings have survived in manuscript form or preserved in various sources. For some specimens, see Abu'l-Qāsim Kāshānī's *Zubdat al-tawārīkh: baksh-i Fāṭimiyān va Nizāriyān.* See also Faquir M. Hunzai, *Shimmering Light: An Anthology of Ismaili Poetry* (London, 1996), pp. 79–84, for Ra'īs Ḥasan; and al-Ṭūsī, *Sayr wa sulūk,* ed. Badakhchani, p. 67, note 16 on Ḥasan Maḥmūd.

26. Graham, 'Abū Sa'īd b. Abi'l-Khayr and the School of Khurāsān,' pp. 106–16.

27. Hermann Landolt, 'Walāya' in Eliade, ed., *The Encyclopedia of Religion,* vol. 15, pp. 316–23, and Corbin, *History of Islamic Philosophy,* pp. 25–30.

28. Al-Qāḍī al-Nu'mān, *The Book of Faith.* Partial English tr. of *Da'ā'im al-Islām,* by Asaf A.A. Fyzee (Bombay, 1974).

29. Nizārī, *Kulliyyāt,* f.261a; *Dīwān,* edited version, vol. 1, p. 186; tr. Hunzai, *Shimmering Light,* p. 87.

30. Nizārī, *Kulliyāt,* f.329b, untitled.

31. Nizārī, *Kulliyāt,* f.146a; *Dīwān,* edited version, vol. 1, p. 1206 (where the last *bayt* is not found).

32. A reference to the Prophetic Tradition, 'If the world were without an Imam for a moment, it would be convulsed with all its people.' See al-Kulaynī, *al-Uṣūl min al-kāfī* (Tehran, 1388/1968), vol. 1, p. 145.

33. The poet is alluding here to the Qur'anic verse, 'One day We shall summon together all human beings with their Imam' (17:71), and the well-known hadith, 'He who dies without knowing the Imam of the time dies in ignorance.' Al-Kulaynī, *Uṣūl,* vol. 1, p. 397.

34. Nizārī, *Kulliyyāt,* f.94a; *Dīwān,* edited version, vol. 1, p. 674. (the last verse is not found in the *Kulliyyāt* ms.), tr. Hunzai, *Shimmering Light,* pp. 91–4.

35. Nizārī, *Kulliyyāt,* f.176b–177a, *Dīwān,* edited version, vol. 1, p.80.

36. Nizārī, *Kulliyyāt,* f.280b, *Tarqībāt wa tarjī'āt* (incorrectly cited by Baiburdi as f.208a).

37. Nizārī, *Kulliyyāt,* f.144a; *Dīwān,* edited version, vol. 1, p. 61.

38. Nizārī, *Kulliyyāt,* f.384b, *Dastūr-nāma; Dīwān,* edited version, p. 263.

39. According to Sami N. Makarem, 'In examining the Ismā'īlī works from the 12th and 13th centuries A.D., we find that they are either a repetition of, or an elaboration on, older works such as *Rasā'īl Ikhwān aṣ-Ṣafā',* Abū Ya'qūb Isḥāq al-Sijistānī's *Tuḥfat al-mustajībīn* and *al-Yanābī',* Ḥamīd ad-Dīn al-Kirmānī's *Rāḥat al-'aql* and other classical works, mainly

of the Fatimid period.' Shihāb al-Dīn Abū Firās, *Ash-Shāfiya: An Ismāʿīlī Poem*, ed. and tr. S.N. Makarem (Beirut, 1966), p. 24.

40. Nizārī, *Kulliyyāt*, f.261a, *Dīwān*, edited version, vol. 1, p. 185, tr. Hunzai, *Shimmering Light*, p. 86.

41. For further discussion on this subject, see Leonard Lewisohn, 'Sufism and Ismāʿīlī Doctrine in the Persian Poetry of Nizārī Quhistānī,' paper presented at the Middle East Studies Association Conference (2001, unpublished).

42. Daftary, *A Short History*, p. 160.

43. Etan Kohlberg, 'Some Imāmī-Shīʿī Views on Taqiyya,' *JAOS*, 95 (1975), pp. 395–402, reprinted in his *Belief and Law in Imāmī Shīʿism* (Aldershot, U.K., 1991), article III; Ayatollah Jaʿfar Sobhani, *Doctrines of Shiʿi Islam: A Compendium of Imami Beliefs and Practices* (London, 2001), pp. 150–4, and R. Strothmann and M. Djebli, 'Taḳiyya,' *EI2*, vol. 10, pp. 134–6.

44. Lalani, *Early Shiʿi Thought*, pp. 88–91, and Ṭabāṭabāʾī, *Shiʿite Islam*, pp. 223–5.

45. Halm, 'The Ismaʿili Oath of Allegiance,' pp. 91–9.

46. Hodgson, *The Venture of Islam*, vol. 2, pp. 311–15.

47. Leo Strauss, *Persecution and the Art of Writing* (Glencoe, Illinois, 1952), pp. 22–37.

48. Ivanow, *Ismaili Literature*, pp. 138.

49. Abū Isḥāq Quhistānī, *Haft bāb-i Bū Isḥāq*, ed. and tr. W. Ivanow (Tehran, 1957), pp. 49–50.

50. Baiburdi, *Zhizn*, pp. 39–40.

51. Nizārī, *Kulliyāt*, f.146a; *Dīwān*, edited version, vol. 1, p. 1206.

52. Nizārī, *Kulliyyāt*, f.166a; *Dīwān*, edited version, vol. 1, p. 1360.

53. Nizārī, *Kulliyyāt*, 373b, *Safar-nāma.*

Chapter 7: Nizārī's *Safar-nāma*: The Journey of a *Dāʿī*

1.The *Safar-nāma* of Nizārī is found in the three extant copies of his *Kulliyyāt* preserved in Russia (St. Petersburg), Tajikistan (Dushambe) and Turkey (Corum). See Chapter 5, note 1 above for more information on these manuscripts.

2. Lewisohn, 'Sufism and Ismāʿīlī Doctrine in the Persian Poetry of Nizārī Quhistānī,' p. 23.

3. Baiburdi, in his work on Nizārī, gives only a brief account of his journey and restricts his analysis of the *Safar-nāma* largely to its historical and ethnographical content. Although he notes the many references

Nizārī makes to religious matters, he says: 'The *Safar-nāma* supplements our ideas about the lives of the cities of Transcaucasia in the 13th century with much valuable information of an historical, social and ethnographical order. Also in his writing, Nizārī rouses considerable interest in the political and cultural study of the lives of the people of these countries.' Baiburdi, *Zhizn*, p. 88.

4. Nāṣir-i Khusraw, *Safar-nāma*, ed. M. Ghanīzāda (Berlin, 1922) and S.M. Dabīr Siyāqī (Tehran, 1977); English trans. W.M. Thackston, Jr., *Nāṣer-e Khosraw's Book of Travels (Safarnama)*, (Albany, NY, 1986). See also Hunsberger, *Nasir Khusraw, The Ruby of Badakhshan*, pp. 91–219, for a detailed analysis of the author's journey.

5. Nizārī, *Kulliyyāt*, f.371a, *Safar-nāma*.

6. On the search for knowledge as a major *leitmotiv* of Muslim societies, see I.R. Netton, *Seek Knowledge: Thought and Travel in the House of Islam* (Richmond, U.K., 1996).

7. Baradin, '*Ḥakīm Nizārī*,' p. 91.

8. Baiburdi, *Zhizn*, p. 89.

9. Muṣaffā, introduction to Nizārī's *Dīwān*, pp. 26, 110.

10. In one of his later poems, possibly written in his years of retirement in Bīrjand, Nizārī dedicates the final verse to Shams al-Dīn Juwaynī, in which he refers to himself as an outcast (*maḥrūm*) and request the *wazīr* for assistance. Muṣaffā, introduction to Nizārī's *Dīwān*, pp. 106–7.

11. Nizārī, *Kulliyyāt*, f. 370b, *Safar-nāma*. It is important to note that the reference to 'awakening heart' is missing in the text supplied by Baiburdi.

12. Nizārī, *Kulliyyāt*, f. 373b, *Safar-nāma*.

13. Nizārī, *Kulliyyāt*, f.371ba, *Safar-nāma*.

14. Nizārī, *Kulliyyāt*, f.385a; *Dastūr-nāma*, edited version, vol. 1, p. 267.

15. Nizārī, *Kulliyyāt*, f.381a, *Safar-nāma*.

16. Baiburdi, *Zhizn*, p. 87.

17. Jaʿfar b. Manṣūr al-Yaman, *The Master and the Disciple*, ed. J.W. Morris, pp. 92–7, *passim*.

18. Nizārī, *Kulliyyāt*, f.63b.

19. Al-Sijistānī's discourse on the concept of *qiyāma* can be found in his *Kitāb al-Iftikhār*, ed. M. Ghālib (Beirut, 1980), '*Fī maʿrifat al-qiyāma*,' pp. 74–91.

20. Naṣīr al-Dīn al-Ṭūsī, *Taṣawwurāt*, pp. 58–9.

21. Corbin, *Cyclical Time and Ismaili Gnosis*, p. 54.

22. Baiburdi, *Zhizn*, p. 89.

23. Hunsberger, *Nasir Khusraw, The Ruby of Badakhshan*, pp. 49–71,

and W. Ivanow, *Problems in Nasir-i Khusraw's Biography* (Bombay, 1956), pp. 21–40.

24. Thackston's introduction to *Nāṣer-e Khosraw's Book of Travels (Safarnāma),* p. xi.

25. Hunsberger, *Nasir Khusraw, The Ruby of Badakhshan,* pp. 188–95.

26. Nizārī, *Kulliyyāt,* f.378b, *Safar-nāma.*

27. See Daftary, *The Ismāʿīlīs,* pp. 369–70, for a summary of Ḥasan-i Ṣabbāḥ's doctrine of *taʿlīm.*

28. Nizārī, *Kulliyyāt,* f.377a, *Safar-nāma.*

29. Al-Ṭūsī, *Sayr wa sulūk,* tr. Badakhchani, *Contemplation and Action,* pp. 50–1.

30. Nizārī, *Kulliyāt,* f.380a, *Safar-nāma.*

31. Nizārī, *Kulliyāt,* f.373b, *Safar-nāma.*

32. Nāṣir-i Khusraw, *Safar-nāma,* tr. Thackston, pp. 99.

33. Rashīd al-Dīn, *Jāmiʿ*, ed., Alizade, pp. 557–8.

34. Boyle, 'The Capture of Isfahan by the Mongols,' in Academia Nazionale dei Lincei, *Atti del convegno internzionale sul tema: La Persia nel medioevo* (Rome, 1971), pp. 331–6; J.E. Woods, 'A Note on the Mongol Capture of Isfahan,' *Journal of Near Eastern Studies,* 36 (1977). pp.49–51.

35. Howorth, *History of the Mongols,* pp. 221–2.

36. Nizārī, *Kullīyat,* f. 371a, *Safar-nāma.*

37. Baiburdi, *Zhizn,* p. 91.

38. Maẓāhir Muṣaffā in his Introduction to Nizārī's *Dīwān,* p. 32, but he provides no conclusive evidence to support his view that Īrānshāh was related to the Ismaili Imam.

39. Nasr, 'Shiʿism and Sufism,' in *Sufi Essays,* pp. 105–6.

40. Trimingham, *The Sufi Orders in Islam,* pp. 181–5.

41. Nizārī, *Kulliyāt,* f.377a, *Safar-nāma.*

42. Nizārī, *Kulliyāt,* f.378a, *Safar-nāma.*

43. On the Ismaili presence in Iṣfahān, see Daftary, *The Ismāʿīlīs,* pp. 121, 336–7, 354–5, 361–2.

44. Naṭanz does not seem to have been mentioned by any Arab geographer before Yāʿqūt, according G. Le Strange, *Lands of the Eastern Caliphate* (London, 1905, repr. 1966), p. 209.

45. Nāṣir-i Khusraw, *Safar-nāma,* tr. Thackston, p. 5.

46. Yāqūt al-Ḥamawī, *Muʿjam al-buldān,* vol. 1, p. 822.

47. W. Barthold, *An Historical Geography of Iran* (Princeton, 1984), p. 218.

48. Baiburdi, in *Zhizn,* p. 92, mistakenly writes March 1281, which would not fit in with Nizārī's subsequent itinerary.

49. J.A. Boyle, 'The Il-Khans of Persia and the Princes of Europe, *Central Asian Journal*, 20 (1976), pp. 2–40.

50. Rashīd al-Dīn, *Jāmi*ʿ, ed. Alizade, p. 162. It seems that Abaqa had intended to invade Syria for some time but had been occupied in a campaign against the rebellious Mongol forces of the Nīkūdarīs who had raided Fars and Kirmān provinces from their base in Afghanistan. Boyle, 'Dynastic and Political History of the Īl-Khāns,' p. 262–3.

51. Amitai-Preiss, *Mongols and Mamlūks*, pp. 189, 194.

52. Nizārī, *Kulliyāt*, f. 371a, *Safar-nāma*.

53. Naṣīr al-Dīn al-Ṭūsī, *Rawḍa-yi taslīm* (*The Paradise of Submission*), a new ed. and English trans. by S.J. Badakhchani (London, forthcoming), section 145.

54. For al-Ṭūsī's discussion on the concept of Paradise, see his 'Fifteenth Deliberation concerning Paradise and paradises, Hell and hells, Purgatories and the paths,' in ibid., sections 137–64.

55. Nizārī, *Kulliyyāt*, f. 371b, *Safar-nāma*.

56. Nizārī, *Kulliyyāt*, f. 371b, *Safar-nāma*.

57. Daftary, *The Ismāʿīlīs*, pp. 166–7.

58. Trimingham, *The Sufi Orders in Islam*, pp. 74–5.

59. Graham, 'Abū Saʿīd b. Abi'l-Khayr and the School of Khurāsān,' p.116–21.

60. For a discussion of the Sufi *samā*ʿ, see also Schimmel, *Mystical Dimensions of Islam*, pp. 178–86; Trimingham, *The Sufi Orders in Islam*, pp. 195–6; and J.L. Michon, 'Sacred Music and Dance in Islam,' in S.H. Nasr, ed., *Islamic Spirituality: Manifestations* (New York, 1991), p. 474.

61. E. Yarshater, 'Wine-drinking in Persian Poetry,' *Studia Islamica*, 27 (1960), pp. 43–53.

62. Nizārī, *Kulliyyāt*, f.374a, *Safar-nāma*.

63. Nizārī, *Kulliyyāt*, f.385a, *Dastur-nāma*; *Dīwān*, edited version, vol. 1, p. 265.

64. Nizārī, *Kulliyyāt*, f.280a, *Safar-nāma*.

65. See Lewisohn, 'Sufism and Ismāʿīlī Doctrine in the Persian Poetry of Nizārī Quhistānī,' p. 10, which also contains an interesting discussion of what he calls the 'bacchanalian verses' of the poet.

66. Nizārī, *Kulliyyāt*, f.371b, *Safar-nāma*.

67. Nizārī, *Kulliyyāt*, f.371b–372a, *Safar-nāma*.

68. Nizāmī's epic has been translated into English by James Atkinson as *Layla and Majunun* (London, 1836, repr. 1968), and R. Gelpe, *The Story of Layla and Majnun* (Leiden, 1977).

69. The most detailed account in English of the life and teachings of

Shams-i Tabrīz and his relationship with Rūmī appears in Franklin D. Lewis, *Rumi: Past and Present, East and West* (Oxford, 2000), pp. 134–202.

70. Shihāb al-Dīn Abū Firās, *Ash-Shāfiya: An Ismāʿīlī Treatise*, ed. and tr. S.N. Makarem (Beirut, 1966), verses 713–733 and 720. There is some doubt on the authorship of this work because Makarem concludes in his introduction, pp. 14–16, that it gives the impression of having been written during the 7th/13th century.

71. This view is supported by Daftary, *The Ismāʿīlīs*, p. 446.

72. Daftary, *The Ismāʿīlīs*, p. 445.

73. For details on this issue see, Nanji, *The Nizārī Ismāʿīlī Tradition*, pp. 62–9; W. Ivanow, 'Shums-i Tabrez of Multān,' in S.M. Abdullah, ed., *Professor Muḥammad Shāfi Presentation Volume* (Lahore, 1955), pp. 109–18; and J.G. Cowan, *Where Two Oceans Meet* (Dorset, UK, 1992), pp. 5–7.

74. Nanji, *The Nizārī Ismāʿīlī Tradition*, p. 63.

75. Nizārī, *Kulliyyāt*, f.385a, *Dastūr-nāma*, edited version, vol. 1, p. 267.

76. Nizārī, *Kulliyyāt*, f.383a, *Safar-nāma.*

77. Ivanow, *Ismāʿīlī Literature*, p. 137.

78. Nizārī, *Kulliyyāt*, f.372a–372b, *Safar-nāma.*

79. Rashīd al-Dīn, *Jāmiʿ*, ed. Alizade, p. 170.

80. J.A. Boyle, 'Dynastic and Political History of the Īl-Khāns,' in *The Cambridge History of Iran*, Volume 5, p. 362.

81. The Mongols invaded Syria for a second time in the summer of 679/1280 with a force of about 50,000 men, including contingents of Armenians, Georgians, Seljuqs from Anatolia and Frankish troops, led by Abaqa's younger brother Mengü Timür and other commanders. After capturing Aleppo, they were decisively defeated by the Mamlūks at the Battle of Hims in October of the following year. For a detailed study of this war, see Amitai-Preiss, *Mongols and Mamlūks*, especially pp. 183–201.

82. Nizārī, *Kulliyyāt*, f.372b, *Safar-nāma.*

83. Le Strange, *Lands of the Eastern Caliphate*, pp. 160–1; Howorth, *History of the Mongols*, p. 136.

84. Howorth mentions that there had been Ismailis in the vicinity of Khoy during the time of the Imam ʿAlāʾ al-Dīn Muḥammad (d. 653/1255), who had also sent out from Alamūt an envoy to Khoy to negotiate with Sultan Jalāl al-Dīn, the Khwārazm-shāh, who had arrived there in 1225 to carry out his conquest of Georgia. *History of the Mongols*, pp. 92–3.

85. Abaqa Khān had selected Alatāq as the main pasture grounds in

summer for the vast herds of cattle which provided food for the Mongol army during its campaigns. Le Strange, *Lands of the Eastern Caliphate*, p. 182.

86. Boyle, 'Dynastic and Political History of the Īl-Khāns,' p. 264.

87. According to V.M. Kurkjian, *A History of Armenia* (New York, 1958), p. 249, Leon III provided a contingent of 25,000 troops for the invasion of Syria.

88. Barthold, *An Historical Geography of Iran*, p. 226.

89. Nizārī, *Kulliyyāt*, f.372b, *Safar-nāma*. The last line reads literally, 'that you would have put your finger in your mouth out of disbelief.'

90. King Dimitri ruled not only Georgia but also other territories for which he owed allegiance to the Mongols. Apparently he was held in high favour by Abaqa Khān. W.T. Allen, *A History of the Georgian People* (New York, 1932), p. 118.

91. Nizārī, *Kulliyyāt*, f.372b–373a, *Safar-nāma*.

92. Gukchah Tangiz is a sweet water lake in Armenia some distance to the north of Dabil. Le Strange, *Lands of the Eastern Caliphate*, p. 183.

93. Ibid., pp. 176–8.

94. Nizārī's description of the armies gathering in the plain of Arrān in September and October of 1280 substantiates the suggestion by Amitai-Preiss that Mongol troops, perhaps only an advanced group, penetrated into northern Syria in September 1280, gaining temporary possession of ʿAyn Tāb, Baghrās and al-Darbassāk and Aleppo. They then withdrew from Syria only to return in full force, under the leadership of Mengü Timür, in the August of the following year. Amitai-Preiss, *Mongols and Mamlūks*, pp. 184–9.

95. In 664/1265, Abaqa Khān and his brother Yoshmut crossed the Kūr river to confront Berke, the ruler of the Golden Horde. Although Berke died during this battle and his troops withdrew to Darband with their booty, the feud did not cease and Abaqa continued to maintain a large military presence in this region under the command of his brother Mengü Timür. Amitai-Preiss, *Mongols and Mamlūks*, p. 183; Howorth, *History of the Mongols*, pp. 224, 264; Rashīd al-Dīn, *Jāmiʿ al-tawarīkh*, tr. Alizade, pp. 102, 104.

96. This location is not mentioned in Persian source, but as Nizārī describes it as a well fortified place, he may be referring here to the castle of Baquyya situated high above the city. Ḥamd Allah Mustawfī, *Nuzhat al-Qulūb*, p. 161.

97. There is no mention of Aniq in Persian sources, nor is this battle in either Rashīd al-Dīn or Waṣṣāf. But Baiburdi states that Aniq was

probably the same as Ani, the capital of Armenia. This seems improbable for two reasons. In 679/1280, the Armenian king Leon III contributed troops for Abaqa's invasion of Syria. Secondly, according to Nizārī, Aniq was close to Darband. This is confirmed by Howorth who tells of a campaign by Arghun Khān in 689/1290 against the people of Darband who had revolted against his rule and then retreated to the strong fortress of Anik. Howorth, *History of the Mongols*, p. 322.

98. Le Strange, *Lands of the Eastern Caliphate*, p. 176.

99. Howorth, *History of the Mongols*, pp. 261, 344.

100. Barthold, *An Historical Geography of Iran*, p. 213; Le Strange, *Lands of the Eastern Caliphate*, p. 222.

101. During the time of Abaqa, the territory between Abhar and Zanjān was known as Qongqur-Oleng (Brown Meadow). Boyle, 'Dynastic and Political History of the Īl-Khāns,' p. 356.

102. Nizārī, *Kulliyyāt*, f.374b, *Safar-nāma.* It is noteworthy that Futūh was the family name of the daughter of Ḥasan-i Ṣabbāḥ and that Ṣadr al-Dīn is also referred to by Nizārī as 'ibn al-Mawlānā,' the appellation of a son of Naṣīr al-Dīn al-Ṭūsī. Personal communication from Jalal H. Badakhchani.

103. Nizārī, *Kulliyyāt*, f.380b, *Safar-nāma.*

104. During the time of the Ismaili Imam Jalāl al-Dīn, Zanjān was given to him as recompense for services rendered to the Oz-Beg of Ādharbāyjān and the Abbasid Caliph. Daftary, *The Ismāʿīlīs*, p. 407.

105. Nizārī, *Kulliyyāt*, f.380b, *Safar-nāma.*

106. Nizārī, *Kulliyāt*, f.378b, *Safar-nāma.*

107. Nizārī, *Kulliyāt*, 383a, *Safar-nāma.*

108. Ḥasan-i Ṣabbāḥ, the founder of the Ismaili state in Persia and *ḥujja* of the hidden Imam, is referred to in Nizārī sources as 'Jesus of the *dawr-i qiyāma.*' See Abū Isḥāq Quhistānī, *Haft bāb*, p. 63, n.2.

109. Nizārī, *Kulliyāt*, 383a, *Safar-nāma.*

Bibliography

Abū Firās, Shihāb al-Dīn al-Maynaqī. *Ash-Shāfiya. An Ismāʿīlī Treatise*, ed. and tr. S.N. Makarem. Beirut, 1966.

Abū Isḥāq Quhistānī. *Haft bāb*, ed. and tr. W. Ivanow. Bombay, 1959.

Ādhār, Luṭf ʿAlī Beg. *Ātashkada*, ed. Ḥasan Sādāt Nāṣirī. Gīlān, 1339/1960.

Allen, W.T. *A History of the Georgian People*. New York, 1932.

Allsen, Terry. *Mongol Imperialism: The Policies of Grand Qan Mongke in China, Russia and the Islamic Lands 1251–1259*. Berkeley, CA, 1987.

Amanat, Abbas. 'The Nuqṭawī Movement of Maḥmūd Pisīkhānī and his Persian Cycle of Mystical-Materialism,' in Daftary, ed., *Mediaeval Ismaʿili History and Thought*, pp. 281–97.

Amir-Moezzi, Mohammad Ali. *The Divine Guide in Early Shiʿism: The Sources of Esotericism in Islam*, tr. D. Streight. Albany, NY, 1994.

Amitai-Preiss, Reuven. *Mongols and Mamlūks: The Mamlūk-Īlkhānid War, 1260–1281*. Cambridge, 1995.

Asani, Ali S. *The Būjh Niranjan: An Ismaili Mystical Poem*. Cambridge, Mass., 1991.

—— *Ecstasy and Enlightenment: The Ismaili Devotional Literature of South Asia*. London, 2002.

Atkinson, James and R. Gelpke, *The Story of Layla and Majnun*. Leiden, 1977.

ʿAṭṭār, Farīd al-Dīn. *Manṭiq al-Ṭayr, The Conference of the Birds*, tr. C.S. Nott. London, 1954.

Aubin, Jean. 'Un Canton Quhistani de l'epoque timouride,' *Revue des Etudes Islamiques*, 35 (1967), pp. 185–204.

Austin, R.W.J. 'The Sophianic Feminine in the Work of Ibn ʿArabi and

Rumi,' in L. Lewisohn, ed., *The Heritage of Sufism*. Oxford, 1992, vol. 2, pp. 233–45.

Baiburdi, Chengiz G. 'Rukopisi Proizvedeniy Nizārī,' in *Kratkie Soobsheniya Instituta Naradov Azii*, 65 (1964), pp. 13–24.

— *Zhizn i tvorchestvo Nizārī-Persidskogo poeta*. Moscow, 1966; Persian tr. M. Ṣadrī, *Zindigī va āthār-i Nizārī*. Tehran, 1370/1991.

Baradin, Chengiz G. 'Ḥakīm-i Nizārī Quhistānī,' *Farhang-i Īrān Zamīn*, 6 (1337/1958), pp.178–203.

Barthold, W. *An Historical Geography of Iran*, tr. Svat Soucek. Princeton, NJ, 1984.

Bausani, Alessandro. 'Religion under the Mongols,' in *The Cambridge History of Iran*, Volume 5, 1968, pp. 538–49.

— 'Ḥurūfiyya,' *EI2*, vol. 3, pp. 600–1.

Bell, Joseph N. *Love Theory in Later Hanbalite Islam*. Albany, NY, 1979.

Bertel's, Y. E. 'Introduction to Nizārī's *Dastūr-nāma*,' *Vostochniy Sbornik*, 1 (1926), pp. 37–104

Bīrjandī, Mujtahid Zāda. *Nasīm-i bahārī dar aḥvāl-i Ḥakīm Nizārī*. Mashhad, 1344/1926.

Bosworth, C. Edmund. 'The Political and Dynastic History of the Iranian World (AD 1000–1217),' in *The Cambridge History of Iran*, Volume 5, pp. 1–202.

— *The History of the Saffarids of Sistan and the Maliks of Nimruz (247/861 to 949/1542–3)*. Costa Mesa, CA, and New York, 1994.

— 'The Isma'ilis of Quhistān and the Maliks of Nīmrūz or Sīstān,' in Daftary, ed., *Mediaeval Ismaili History and Thought*, pp. 221–9.

Boyle, John A. 'Dynastic and Political History of the Īl-Khāns,' in *The Cambridge History of Iran*, Volume 5, pp. 303–421.

— 'The Capture of Isfahan by the Mongols,' in *Atti del convegno internazionale sul Tema, La Persia nel Medioevo*. Rome, 1971, pp. 331–6.

— 'The Ismā'īlīs and the Mongol Invasions,' in Nasr, ed., *Ismā'īlī Contributions to Islamic Culture*, pp. 7–22.

Brett, Michael. *The Rise of the Fatimids: The World of the Mediterranean and the Middle East in the Fourth Century of the Hijra, Tenth Century C.E.* Leiden, 2001.

Browne, Edward G. *A Literary History of Persia*. Cambridge, 1928.

The Cambridge History of Iran, Volume 4, *The Period from the Arab Invasion to the Invasion of the Saljūqs*, ed. R.N. Frye. Cambridge, 1975.

The Cambridge History of Iran, Volume 5, *The Saljūq and Mongol Periods*, ed. John A. Boyle, Cambridge, 1968.

Canard, Marius. 'Daʿwa,' *EI2*, vol. 3, pp. 168–70.
—— 'Fāṭimids,' *EI2*, vol. 2, pp. 850–62.
Corbin, Henry, ed. and tr. *Trilogie Ismaélienne.* Tehran and Paris, 1961.
—— 'Huitième centenaire d'Alamut,' *Mercure de France* (Feb., 1965), pp. 285–304.
—— *Creative Imagination in the Ṣūfism of Ibn ʿArabī.* Princeton, NJ, 1969.
—— 'L'Initiation Ismaélienne ou l'ésoterisme et le Verbe,' *Eranos Jahrbuch*, 39 (1970), pp. 41–142; repr. in his *L'Homme et son ange.* Paris, 1983, pp. 81–205.
—— 'Nāṣir-i Khusrau and Iranian Ismāʿīlīsm,' in *The Cambridge History of Iran*, Volume 4, pp. 520–42.
—— 'The Ismāʿīlī Response to the Polemic of Ghazālī,' in Nasr, ed., *Ismāʿīlī Contributions to Islamic Culture*, pp. 69–98.
—— *Cyclical Time and Ismaili Gnosis*, tr. R. Manheim and J.W. Morris. London, 1983.
—— *History of Islamic Philosophy*, tr. P. Sherard. London, 1993.
Dabashi, Hamid. 'The Philospher/Vizier Khwāja Naṣīr al-Dīn al-Ṭūsī and the Ismaʿilis,' in Daftary, ed., *Mediaeval Ismaʿili History and Thought*, pp. 231–45.
—— *Truth and Narrative: The Untimely Thoughts of ʿAyn al-Quḍāt al-Hamadhānī.* London, 1999.
Daftary, Farhad. *The Ismāʿīlīs: Their History and Doctrines.* Cambridge, 1990.
—— 'The Earliest Ismāʿīlīs,' *Arabica*, 38 (1991), pp. 214–45.
—— 'Persian Historiography of the Early Nizārī Ismāʿīlīs,' *Iran*, 30 (1992), pp. 91–7.
—— 'A Major Schism in the Early Ismāʿīlī Movement,' *Studia Islamica*, 77 (1993), pp. 123–39.
—— *The Assassin Legends: Myths of the Ismaʿilis.* London, 1994.
—— 'Dawr,' *Encyclopaedia Iranica*, vol. 7, pp. 151–3.
—— 'Ḥasan-i Ṣabbāḥ and the Origins of the Nizārī Ismaʿili Movement,' in Daftary, ed., *Mediaeval Ismaʿili History and Thought*, pp. 181–204.
—— ed., *Mediaeval Ismaʿili History and Thought.* Cambridge, 1996.
—— *A Short History of the Ismailis: Traditions of a Muslim Community.* Edinburgh, 1998.
—— 'The Ismaili *Daʿwa* outside the Fatimid *Dawla*' in Marianne Barrucand, ed., *L'Egypte Fatimide: son art et son histoire.* Paris, 1999, pp. 29–43.
—— 'Ismāʿīlī-Sufi Relations in Early Post-Alamūt and Safavid Persia,' in L. Lewisohn and D. Morgan, ed., *The Heritage of Sufism.* Oxford, 1999, vol. 3, pp. 275–89.

Dawlatshāh b. ʿAlāʾ al-Dawla. *Tadhkirat al-shuʿarāʾ*, ed. E.G. Browne. London, 1901.
De Bruijn, J.T.P. 'Ḥamīd al-Dīn al-Kirmānī,' *EI2*, vol. 5, pp. 166–7.
— 'Nizārī Ḳuhistānī,' *EI2*, vol. 7, pp. 83–4
De Meynard, C.B. *Dictionnaire Geographique, Historique et Litteraire de Perse et des Contrees Adjacentes.* Amsterdam, 1970.
Donaldson, Dwight M. *The Shiʿite Religion: A History of Islam in Persia and Irak.* London, 1933.
Durri, J. 'Baʿze maʿlumot dar borayi Nizori,' *Sharqi Surkh* (1958–59), pp. 140–54.
Esmail, Aziz and Azim Nanji. 'The Ismāʿīlīs in History,' in Nasr, ed., *Ismāʿīlī Contributions to Islamic Culture*, pp. 225–65.
Fidāʾī Khurāsānī, Muḥammad b. Zayn al-ʿĀbidīn. *Kitāb-i Hidāyat al-muʾminīn al-ṭālibīn*, ed. A.A. Semenov. Moscow, 1959.
Gardet, Louis. 'Ḳiyāma,' *EI2*, vol. 5, pp. 235–8.
Ghālib, Muṣṭafā. *Aʿlām al-Ismāʿīliyya.* Beirut, 1964.
— *The Ismailis of Syria.* Beirut, 1970.
Graham, Terry. 'Abū Saʿīd b. Abi'l-Khayr and the School of Khurāsān,' in L. Lewisohn, ed., *The Heritage of Sufism.* Oxford, 1999, vol. 1, pp. 83–135.
Ḥāfiẓ-i Abrū, ʿAbd Allāh b. Luṭf ʿAlī. *Majmaʿ al-tawārīkh al-sulṭāniyya: qismat-i khulafāʾ-i ʿAlawiyya-i Maghrib va Miṣr va Nizāriyān va rafīqān*, ed. M. Mudarrisī Zanjānī. Tehran, 1364/1985.
Haft bāb-i Bābā Sayyidna, ed. and tr. W. Ivanow in his *Two Early Ismaili Treatises.* Bombay, 1933, pp. 4–44. English tr. Marshall G.S. Hodgson in his *The Order of Assassins.* The Hague, 1955, pp. 279–324.
Halm, Heinz. 'Die Sīrat Ibn Haušab: Die ismailitische daʿwa im Jemen und die Fatimiden,' *Die Welt des Orients*, 12 (1981), pp. 107–35.
— *Shiism*, tr. J. Watson. Edinburgh, 1991.
— 'The Ismaʿili Oath of Allegiance (*ʿahd*) and the "Sessions of Wisdom" (*majālis al-ḥikma*) in Fatimid Times,' in Daftary, ed., *Mediaeval Ismaʿili History and Thought*, pp. 91–115.
— *The Empire of the Mahdi: The Rise of the Fatimids*, tr. M. Bonner. Leiden, 1996.
— *The Fatimids and their Traditions of Learning.* London, 1997.
— 'Dawr,' *EI2*, *Supplement*, pp. 206–7.
Ḥamd Allāh Mustawfī Qazwīnī. *The Geographical Part of the Nuzhat al-Qulūb*, ed. and tr. G. Le Strange. Leiden and London, 1915–19.
— *Taʾrīkh-i guzīda*, ed. ʿAbd al-Ḥusayn Navāʾī. Tehran, 1339/1960.
Hamdani, Abbas. 'Evolution of the Organisational Structure of the Faṭimī

Da'wah,' *Arabian Studies*, 3 (1976), pp. 85–114.

al-Hamdānī, Husain F. 'History of the Ismā'īlī *Da'wat* and its Literature during the Last Phase of the Fāṭimid Empire,' *JRAS* (1932), pp. 126–36.

—— 'Some Unknown Ismā'īlī Authors and their Works,' *JRAS* (1933), pp. 359–78.

Hammer-Purgstall, Joseph von. *The History of the Assassins*, tr. O.C. Wood. London, 1835; repr., New York, 1968.

al-Harawī, Sayf b. Muḥammad. *Ta'rīkh nāma-yi Harāt*, ed. M. Zubayr al-Ṣiddīqī. Calcutta, 1944; repr. Tehran, 1973.

Ḥasan, Ḥasan I. *Ta'rīkh al-dawla al-Fāṭimiyya*. 3rd ed., Cairo, 1964.

Hidāyat, Riḍā Qulī Khān. *Majmā' al-fuṣahā*, ed. M. Muṣaffā. Tehran, 1336–40/1957–61.

Hodgson, Marshall G.S. 'How did the Early Shī'a become Sectarian?' *JAOS*, 75 (1955), pp. 1–13.

—— *The Order of Assassins*. The Hague, 1955.

—— 'The Ismā'īlī State' in *The Cambridge History of Iran*, Volume 5, pp. 422–82.

—— *The Venture of Islam: Conscience and History in a World Civilization*. Chicago, 1974.

—— 'Bāṭiniyya,' *EI2*, vol. 1, pp. 1098–100.

—— 'Dā'ī,' *EI2*, vol. 2, pp. 97–8.

Hollister, John N. *The Shi'a of India*. London, 1953.

Howorth, Henry. *History of the Mongols*. New York, 1888.

Hunsberger, Alice C. *Nasir Khusraw, The Ruby of Badakhshan: A Portrait of the Persian Poet, Traveller and Philosopher*. London, 2000.

Hunzai, Faquir, tr. *Shimmering Light: An Anthology of Ismaili Poetry*, ed. Kutub Kassam. London, 1996.

Ibn al-Athīr, 'Izz al-Dīn 'Alī b. Muḥammad. *al-Kāmil fi'l-ta'rīkh*, ed. C.J. Tornberg. Leiden, 1851–76; repr. Beirut, 1965–7.

Ibn al-Haytham, Abū 'Abd Allāh Ja'far. *Kitāb al-Munāẓarat*, ed. and tr. W. Madelung and P.E. Walker as *The Advent of the Fatimids: A Contemporary Shi'i Witness*. London, 2000.

Ibn Khaldūn, 'Abd al-Raḥmān. *The Muqaddimah, An Introduction to History*, tr. Franz Rosenthal. New York, 1958.

Ibn Ẓāfir, Jamāl al-Dīn 'Alī. *Akhbār al-duwwal al-munqaṭi'a, La Section consacrée aux Fatimides*, ed. A. Ferré. Cairo, 1972.

Idrīs 'Imād al-Dīn b. al-Ḥasan. *'Uyūn al-akhbār wa-funūn al-āthār*, vol. 4, ed. M. Ghālib, Beirut, 1973.

Iqbal, 'Abbās. *Ta'rīkh-i mufaṣṣal-i Īrān*. Tehran, 1341/1962.

Isfizārī, Muʿīn al-Dīn Muḥammad. *Rawḍat-i jannāt fi awṣāf-i madīnat-i Harāt*, ed. M. Kāẓim Imām. Tehran, 1338/1959.

Ivanow, W. 'Ismailitica,' in *Memoirs of the Asiatic Society of Bengal*, 8 (1922), pp. 1–76.

—— 'Imam Ismail,' *Journal and Proceedings of the Asiatic Society of Bengal*, NS, (1923), pp. 305–310.

—— 'An Ismailitic Work by Nasiru'd-din Tusi,' *JRAS* (1931), pp. 527–64.

—— 'An Ismaili Interpretation of the Gulshani Raz,' in *JBBRAS*, NS, 8 (1932), pp. 68–78.

—— ed. *Two Early Ismaili Treatises*. Bombay, 1933.

—— *A Guide to Ismaili Literature*. London, 1933.

—— 'A Forgotten Branch of the Ismailis,' *JRAS* (1938), pp. 57–79.

—— 'Tombs of Some Persian Ismaili Imams,' *JBBRAS*, NS, 14 (1938), pp. 49–62.

—— 'The Organization of the Fatimid Propaganda,' *JBBRAS*, NS, 15 (1939), pp. 1–35.

—— 'Ismailis and Qarmatians,' *JBBRAS*, NS, 16 (1940), pp. 43–85.

—— 'Early Shīʿite Movements,' *JBBRAS*, NS, 17 (1941), pp. 1–23.

—— *Ismaili Tradition Concerning the Rise of the Fatimids*. London, etc., 1942.

—— *The Alleged Founder of Ismailism*. Bombay, 1946.

—— *Brief Survey of the Evolution of Ismailism*. Leiden, 1952.

—— *Studies in Early Persian Ismailism*. 2nd ed., Bombay, 1955.

—— *Problems in Nasir-i Khusraw's Biography*. Bombay, 1956.

—— *Ibn al-Qaddāḥ (The Alleged Founder of Ismailism)*. 2nd rev. ed., Bombay, 1957.

—— 'Shums Tabrez of Multān,' in S.M. Abdullah, ed., *Professor Muḥammad Shāfi Presentation Volume*. Lahore, 1955, pp. 109–118.

—— *Alamut and Lamasar: Two Mediaeval Ismaili Strongholds in Iran*. Tehran, 1960.

—— *Ismaili Literature: A Bibliographical Survey*. Tehran, 1963.

—— 'Hakim Nizari Kohistani,' *Africa Ismaili*, Nairobi (Sept., 1969), pp. 6–7.

—— 'Ismailism and Sufism,' *Ismaili Bulletin*, vol. 1, no.12 (Karachi, 1975), pp. 3–6.

Jafri, S.Husain M. *Origins and Early Development of Shīʿa Islam*. London, 1979.

Jāmī, Nūr al-Dīn ʿAbd al-Raḥmān. *Bahāristān*, tr. Ottocar Maria Freihern. Wien, 1846.

—— *Bahāristān-i rasāʾil-i Jāmī*, ed. Aʿalā Afṣahzād et al. Tehran, 1379/2000.

Jiwa, Shainool. 'The Initial Destination of the Fatimid Caliphate: The Yemen or Maghrib?' *British Society for Middle Eastern Studies, Bulletin*, 13 (1986), pp. 15–26.

Juwaynī, 'Alā' al-Dīn 'Aṭā-Malik. *Ta'rīkh-i jahān gushāy*, ed. M. Qazwīnī. Leiden-London, 1912–37. English tr. J.A. Boyle, *The History of the World-Conqueror*. Manchester, 1958.

Juzjānī, Minhāj al-Dīn 'Uthmān b. Sirāj. *Tabaqāt-i Nāṣirī*, tr. H.G. Raverty, The *Ṭabaḳāt-i-Nāṣirī: A General History of the Muhammadan Dynasties of Asia*. London, 1881–99; repr. New Delhi, 1970.

Kāshānī, Abu'l-Qāsim 'Abd Allāh b. 'Alī. *Zubdat al-tawārīkh: bakhsh-i Fāṭimiyān va Nizāriyān*, ed. M.T. Dānishpazhūh. 2nd ed., Tehran, 1366/1987.

Kassam, Tazim R. *Songs of Wisdom and Circles of Dance: Hymns of the Satpanth Ismā'īlī Muslim Saint, Pīr Shams*. Albany, NY, 1995.

Khayrkhwāh-i Harātī, Muḥammad Riḍā b. Sulṭān Ḥusayn. *Kalām-i pīr, A Treatise on Ismaili Doctrine also (wrongly) called Haft Babi Shah Sayyid Nasir*, ed. and tr. W. Ivanow. Bombay, 1935.

Khwānd Amīr, Ghiyāth al-Dīn b. Humām al-Dīn. *Ḥabīb al-siyar*, ed. J. Humā'ī. Tehran, 1333/1954.

al-Kirmānī, Ḥamīd al-Dīn Aḥmad. *Rāḥat al-'aql*, ed. M.K. Ḥusayn and M.M. Ḥilmī. Cairo, 1953.

—— *al-Maṣābīḥ fī ithbāt al-imāma*, ed. M. Ghālib. Beirut, 1969.

Kohlberg, Etan. 'Some Imāmī-Shī'ī Views on Taqiyya,' *JAOS*, 95 (1975), pp. 395–402; repr. in his *Belief and Law in Imāmī Shī'ism*. Aldershot, 1991, article III.

Kramers, J.H. 'Ḳūhistān,' *EI2*, vol. 5, pp. 354–6.

Krenkow, F. 'Ṣulayḥī,' *EI*, vol. 4, pp. 515–17.

Al-Kulaynī, Muḥammad b. Ya'qūb. *Al-Uṣūl min al-kāfī*. Tehran, 1388/1968.

Kurkjian, V.M. *A History of Armenia*. New York, 1958.

Lalani, Arzina R. *Early Shī'ī Thought: The Teachings of Imam Muḥammad al-Bāqir*. London, 2000.

Landolt, Hermann. 'Walāya,' in M. Eliade, ed., *The Encyclopedia of Religion*. New York and London, 1987, vol. 15, pp. 316–23.

Le Strange, Guy. *Lands of the Eastern Caliphate*. London, 1905; repr. 1966.

Lewis, Bernard. *The Origins of Ismā'īlism: A Study of the Historical Background of the Fāṭimid Caliphate*. Cambridge, 1940.

—— *The Assassins: A Radical Sect in Islam*. London, 1967.

Lewisohn, Leonard. 'Overview: Iranian Islam and Persianate Sufism,' in L. Lewisohn, ed., *The Heritage of Sufism*, vol. 2. Oxford, 1999, pp. 11–43.

—— and David Morgan, ed. *The Heritage of Sufism*, vol. 3, Oxford, 1999.
Madelung, Wilferd. 'Das Imamat in der frühen ismailitischen Lehre,' *Der Islam*, 37 (1961), pp.43–135.
—— 'Aspects of Ismāʿīlī Theology: The Prophetic Chain and the God Beyond Being,' in Nasr, ed., *Ismāʿīlī Contributions to Islamic Culture*, pp. 51–65; reprinted in his *Religious Schools and Sects in Medieval Islam*. London, 1985, article XVII.
—— 'Naṣīr ad-Dīn Ṭūsī's Ethics between Philosophy, Shiʿism and Sufism,' in Richard G. Hovannisian, ed., *Ethics in Islam*. Malibu, CA, 1985, pp. 85–101.
—— 'Ismāʿīliyya,' *EI2*, vol. 4, pp. 198–206.
—— 'al-Mahdī,' *EI2*, vol. 5, pp. 1230–8.
—— 'Manṣūr al-Yaman,' *EI2*, vol. 6, pp. 438–9.
Maḥjūb, Muḥammad Jaʿfar. 'Chivalry and Early Persian Sufism,' in L. Lewisohn, ed., *The Heritage of Sufism*. Oxford, 1999, vol.1, pp. 549–81.
Makarem, Sami N. *Doctrine of the Ismāʿīlīs*. Beirut, 1972.
Marʿashī, Ẓahīr al-Dīn. *Ta'rīkh-i Gīlān va Daylamistān*, ed. H.L. Rabino. Rasht, 1330/1912.
Massignon, Louis. 'Time in Islamic Thought,' in *Man and Time, Papers from the Eranos Yearbooks*. New York, 1957, pp. 108–114.
Michon, Jean-Louis. 'The Spiritual Practices of Sufism,' in S.H. Nasr, ed., *Islamic Spirituality: Foundations*. London, 1987, pp. 265–93.
—— 'Sacred Music and Dance in Islam,' in S.H. Nasr, ed., *Islamic Spirituality: Manifestations*. New York, 1991, pp. 469–505.
Minasian, Caro O. *Shah Diz of Ismaʿili Fame: Its Siege and Destruction*. London, 1971.
Mīrkhwānd, Muḥammad b. Khwāndshāh, *Rawḍat al-ṣafā'*. Tehran, 1338–9/1960.
Mitha, Farouk. *al-Ghazālī and the Ismailis: A Debate on Reason and Authority in Medieval Islam*. London, 2001.
Momen, Moojan. *An Introduction to Shiʿi Islam*. New Haven, CT, 1985.
Morgan, David. *The Mongols*. Oxford, 1986.
Mujtahid Zāda, 'Alī R. *Ḥakim Nizārī Quhistānī*. Mashhad, 1926.
Muscati, Jawad and Khan Bahadur A.M. Moulvi. *Life and Lectures of the Grand Missionary al-Muayyad fid-Dīn al-Shirazi*. Karachi, 1966.
Nanji, Azim. *The Nizārī Ismāʿīlī Tradition in the Indo-Pakistan Subcontinent*. Delmar, NY, 1978.
—— 'Ismāʿīlism,' in S.H. Nasr, ed., *Islamic Spirituality: Foundations*. London, 1987, pp. 179–98.

—— 'Assassins,' in M. Eliade, ed., *The Encyclopaedia of Islam.* London-New York, 1987, vol. 1, p. 470.

Nāṣir-i Khusraw. *Forty Poems from the Dīvān,* tr. P.L. Wilson and G.R. Aavani. Tehran, 1977.

—— *Jāmiʿ al-ḥikmatayn,* ed. H. Corbin and M. Muʿīn. Tehran and Paris, 1953.

—— *Khwān al-ikhwān,* ed. Y. al-Khashshāb. Cairo, 1940.

—— *Safar-nāma,* ed. M. Ghanīzāda. Berlin, 1922; ed. S.M. Dabīr Siyāqī. Tehran, 1977; English tr. W.M. Thackston Jr., *Nāṣer-e Khosraw's Book of Travels (Safarnāma),* Albany, NY, 1986.

—— *Wajh-i dīn,* ed. G.R. Aavani. Tehran, 1977.

Nasr, S. Hossein. *An Introduction to Islamic Cosmological Doctrines.* Cambridge, Mass., 1964.

—— *Sufi Essays.* London, 1972.

—— ed. *Ismāʿīlī Contributions to Islamic Culture.* Tehran, 1977.

—— ed. *Islamic Spirituality: Foundations.* London, 1987.

Netton, Ian R. *Muslim Neoplatonists: An Introduction to the Thought of the Brethren of Purity (Ikhwān al-Ṣafā').* London, 1982.

—— *Seek Knowledge: Thought and Travel in the House of Islam.* Richmond, Surrey, 1996.

al-Nīsābūrī, Aḥmad b. Ibrāhīm. *Istitār al-Imām,* ed. W. Ivanow in *Bulletin of the Faculty of Arts, University of Egypt,* 4, Part 2 (1936), pp. 93–107, English tr. in W. Ivanow, *Ismaili Traditions Concerning the Rise of the Fatimids.* London etc., 1942, pp. 157–83.

Niẓām al-Mulk, Abū ʿAlī Ḥasan. *Siyar al-mulūk (Siyāsat-nāma,)* English tr. H. Darke, *The Book of Government or Rules for Kings.* London, 1960.

Nizārī Quhistānī, Saʿd al-Dīn b. Shams al-Dīn. *Dastūr-nāma,* ed. and tr. into Russian by E. Bertel's in *Vostochniy Sbornik,* 1 (1926), pp. 37ff.

—— *Dīwān,* ed. M. Muṣaffā. Tehran, 1371–73/1992–4.

—— *Kulliyyāt.* MS, The Institute of Oriental Studies, St. Petersburg.

al-Nuʿmān b. Muḥammad, al-Qāḍī Abū Ḥanīfa. *Asās al-ta'wīl,* ed. ʿĀ. Tāmir. Beirut, 1960.

—— *Daʿā'im al-Islām,* ed. A.A.A. Fyzee. Cairo, 1951–61. Partial English tr., A.A.A. Fyzee, *The Book of Faith.* Bombay, 1974.

—— *Iftitāḥ al-daʿwa,* ed. Farhat Dachraoui. Tunis, 1975.

—— *Sharḥ al-akhbār,* ed. S.M. al-Ḥusaynī al-Jalālī. Qumm, 1409–12/1988–92. Partial English tr. in W. Ivanow, 'Early Shiʿite Movements,' *JBBRAS,* NS, 17 (1941), pp. 1–23.

Nurbakhsh, Jawad. *Sufi Symbolism.* London, 1986.

Petrushevsky, I.P. 'The Socio-Economic Conditions in Iran under the Īl-

Khāns,' in *The Cambridge History of Iran*, Volume 5, pp. 483–537.
Poonawala, Ismail K. *Biobibliography of Ismāʿīlī Literature.* Malibu, CA, 1977.
Pourjavady, Nasrollah and P.L. Wilson. 'Ismāʿīlīs and Niʿmatullāhīs,' *Studia Islamica*, 41 (1975), pp. 113–35
Rabino, Hyacinth L. 'Rulers of Gilan,' *JRAS* (1920), pp.277–96.
Rahman, F. *Islam.* New York, 1963.
Rashīd al-Dīn Faḍl Allāh. *Jāmiʿ al-tawārīkh*, ed. A.A. Alizade. Baku, 1957.
—— *Jāmiʿ al-tawārīkh: qismat-i Ismāʿīliyān va Fāṭimiyān va Nizāriyān va dāʿīyān va rafīqān*, ed. M.T. Dānishpazhūh and M. Mudarrisī Zanjāni. Tehran, 1338/1959.
Rāzī, Amīn Aḥmad. *Haft iqlīm*, ed. Javād Fāḍil. Tehran, n.d.
Rosenthal, Franz. *A History of Muslim Historiography.* Leiden, 1968.
Rypka, Jan. 'Poets and Prose Writers of the Late Saljūq and Mongol Periods,' in *The Cambridge History of Iran*, Volume 5, pp. 550–625.
—— *History of Iranian Literature*, ed. Karl Jahn. Dordrecht, 1968.
Sachedina, A.A. *Islamic Messianism: The Idea of the Mahdi in Twelver Shiʿism.* Albany, NY, 1981.

Saunders, J.J. *The History of the Mongol Conquests.* London, 1977.
Savory, R.M. 'Khoi, Khūy,' *EI2*, vol. 5, pp. 28–29.
Schimmel, Annemarie. *Mystical Dimensions of Islam.* Chapel Hill, NC, 1975.
—— 'Aspects of Mystical Thought in Islam,' in Yvonne Yazbeck Haddad, et al., *The Islamic Impact.* Syracuse, NY, 1984.
—— *Make a Shield from Widsom: Selected Verses from Nāṣir-i Khusraw's Dīvān.* Rev. ed., London, 2001.
Seltzar, Leon, ed. *The Columbia Gazetteer of the World.* New York, 1952.
Shackle, Christopher and Zawahir Moir. *Ismaili Hymns from South Asia: An Introduction to the Ginans.* London, 1992.
al-Shahrastānī, Abu'l-Fatḥ Muḥammad b. ʿAbd al-Karīm. *Kitāb al-Milal wa'l-niḥal*, ed. A. Fahmī Muḥammad. Cairo, 1948; partial English tr. A.K. Kazi and J.G. Flynn, *Muslim Sects and Divisions.* London, 1984.
al-Sijistānī, Abū Yaʿqūb. *Ithbāt al-nubūʾāt*, ed. ʿĀ. Tāmir. Beirut, 1966.
—— *Kashf al-maḥjūb*, ed. H. Corbin. Tehran and Paris, 1949; partial English tr. H. Landolt, *Unveiling the Hidden*, in S.H. Nasr and M. Aminrazavi, ed., *An Anthology of Philosophy in Persia.* Oxford, 2001, vol. 2, pp. 70–124.
—— *Kitāb al-Iftikhār*, ed. M. Ghālib. Beirut, 1980.
—— *Kitāb al-Yanābīʿ*, ed. and French tr. H. Corbin in his *Trilogie Ismaélienne.* Tehran and Paris, 1961, text pp. 1–97, translation pp. 1–127. Eng-

lish tr. Paul E. Walker as *The Book of Wellsprings* in his *The Wellsprings of Wisdom*. Salt Lake City, 1994, pp. 37–111.

—— *Tuhfat al-mustajībīn*, in *Khams rasā'il al-Ismā'īliyya*, ed. 'Ā. Tāmir. Salamiyya, 1956, pp.145–56.

Silvestre de Sacy, Antoine Isaac. 'Mémoire sur la dynastie des Assassins,' *Mémoires de l'Institut Royal de France*, 4 (1818), pp.1–84; English tr. 'Memoir on the Dynasty of the Assassins,' in Daftary, *The Assassin Legends*, pp.136–88.

Sobhani, Ayatollah Ja'far. *Doctrines of Shi'i Islam: A Compendium of Imami Beliefs and Practices*, tr. and ed. Reza Shah-Kazemi. London, 2001.

Sprenger, A. *A Catalogue of the Persian Manuscripts of the King of Oudh*. Calcutta, 1854.

Stark, Freya. *The Valleys of the Assassins*. London, 1934.

Stern, Samuel M. 'Ismā'īlī Propaganda and Fatimid Rule in Sind,' *Islamic Culture*, 23 (1949), pp. 298–307, reprinted in his *Studies*, pp. 177–188.

—— 'The Epistle of the Fatimid Caliph al-Āmir (*al-Hidāya al-Āmiriyya*)—its date and its purpose,' *JRAS* (1950), pp. 20–31.

—— 'The Early Ismā'īlī Missionaries in North-West Persia and in Khurāsān and Transoxania,' *Bulletin of the School of Oriental and African Studies*, 23 (1960), pp. 59–60, reprinted in his *Studies*, pp. 189–233.

—— 'Cairo as a Centre of the Ismā'īlī Movement,' *Colloque international sur l'histoire du Caire*. Cairo, 1972, pp. 437–50, reprinted in his *Studies*, pp. 234–56.

—— *Studies in Early Ismā'īlism*. Jerusalem and Leiden, 1983.

Strauss, Leo. *Persecution and the Art of Writing*. Glencoe, Ill., 1952.

Strothmann, R. and M. Djebli. 'Taḳiyya,' *EI2*, vol. 10, pp. 134–36.

Ṭabāṭabā'ī, Muḥammad Ḥusayn. *Shi'ite Islam*, ed. and tr. S.H. Nasr. London, 1975.

Tāmir, 'Ārif. 'Furū' al-shajara al-Ismā'īliyya al-Imāmiyya,' *al-Mashriq*, 51 (1957), pp. 581–612.

—— *al-Imāma fi'l-Islām*. Beirut, 1964.

Ta'rīkh-i Sīstān, ed. M.T. Bahār. Tehran, 1314/1935; English tr. M. Gold. Rome, 1976.

Trimingham, J. Spencer. *The Sufi Orders in Islam*. Oxford, 1971.

al-Ṭūsī, Naṣīr al-Dīn Muḥammad. *Rawḍat al-taslīm, yā taṣawwurāt*, ed. and tr. W. Ivanow. Leiden, 1950; French tr. C. Jambet, *La Convocation d'Alamût: Somme de philosophie Ismaélienne*. Lagrasse, 1996.

—— *Sayr wa sulūk*, ed. and tr. J. Badakhchani as *Contemplation and Action: The Spiritual Autobiography of a Muslim Scholar*. London, 1998.

Walker, Paul E. 'An Early Ismaili Interpretation of Man, History and Salvation,' *Ohio Journal of Religious Studies*, 3 (1975), pp. 29–35.

—— 'Eternal Cosmos and the Womb of History: Time in Early Ismaili Thought,' *International Journal of Middle East Studies*, 9 (1978), pp. 355–66.

—— *Early Philosophical Shiism. The Ismaili Neoplatonism of Abū Ya'qūb al-Sijistānī*. Cambridge, 1993.

—— 'The Ismaili *Da'wa* in the Reign of the Fatimid Caliph al-Ḥākim,' *Journal of the American Center in Egypt*, 30 (1993), pp.161–82.

—— *Abū Ya'qūb al-Sijistānī: Intellectual Missionary*. London, 1996.

—— *Ḥamīd al-Dīn al-Kirmānī: Ismaili Thought in the Age of al-Ḥakim*. London, 1999.

Waṣṣāf, 'Abd Allah b. Faḍl Allah. *Ta'rīkh-i Waṣṣāf*, ed. 'A. Āyatī. Tehran, n.d.

Willey, Peter. *The Castles of the Assassins*. London, 1963.

Woods, J.E. 'A Note on the Mongol Capture of Isfahan,' *Journal of Near Eastern Studies*, 36 (1977) pp.49–51.

Yāqūt al-Ḥamawī, Shihāb al-Dīn Abū 'Abd Allāh. *Mu'jam al-buldān*, ed. F. Wüstenfeld. Leipzig, 1866–73.

Yarshater, Ehsan. 'Wine-Drinking in Persian Poetry,' *Studia Islamica*, 27 (1960), pp. 43–53.

Index